Additional Practice Workbook

GRADE 3 TOPICS 1–16

enVision® Mathematics

Savvas Learning Company LLC, 15 East Midland Avenue, Paramus, NJ 07652

ISBN-13: 978-0-13-495378-6
ISBN-10: 0-13-495378-9
4 20

Grade 3 Topics 1–16

Topic 1
Understand Multiplication and Division of Whole Numbers

Lesson 1-1 1
Lesson 1-2 3
Lesson 1-3 5
Lesson 1-4 7
Lesson 1-5 9
Lesson 1-6 11

Topic 2
Multiplication Facts: Use Patterns

Lesson 2-1 13
Lesson 2-2 15
Lesson 2-3 17
Lesson 2-4 19
Lesson 2-5 21
Lesson 2-6 23

Topic 3
Apply Properties: Multiplication Facts for 3, 4, 6, 7, 8

Lesson 3-1 25
Lesson 3-2 27
Lesson 3-3 29
Lesson 3-4 31
Lesson 3-5 33
Lesson 3-6 35
Lesson 3-7 37

Topic 4
Use Multiplication to Divide: Division Facts

Lesson 4-1 39
Lesson 4-2 41
Lesson 4-3 43
Lesson 4-4 45
Lesson 4-5 47
Lesson 4-6 49
Lesson 4-7 51
Lesson 4-8 53
Lesson 4-9 55

Topic 5
Fluently Multiply and Divide within 100

Lesson 5-1 57
Lesson 5-2 59
Lesson 5-3 61
Lesson 5-4 63
Lesson 5-5 65
Lesson 5-6 67

Topic 6
Connect Area to Multiplication and Addition

Lesson 6-1 69
Lesson 6-2 71
Lesson 6-3 73
Lesson 6-4 75
Lesson 6-5 77
Lesson 6-6 79
Lesson 6-7 81

Topic 7
Represent and Interpret Data

Lesson 7-1 83
Lesson 7-2 85
Lesson 7-3 87
Lesson 7-4 89
Lesson 7-5 91

Topic 8
Use Strategies and Properties to Add and Subtract

Lesson 8-1 93
Lesson 8-2 95
Lesson 8-3 97
Lesson 8-4 99
Lesson 8-5 101
Lesson 8-6 103
Lesson 8-7 105
Lesson 8-8 107

Topic 9
Fluently Add and Subtract within 1,000

Lesson 9-1 109
Lesson 9-2 111
Lesson 9-3 113
Lesson 9-4 115
Lesson 9-5 117
Lesson 9-6 119
Lesson 9-7 121

Topic 10
Multiply by Multiples of 10

Lesson 10-1 123
Lesson 10-2 125
Lesson 10-3 127
Lesson 10-4 129

Topic 11
Use Operations with Whole Numbers to Solve Problems

Lesson 11-1 131
Lesson 11-2 133
Lesson 11-3 135
Lesson 11-4 137

Topic 12
Understand Fractions as Numbers

Lesson 12-1 139
Lesson 12-2 141
Lesson 12-3 143
Lesson 12-4 145
Lesson 12-5 147
Lesson 12-6 149
Lesson 12-7 151
Lesson 12-8 153

Topic 13
Fraction Equivalence and Comparison

Lesson 13-1 155
Lesson 13-2 157
Lesson 13-3 159
Lesson 13-4 161
Lesson 13-5 163
Lesson 13-6 165
Lesson 13-7 167
Lesson 13-8 169

Topic 14
Solve Time, Capacity, and Mass Problems

Lesson 14-1 171
Lesson 14-2 173
Lesson 14-3 175
Lesson 14-4 177
Lesson 14-5 179
Lesson 14-6 181
Lesson 14-7 183
Lesson 14-8 185
Lesson 14-9 187

Topic 15
Attributes of Two-Dimensional Shapes

Lesson 15-1 189
Lesson 15-2 191
Lesson 15-3 193
Lesson 15-4 195

Topic 16
Solve Perimeter Problems

Lesson 16-1 197
Lesson 16-2 199
Lesson 16-3 201
Lesson 16-4 203
Lesson 16-5 205
Lesson 16-6 207

Name ____________

Additional Practice 1-1
Relate Multiplication and Addition

Another Look!

Each group below has the same number of squares. There are 5 groups of 4 squares.

20 squares

4	4	4	4	4

An addition equation or a multiplication equation can represent the total number of squares.

$4 + 4 + 4 + 4 + 4 = 20$

$5 \times 4 = 20$

Complete **1** and **2**. Use the pictures to help.

1.  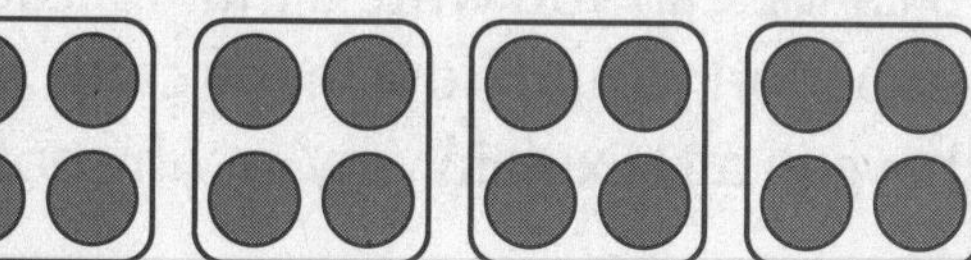 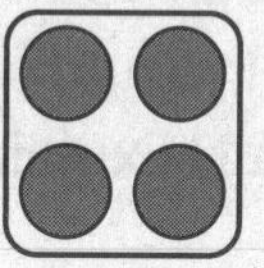 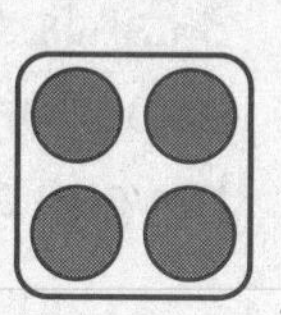

4 groups of ____

$4 + 4 + 4 + 4 =$ ____

$4 \times$ ____ $=$ ____

2. 32

8	8	8	8

____ groups of 8

____ + ____ + ____ + ____ = 32

____ $\times 8 =$ ____

In **3** and **4**, write the addition equation as a multiplication equation.

3. $3 + 3 + 3 + 3 + 3 = 15$

4. $7 + 7 + 7 = 21$

In **5–8**, write the multiplication equation as an addition equation.

5. $5 \times 5 = 25$

6. $6 \times 2 = 12$

7. $3 \times 4 = 12$

8. $5 \times 6 = 30$

9. Jan buys 3 bags of beads. Each bag contains 7 beads. Complete the bar diagram and write an addition equation and a multiplication equation to show how many beads Jan buys. How are the two equations related?

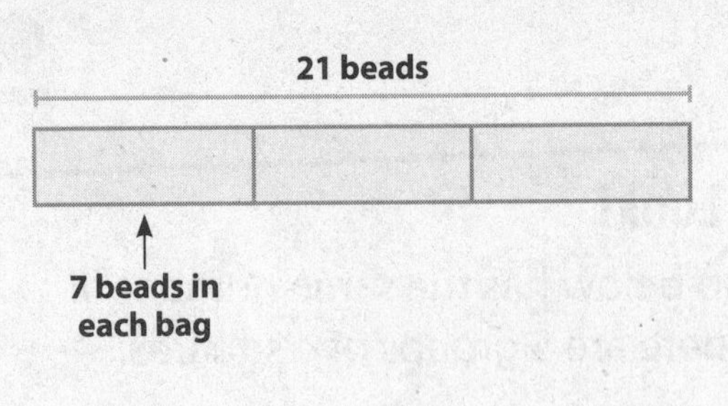

10. Misha buys 4 boxes of 6 markers each. He writes this addition equation to show how many markers he buys: $6 + 6 + 6 + 6 = 24$. What multiplication equation can Misha write to represent this situation?

11. enVision® STEM Some scientists think that geese fly in a V-shaped group to save energy. Ellen sees 3 groups. Each group has 9 geese. How many geese does she see in all? Write an addition equation and a multiplication equation.

12. Critique Reasoning Carrie draws this picture to show 3 groups of 3.

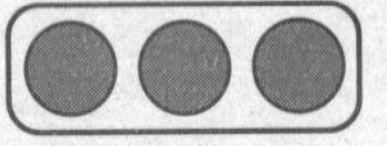  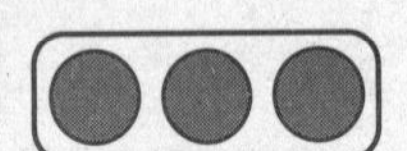

Is Carrie's picture correct? Explain why or why not.

13. Higher Order Thinking Marion has 4 cards, Jake has 4 cards, and Sam has 3 cards. Can you write a multiplication equation to find how many cards they have in all? Explain why or why not.

Assessment Practice

14. Martin has 15 coins. He arranges the coins in equal piles. Which sentences could Martin use to describe his piles? Select all that are correct.

- ☐ Martin arranged 3 piles of 5 coins.
- ☐ Martin arranged 2 piles of 7 coins.
- ☐ Martin arranged 3 piles of 6 coins.
- ☐ Martin arranged 5 piles of 3 coins.
- ☐ Martin arranged 8 piles of 2 coins.

15. Anthony sorts 8 shirts into equal groups. Which sentences could Anthony use to describe his groups? Select all that are correct.

- ☐ Anthony sorted 2 groups of 3.
- ☐ Anthony sorted 2 groups of 4.
- ☐ Anthony sorted 4 groups of 4.
- ☐ Anthony sorted 2 groups of 2.
- ☐ Anthony sorted 4 groups of 2.

Name ____________

Practice Video Tools Games

Additional Practice 1-2
Multiplication on the Number Line

Another Look!

There are 4 fruit bars in a package. Abby buys 5 packages. How many fruit bars does she buy?

Use a number line. Skip count by 4s, five times.

You can use a number line to show 5×4.

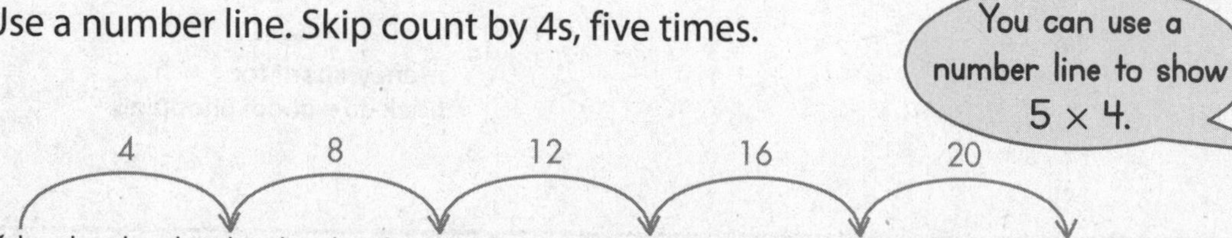

Number of jumps: 5

Number in each jump: 4

$5 \times 4 = 20$ Abby buys 20 fruit bars.

In **1–3**, use the number line.

1. Jack puts 2 photos on each of 7 pages of his photo album. How many photos does he use? Complete the jumps on the number line by adding arrows.

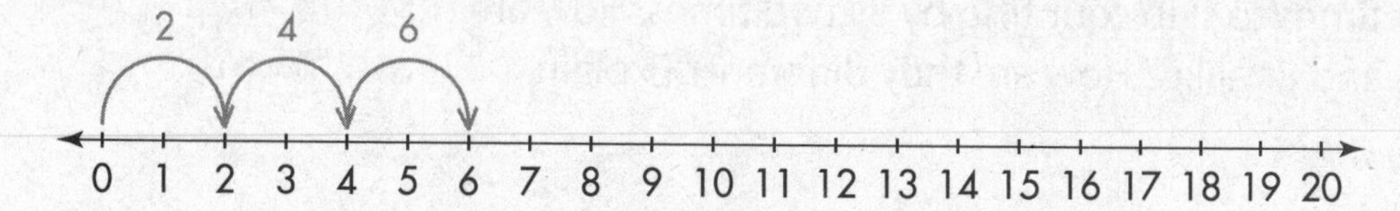

Number of jumps: ____

Number in each jump: ____

____ × ____ = ____

Jack uses ____ photos.

2. Why do you skip count by 2s on the number line?

3. Why do you make 7 jumps on the number line?

4. Tony buys 7 packages of mini-muffins. There are 3 mini-muffins in each package. How many mini-muffins does Tony buy? Use the number line to help find the answer.

0 1 2 3 4 5 6 7 8 9 10 11 12 13 14 15 16 17 18 19 20 21 22

5. Mrs. Calvino's classroom has 6 rows of desks. Each row has 4 desks. Explain how to use skip counting to find how many desks there are.

6. Alyssa has saved \$77 from mowing lawns. She spends \$34 on back-to-school shopping. How much of her savings does Alyssa have left?

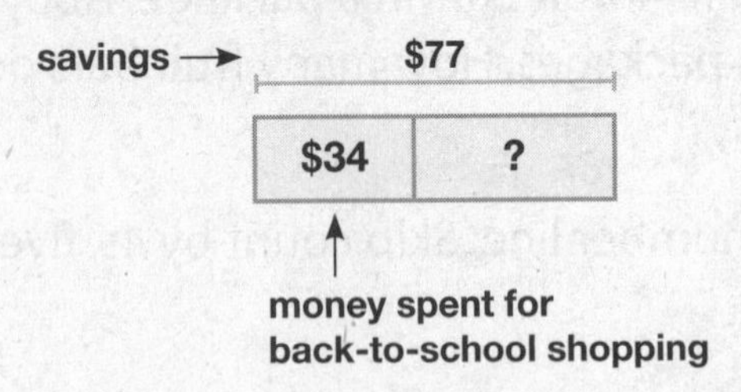

7. Critique Reasoning Tina drew this number line to show $5 \times 3 = 15$.

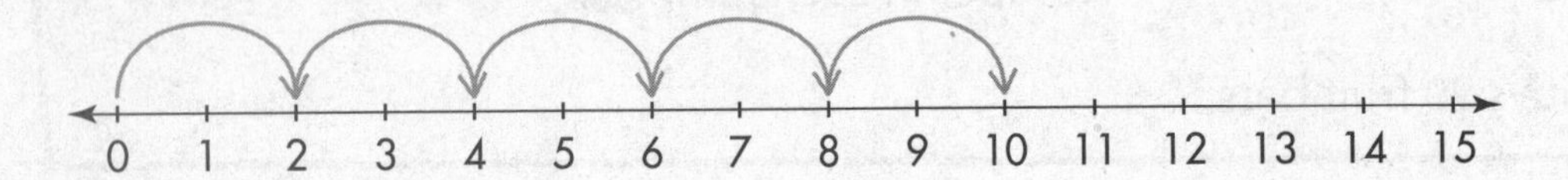

Is her number line correct? Why or why not?

8. Higher Order Thinking Use the number line to compare skip counting by 4s four times to skip counting by 8s two times. How are skip counting by 4s and 8s alike? How are they different? Explain.

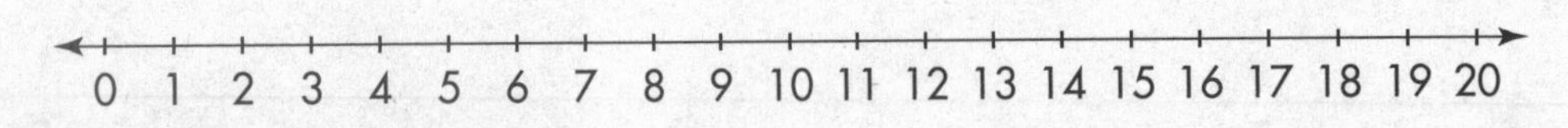

Assessment Practice

9. Which of the following contexts does the number line and the expression 7×2 represent?

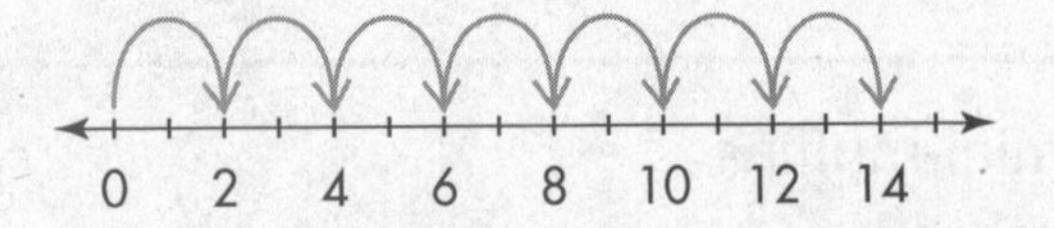

Ⓐ 7 boxes with 7 gifts in each

Ⓑ 7 boxes with 2 gifts in each

Ⓒ 2 boxes with 2 gifts in each

Ⓓ 2 boxes with 7 gifts in each

10. Which of the following contexts does the number line and the expression 4×4 represent?

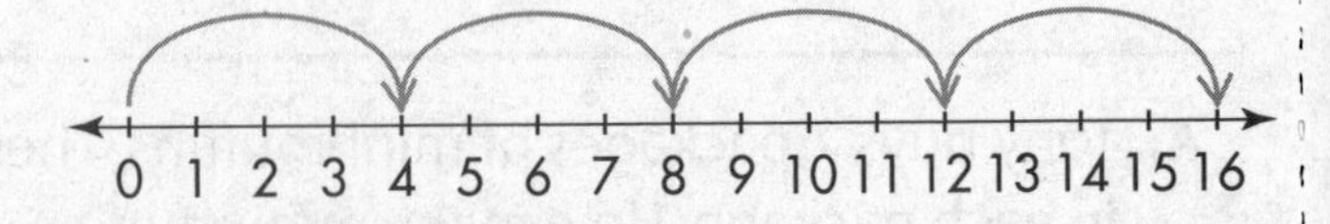

Ⓐ 4 bags with 5 books in each

Ⓑ 3 bags with 4 books in each

Ⓒ 4 bags with 4 books in each

Ⓓ 5 bags with 4 books in each

Name ____________________

Practice Video Tools Games

Additional Practice 1-3
Arrays and Properties

Another Look!

Scott arranges some apples into arrays.
How many apples are in each array?

$3 \times 2 = 6$ $2 \times 3 = 6$

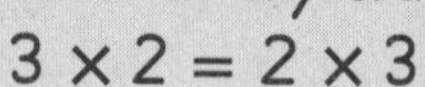

You can use the Commutative Property of Multiplication to multiply numbers in any order.
$3 \times 2 = 2 \times 3$

There are 6 apples in each array.

In **1–3**, fill in the blanks to show skip counting and multiplication for each array.

1.

3, ___, ___

$3 \times$ ___ $= 9$

2.

___, ___

$2 \times$ ___ $=$ ___

3.

___, ___, 15

___ $\times$ ___ $= 15$

In **4** and **5**, draw arrays. Write and solve a multiplication equation for each array.

4. 3×4 4×3

5. 2×5 5×2

6. Karen arranges 24 star stickers in the array shown below. Use counters to help complete the table to show other arrays Karen can make with the same number of star stickers.

Number of Rows of Stars		Number of Stars in Each Row		Total Number of Stars
4	×	6	=	24
	×		=	
	×		=	
	×		=	
	×		=	
	×		=	
	×		=	
	×		=	

7. Construct Arguments Scott puts some sports stickers in rows. He makes 6 rows with 5 stickers in each row. If he puts the same number of stickers in 5 equal rows, how many stickers would be in each row? How do you know?

A good math explanation can include words, numbers, and symbols.

8. Higher Order Thinking Vince has 16 beads. How many different arrays can Vince draw to represent the total number of beads he has? List the sizes of the arrays.

Assessment Practice

9. An equation is shown.

$4 \times 9 = 9 \times \square$

Use the Commutative Property of Multiplication to find the missing factor.

Ⓐ 4

Ⓑ 9

Ⓒ 36

Ⓓ 49

10. Using the Commutative Property of Multiplication, which of the following expressions is equivalent to 7×8?

Ⓐ $8 + 8 + 8 + 8 + 8 + 8 + 8$

Ⓑ 8×7

Ⓒ $7 + 7 + 7 + 7 + 7 + 7 + 7$

Ⓓ $8 + 7$

Name ____________________

Practice Video Tools Games

Additional Practice 1-4
Division: How Many in Each Group?

Another Look!

A.J. has 15 T-shirts. He sorted them equally into 5 laundry bins. How many T-shirts did A.J. put in each bin? You can use a bar diagram to solve.

15 T-shirts → 15

5 bins → | 3 | 3 | 3 | 3 | 3 |

↑ 3 T-shirts in each bin

There are 15 T-shirts. There are 5 equal groups.
There are 3 T-shirts in each group.
So, $15 \div 5 = 3$.

A.J. put 3 T-shirts in each laundry bin.

In **1**, use the bar diagram to help divide.

1. There are 12 tennis balls that need to be packaged equally into 4 cans.

How many tennis balls will be in each can?

12 tennis balls → 12

4 cans → | ? | ? | ? | ? |

↑ ? tennis balls in each can

There are ____ tennis balls.
There are ____ groups.
There are ____ tennis balls in each group.
$12 \div$ ____ $=$ ____

In **2–7**, put an equal number of objects in each group. Use counters or draw a picture to solve. Write the unit for each answer.

2. Sort 16 apples equally into 2 baskets. How many apples are in each basket?

3. Arrange 20 chairs equally at 4 tables. How many chairs are at each table?

4. Seven rabbits share 21 carrots equally. How many carrots does each rabbit get?

5. Five children share 25 dimes equally. How many dimes does each child get?

6. Divide 14 books equally on 2 shelves. How many books are on each shelf?

7. Twenty-four people divide among 3 elevators equally. How many people are in each elevator?

8. **Construct Arguments** Can you divide 14 shirts into 2 equal piles? Why or why not?

9. In February 2015, there were 28 days, all in complete weeks. There are 7 days in a complete week. How many weeks were there in February 2015?

10. Ron and Pam each have 20 pennies. Ron puts his pennies into 4 equal groups. Pam puts her pennies into 5 equal groups. Who has more pennies in each group? Explain.

11. Write the division equation that matches the bar diagram.

16			
?	?	?	?

12. **Algebra** There are 92 students in the third and fourth grades at Johnsonville Elementary. Forty-seven of these students are in fourth grade. Write an equation to find how many third graders there are. Use a question mark to represent the unknown number and solve.

13. **Higher Order Thinking** Kyra has a rock collection. When she puts her rocks into 2 equal piles, there are no rocks left over. When she puts her rocks into 3 equal piles, there are still no rocks left over. When she puts her rocks into 4 equal piles, there are still no rocks left over. How many rocks could Kyra have?

Assessment Practice

14. Which of the following contexts does the expression $30 \div 6$ represent?

Ⓐ 30 beads arranged in 30 equal groups

Ⓑ 6 beads arranged in 30 equal groups

Ⓒ 30 beads arranged in 6 equal groups

Ⓓ 30 beads arranged in 3 equal groups

15. Which of the following contexts does the expression $18 \div 2$ represent?

Ⓐ 18 cubes arranged in 2 equal piles

Ⓑ 18 cubes arranged in 18 equal piles

Ⓒ 2 cubes arranged in 18 equal piles

Ⓓ 18 cubes arranged in 6 equal piles

Name ________________

Practice Video Tools Games

Additional Practice 1-5
Division: How Many Equal Groups?

Another Look!

Layla has 20 raffle tickets.
There are 5 tickets in each book.
How many books of raffle tickets does Layla have? Find $20 \div 5 = \square$.

$20 - 5 = 15$
$15 - 5 = 10$
$10 - 5 = 5$
$5 - 5 = 0$

There are four groups of 5 in 20.

You subtracted 5 four times. So, $20 \div 5 = 4$.

Layla has 4 books of raffle tickets.

In **1**, use repeated subtraction to help solve.

1. Ryan has 10 markers.
There are 5 markers in each box.
How many boxes of markers are there?
Find $10 \div 5 = \square$.

$10 - 5 = $ ____

$5 - $ ____ $=$ ____

I subtracted 5 two times.

So, ____ $\div$ ____ $=$ ____.

Ryan has ____ boxes of markers.

In **2** and **3**, use bar diagrams or counters or draw a picture to solve.

2. There are 16 books. The librarian arranged 4 books on each shelf. How many shelves are there?

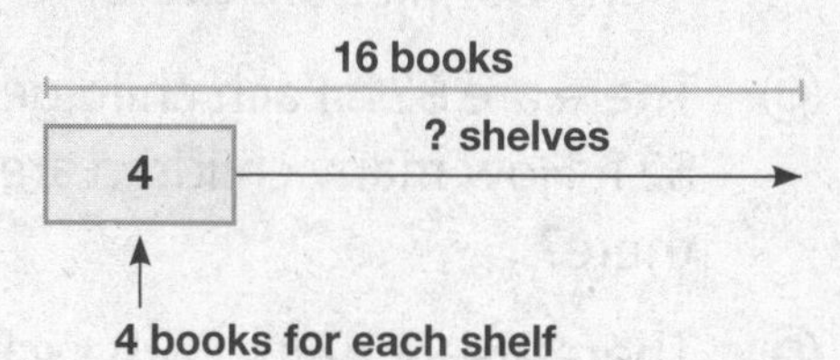

3. Joseph had 28 paintbrushes to give to 4 members of the Art Club. He wanted to give an equal number of brushes to each member. How many brushes did each member get?

4. Daniel has to carry 32 boxes to his room. He can carry 4 boxes on each trip. How many trips will Daniel take? Show your work.

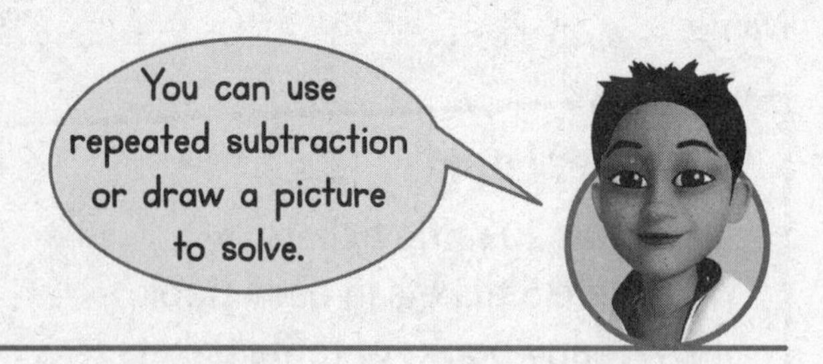

5. Model with Math The United States Mint released 5 state quarters every year. There are 50 states. How many years did it take for all 50 state quarters to be released? Write and solve an equation.

6. Write an equation that represents the bar diagram below.

40				
8	8	8	8	8

7. Number Sense Compare 249 and 271. Write the greater number in word form.

8. Higher Order Thinking A newspaper has more than 30 pages and fewer than 40 pages. The newspaper is divided into sections, and each section has exactly 8 pages. How many sections does the newspaper have?

Assessment Practice

9. A store clerk writes $20 \div 4$. Which problem could the clerk's expression represent?

Ⓐ There are 20 bananas. Each bunch has 10 bananas. How many bunches are there?

Ⓑ There are 20 mugs. Each shelf has 4 mugs. How many shelves have mugs?

Ⓒ There are 20 cans. Each shelf has 2 cans. How many shelves have cans?

Ⓓ There are 4 apples. Each bag has 2 apples. How many bags are there?

10. Tamara writes $21 \div 3$. Which problem could Tamara's expression represent?

Ⓐ There are 21 dolls. Each friend has 3 dolls. How many friends are there?

Ⓑ There are 4 carrots. Each bunny gets 1 carrot. How many bunnies are there?

Ⓒ There are \$21. Each child gets \$21. How many children are there?

Ⓓ There are 21 pens. Each sack has 1 pen. How many sacks are there?

Name ______________________

Additional Practice 1-6
Use Appropriate Tools

Another Look!

Mal downloads 4 songs each week for 5 weeks. Then he sorts the songs into equal groups. There are 10 songs in each group. How many groups are there?

Tell how you can use tools to help solve the problem.

- I can decide which tool is appropriate.
- I can use a tool to represent the situation.
- I can use the tool correctly.

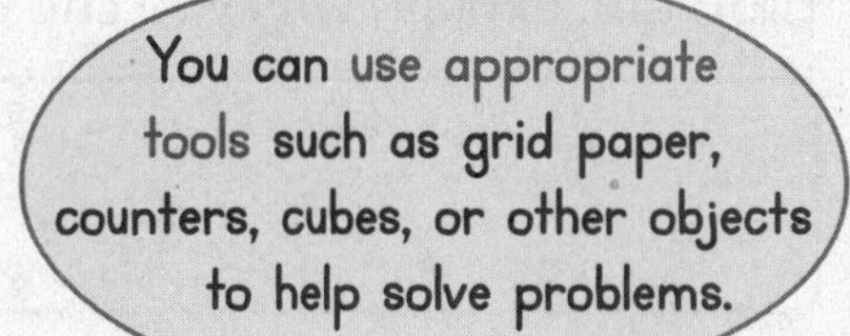

Solve the problem. Explain how you used the tool you chose.

I can use grid paper. Each shaded square represents 1 song.

I shade 4 squares for each week. There are 20 songs. Then I separate them into groups of 10. There are 2 groups.

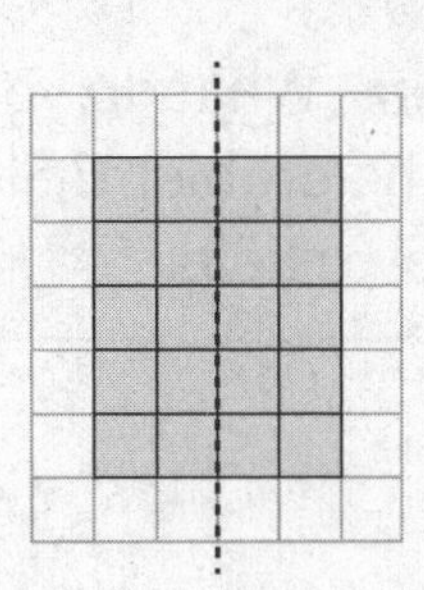

Use Appropriate Tools

Niko bought 4 stamps each week for 3 weeks. He wants to put 6 stamps on each page of his album. How many pages will Niko use?

1. Tell how you can use tools to help solve the problem.

2. Choose a tool to represent the problem. Explain why you chose that tool.

3. Solve the problem. Explain how you used the tool you chose.

Performance Task

Summer Jobs

The table at the right shows how much Tony earns per hour for his summer jobs. One day, Tony spends 3 hours running errands. He wants to use the money from this job to buy two banners.

DATA

Tony's Summer Jobs

Job	Hourly Pay
Walking Dogs	$8
Mowing Lawns	$10
Running Errands	$6

4. **Use Appropriate Tools** Choose a tool to represent the problem. Explain why you chose that tool.

5. **Make Sense and Persevere** What do you need to find out before you can solve the problem? Show a way to find this. You can use a tool to help.

6. **Reasoning** Does Tony have enough money? Use what you know to solve the problem.

7. **Make Sense and Persevere** Did you need all the information in the table to solve the problem? Explain.

8. **Construct Arguments** Tony decides not to buy the banners. Does he have enough money to buy one cap instead? Explain why or why not.

Name ____________________

Practice Video Tools Games

Additional Practice 2-1

2 and 5 as Factors

Another Look!

When you multiply by 2, you can use a doubles fact. For example, 2 × 6 is the same as adding 6 + 6. Both equal 12.

When you multiply by 5, you can use a pattern to find the product.

2s Facts (DATA)

2 × 0 = 0	2 × 5 = 10
2 × 1 = 2	2 × 6 = 12
2 × 2 = 4	2 × 7 = 14
2 × 3 = 6	2 × 8 = 16
2 × 4 = 8	2 × 9 = 18

5s Facts (DATA)

5 × 0 = 0	5 × 5 = 25
5 × 1 = 5	5 × 6 = 30
5 × 2 = 10	5 × 7 = 35
5 × 3 = 15	5 × 8 = 40
5 × 4 = 20	5 × 9 = 45

Each multiple of 2 ends in 0, 2, 4, 6, or 8.

Each multiple of 5 ends in 0 or 5.

In **1–17**, find the missing sum, product, or factor.

1. 2 × 5 = ?
5 + 5 = ____
2 × 5 = ____

2. 2 × 4 = ?
4 + 4 = ____
2 × 4 = ____

3. 1 × 2 = ?
1 + 1 = ____
2 × 1 = ____

4. 5 × ____ = 25

5. 3 × 5 = ____

6. 35 = 7 × ____

7. ____ × 8 = 16

8. 5 × 9 = ____

9. 2 × 7 = ____

10. 5 × 4

11. 1 × 5

12. 2 × 0

13. 8 × 2

14. What is 9 times 2? ____

15. What is 5 times 8? ____

16. What is 6 times 2? ____

17. What is 5 times 0? ____

18. Georgia is making sock puppets. Each pair of socks costs $2. Georgia bought 6 pairs of socks. How much did she spend? Draw a number line to solve.

19. A-Z **Vocabulary** Write an equation where 45 is the product.

20. **Reasoning** There are 5 school days in each week. How many school days are in 9 weeks? Explain.

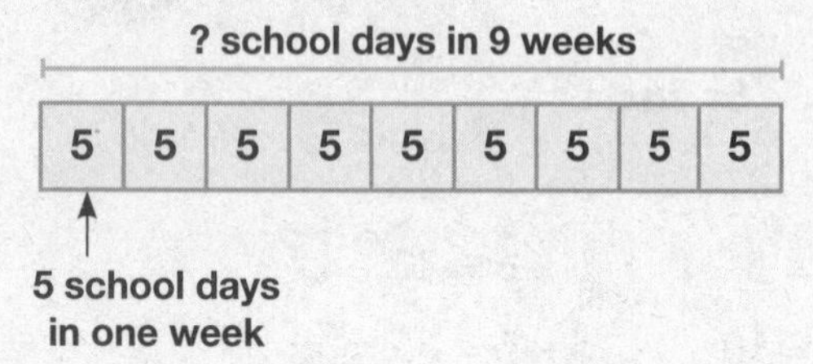

21. Tara walks 2 miles each day. How many miles does Tara walk in a week? How did you find the answer?

22. Mika drew this shape. What is the name of the shape Mika drew? Mika then drew a shape that has 2 fewer sides. What is the name of that shape?

23. **Higher Order Thinking** How can adding doubles help you multiply by 2? Give an example.

Assessment Practice

24. Derek, Sean, and Rebecca are triplets. If they have 5 toes on each of their feet, how many toes do Derek, Sean, and Rebecca have altogether?

Ⓐ 20

Ⓑ 25

Ⓒ 30

Ⓓ 35

25. Caitlin has 3 pairs of glasses. How many lenses are on all of Caitlin's glasses?

Ⓐ 2

Ⓑ 4

Ⓒ 6

Ⓓ 8

Name ______________________

Practice Video Tools Games

Additional Practice 2-2
9 as a Factor

Another Look!

9s Facts
$0 \times 9 = 0$
$1 \times 9 = 9$
$2 \times 9 = 18$
$3 \times 9 = 27$
$4 \times 9 = 36$
$5 \times 9 = 45$
$6 \times 9 = 54$
$7 \times 9 = \blacksquare$
$8 \times 9 = \blacksquare$
$9 \times 9 = \blacksquare$

DATA

The table shows patterns in the 9s facts.

Start with $1 \times 9 = 9$.

When you add ten, you increase the tens place by 1.

When you subtract 1, you decrease the ones place by 1.

Find 7×9.

For each group of 9, add 1 ten and subtract 1 one.

For 7 groups of 9, add 7 tens and subtract 7 ones.

$7 \times 9 = 7$ tens $-$ 7 ones
$7 \times 9 = 70 - 7$
$7 \times 9 = 63$

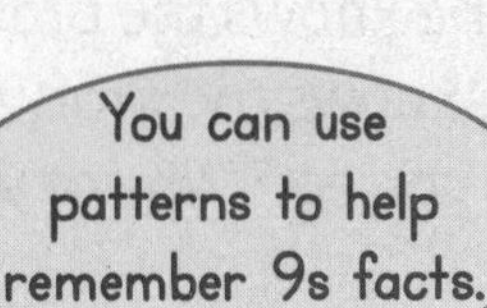

In **1–10**, solve each equation.

1. $9 \times 0 =$ ____

2. $9 \times$ ____ $= 54$

3. $81 = 9 \times$ ____

4. $\begin{array}{r} 9 \\ \times 8 \\ \hline \end{array}$

5. $\begin{array}{r} 7 \\ \times 9 \\ \hline \end{array}$

6. $\begin{array}{r} 4 \\ \times 9 \\ \hline \end{array}$

7. $\begin{array}{r} 2 \\ \times 9 \\ \hline \end{array}$

8. Find 6 times 9.

9. Find 5 times 9.

10. Find 0 times 9.

11. Paula's hair was put into 9 braids. Each braid used 4 beads. How many beads were used? Explain how you found the product.

12. Algebra Tony has 9 sets of baseball cards. Each set contains 6 cards. Write 2 equations that Tony could use to find how many cards he has.

13. Sasha says if she knows the product of 9×8, she also knows the product of 8×9. Is Sasha correct? Why or why not?

14. Make Sense and Persevere Dustin had \$52. He got \$49 more, and then he spent some money. Dustin has \$35 left. How much money did Dustin spend?

15. Higher Order Thinking Jordan received 9 text messages last week. She received 3 times more text messages this week than last week. How many text messages did Jordan receive this week?

16. Rita bought 5 pairs of socks. Each pair cost \$4. How much did Rita spend on socks? Explain how you know.

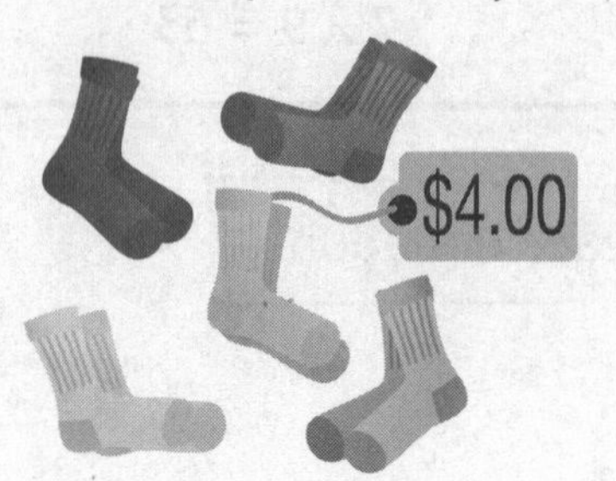

Assessment Practice

17. The zoo has 3 enclosures with 9 northern mockingbirds in each enclosure. How many mockingbirds does the zoo have?

Ⓐ 9
Ⓑ 27
Ⓒ 72
Ⓓ 99

18. Natalia arranged her oranges into an array with 2 oranges in each of 9 rows. How many oranges are in Natalia's array?

Ⓐ 9
Ⓑ 18
Ⓒ 27
Ⓓ 36

Name ____________

Additional Practice 2-3

Apply Properties: Multiply by 0 and 1

Another Look!

Zero and one have special multiplication properties.

The Identity (One) Property of Multiplication

When you multiply a number by 1, the product is that number.

Examples:

$4 \times 1 = 4$ $\quad 16 \times 1 = 16$

$1 \times 9 = 9$ $\quad 13 \times 1 = 13$

$51 \times 1 = 51$ $\quad 1 \times 48 = 48$

The Zero Property of Multiplication

When you multiply a number by 0, the product is 0.

Examples:

$5 \times 0 = 0$ $\quad 123 \times 0 = 0$

$17 \times 0 = 0$ $\quad 0 \times 58 = 0$

$0 \times 51 = 0$ $\quad 74 \times 0 = 0$

In **1–6**, draw a picture to represent the multiplication fact and then solve.

1. $1 \times 3 =$ ____ **2.** $0 \times 6 =$ ____ **3.** $9 \times 0 =$ ____

4. $5 \times 0 =$ ____ **5.** $1 \times 7 =$ ____ **6.** $0 \times 4 =$ ____

In **7–10**, find each product.

7. 7×1 **8.** 8×0 **9.** 8×1 **10.** 10×0

In **11–13**, write <, >, or = in each ◯ to compare.

11. 0×4 ◯ 0×4 **12.** 1×8 ◯ 6×1 **13.** 1×5 ◯ 5×1

14. **Number Sense** Chen says the product of 4×0 is the same as the sum of $4 + 0$. Is Chen correct? Explain.

15. **Model with Math** Sara has 7 boxes for holding seashells. There are 0 shells in each box. How many shells does Sara have? Tell what math you used to find the answer.

16. Bob made a picture graph of the marbles he and his friends have. How many more marbles does Bob have than Kayla? Explain how you found the answer.

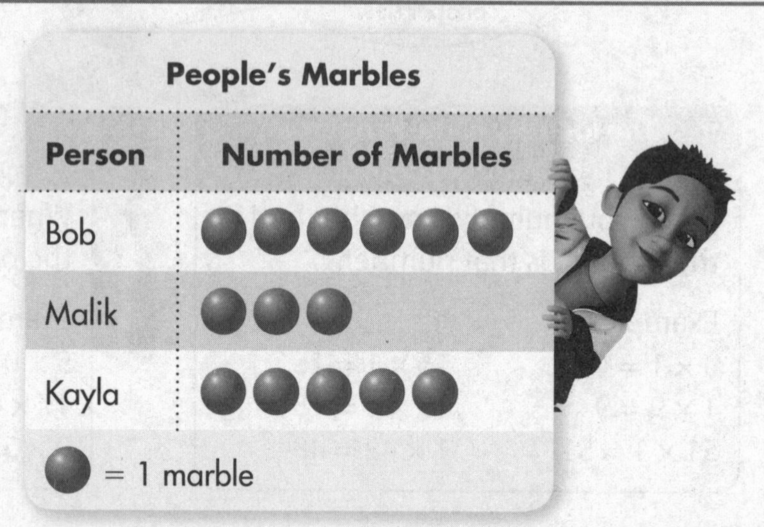

17. Kirsten has 6 coins. She puts the same number of coins in each of 3 envelopes. How many coins does Kirsten put in each envelope?

6 coins

3 envelopes → | ? | ? | ? |

? coins in each envelope

18. **Higher Order Thinking** Chef Morgan's restaurant has 24 tables. Fifteen of the tables each have one flower in a vase. The remaining tables have 5 flowers in each vase. How many flowers are there? Show how you found the answer.

Assessment Practice

19. Use the Zero Property and the Identity Property of Multiplication to select all the correct equations.

- ☐ $2 \times 1 = 1$
- ☐ $0 \times 4 = 0$
- ☐ $1 \times 3 = 3$
- ☐ $0 \times 2 = 0$
- ☐ $4 \times 1 = 4$

20. Use the Zero Property and the Identity Property of Multiplication to select all the correct equations.

- ☐ $0 \times 0 = 1$
- ☐ $1 \times 7 = 1$
- ☐ $5 \times 1 = 5$
- ☐ $0 \times 1 = 0$
- ☐ $1 \times 3 = 1$

Name ______________________

Additional Practice 2-4
Multiply by 10

Another Look!

The table shows multiplication facts for 10.

10s Facts (DATA)

$10 \times 0 = 0$	$10 \times 5 = 50$
$10 \times 1 = 10$	$10 \times 6 = 60$
$10 \times 2 = 20$	$10 \times 7 = 70$
$10 \times 3 = 30$	$10 \times 8 = 80$
$10 \times 4 = 40$	$10 \times 9 = 90$
	$10 \times 10 = 100$

All multiples of 10 in the table end with zero.

Find 5×10.

To find the answer, you can use a number line, place value, or you can use patterns.

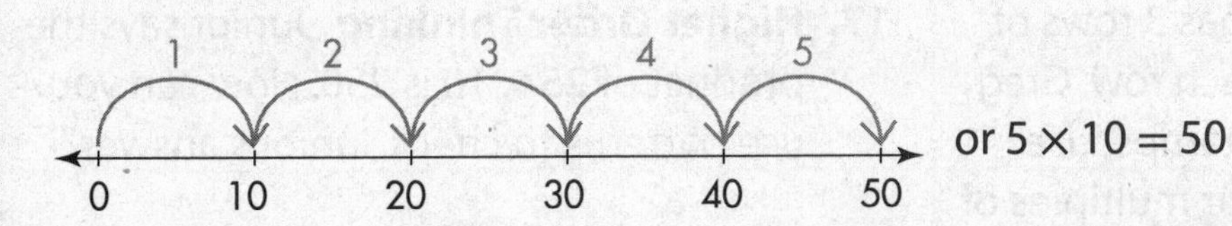

or $5 \times 10 = 50$

In 1 and 2, use the number lines to help find the product.

1. $2 \times 10 =$ ____

2. $4 \times 10 =$ ____

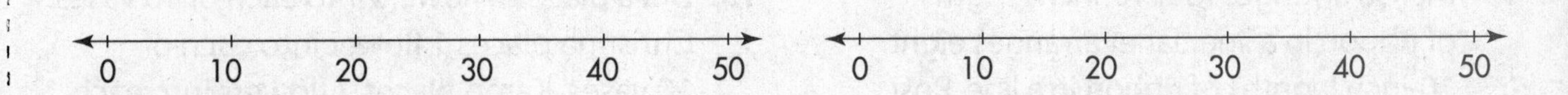

In 3–12, find the product.

3. $10 \times 6 =$ ____

4. $10 \times 10 =$ ____

5. $0 \times 10 =$ ____

6. $1 \times 10 =$ ____

7. $10 \times 3 =$ ____

8. $9 \times 10 =$ ____

9. $\begin{array}{r} 10 \\ \underline{\times 1} \end{array}$

10. $\begin{array}{r} 10 \\ \underline{\times 3} \end{array}$

11. $\begin{array}{r} 10 \\ \underline{\times 8} \end{array}$

12. $\begin{array}{r} 10 \\ \underline{\times 7} \end{array}$

13. Joey made this graph to show how many incorrect answers students got on a test. How many students got 3 answers incorrect? How do you know?

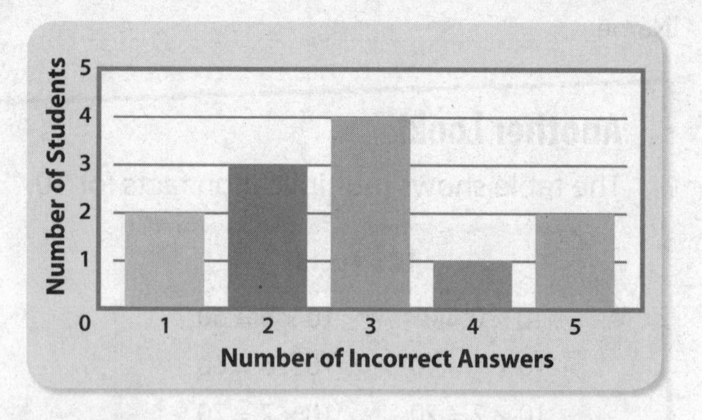

14. **enVision® STEM** Julie sees a ride that spins 10 turns each minute. She says it will spin 40 turns in 4 minutes. Is Julie correct? Explain.

15. **Vocabulary** Define *multiple of 10.*

16. **Critique Reasoning** Greg has 3 rows of stamps with 10 stamps in each row. Greg says there are a total of 35 stamps. Use what you have learned about multiples of 10 to explain why Greg is incorrect.

17. **Higher Order Thinking** Junior says the product of 25×10 is 250. How can you use patterns to check Junior's answer?

Assessment Practice

18. Marcia arranges four 10-inch lengths of ribbon in a line. Janet arranges eight 10-inch lengths of ribbon in a line. Rosi arranges nine 10-inch lengths of ribbon in a line. Select numbers to complete the equations that represent the lengths of the ribbons.

4 8 9 10 40 80

$4 \times 10 = \square$

$\square \times 10 = 80$

$9 \times \square = 90$

19. Delia places 2 flowers into each of 10 vases. Christina places 1 flower into each of 10 vases. Karen places 7 flowers into each of 10 vases. Select numbers to complete the equations that represent the flower arrangements.

1 2 7 10 20 70

$\square \times 2 = 20$

$10 \times \square = 10$

$10 \times 7 = \square$

Name ____________________

Practice Video Tools Games

Additional Practice 2-5

Multiplication Facts: 0, 1, 2, 5, 9, and 10

Another Look!

How many apples are in 5 baskets with 3 apples each?

5 groups of 3 and 3 groups of 5 both have the same number of items: $5 \times 3 = 3 \times 5$.

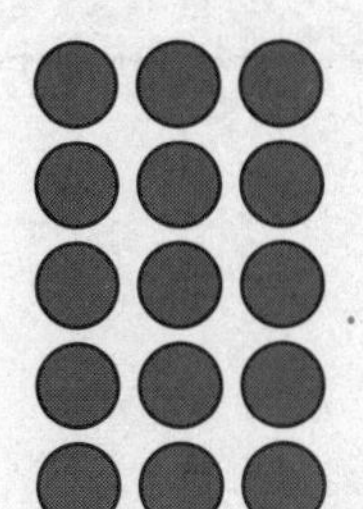

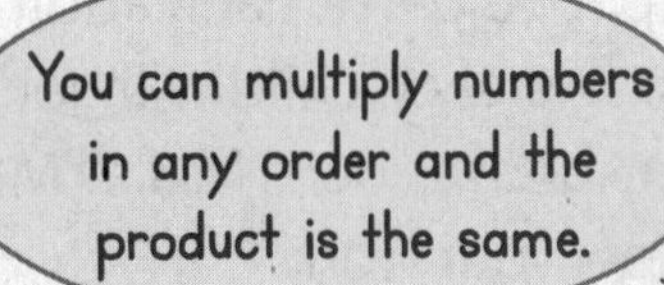

Use a pattern to multiply by 5.

5, 10, 15

$3 \times 5 = 15$

Also, $5 \times 3 = 15$.

In **1–3**, use a pattern to find each product.

1. 7×2 2, 4, ____, ____, ____, ____, ____

$7 \times 2 =$ ____

2. 10×5 ____, ____, ____, ____, ____, ____, ____, ____, ____, ____

$10 \times 5 =$ ____

3. 5×10 ____, ____, ____, ____, ____

$5 \times 10 =$ ____

You can use a pattern to multiply.

In **4–9**, find each product.

4. $2 \times 9 =$ ____

5. $5 \times 8 =$ ____

6. ____ $= 3 \times 2$

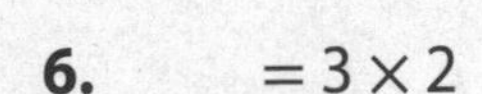

7. $9 \times 1 =$ ____

8. ____ $= 10 \times 10$

9. $0 \times 0 =$ ____

10. Cassy has 9 books on her bookshelf and 3 books on her desk. She wants to know how many books she has in all. What operation should she use? Explain.

11. Ginger found 3 quarters, 2 dimes, and 3 pennies. How much money did she find?

12. Higher Order Thinking Mrs. O'Malley is setting up for a party. Each adult will get 2 glasses, and each child will get 1 glass. How many glasses does Mrs. O'Malley need? Show your work.

Party Guests	
Adults	8
Children	5

13. Norris wrote the equation $7 \times 9 = 63$. Blake wrote the equation $7 \times 9 = 9 \times 7$. Who wrote a correct equation? Explain.

14. Use Appropriate Tools Jana wants to multiply 8×5. Explain what tool she could use to help find the answer. Then solve the problem.

Assessment Practice

15. Vimalesh plants 2 rows of 9 palm trees. Which equation can you use to find the number of palm trees Vimalesh plants?

Ⓐ $2 + 9 = ?$

Ⓑ $2 \times 2 = ?$

Ⓒ $2 \times 9 = ?$

Ⓓ $2 + 2 = ?$

Name ______________________

Practice Video Tools Games

Additional Practice 2-6
Model with Math

Another Look!

Ron has 6 bags. He puts 2 red, 3 yellow, and 4 blue marbles in each bag. How many marbles does Ron have in all?

Explain how you can use the math you know to solve the problem.

- I can find and answer any hidden questions.
- I can use bar diagrams and equations to represent and solve the problem.

You can model with math by using bar diagrams to show the whole and the parts.

Solve the problem.

Find the hidden question:
How many marbles are in each bag?

? marbles in each bag

2	3	4

$2 + 3 + 4 = 9$ marbles in each bag

Use the answer to solve the problem.

? marbles

9	9	9	9	9	9

$6 \times 9 = 54$ marbles in all

Model with Math

Paul has 7 piles of sports cards. There are 3 basketball, 3 football, and 4 baseball cards in each pile. How many total sports cards does Paul have?

1. Explain how you can use the math you know to solve the problem.

2. What is the hidden question you need to answer before you can solve the problem?

3. Solve the problem. Complete the bar diagrams. Show the equations you used.

? sports cards in each pile

___	___	___

? sports cards

___	___	___	___	___	___	___

Jase's Farm

Jase's farm has 9 chickens, each of which laid 3 eggs. Jase's farm has 4 horses. Edna's farm has chickens that laid a total of 23 eggs. Jase wonders whose chickens laid more eggs.

? total chicken eggs

Jase's farm	3	3	3	3	3	3	3	3	3

4. **Make Sense and Persevere** What is a good plan to find whose chickens laid more eggs?

5. **Reasoning** What do you notice in the numbers shown in the bar diagram above? How can this help you solve the problem?

Model with math. When you write equations, think about which operations you can use.

6. **Model with Math** Use equations to show if Jase's or Edna's chickens laid more eggs. How many more eggs did those chickens lay?

7. **Use Appropriate Tools** Lucio says he can use counters to represent the number of eggs laid. Explain how he could do this to find out whose chickens laid more eggs.

Name ______________________

Additional Practice 3-1

The Distributive Property

Another Look!

The array below shows 6×4 or 6 rows of 4 circles.

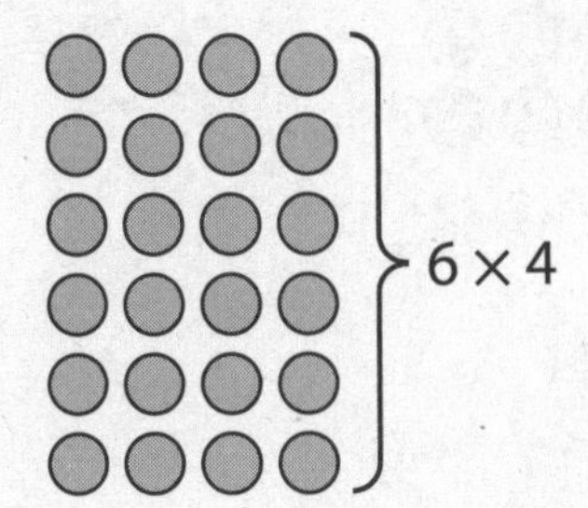

You can draw a line to break **6** rows of 4 circles into **2** rows of 4 circles and **4** rows of 4 circles.

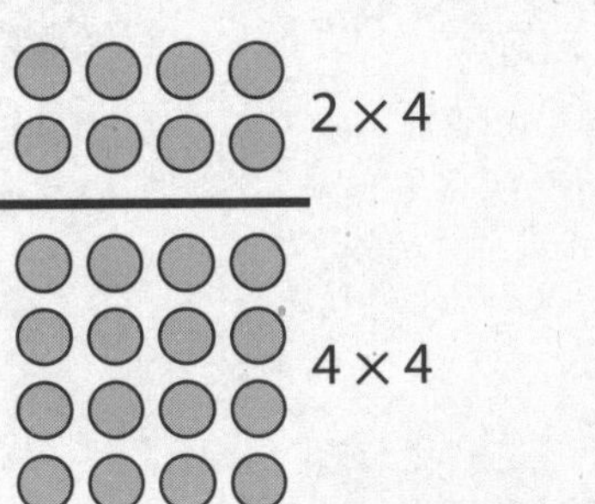

With the Distributive Property, you can break apart a multiplication fact into the sum of two other facts.

In **1** and **2**, draw a line to separate each array into two smaller arrays. Write the new facts.

1. $4 \times 3 = (\_\_\_ \times \_\_\_) + (\_\_\_ \times \_\_\_)$

2. $5 \times 6 = (\_\_\_ \times \_\_\_) + (\_\_\_ \times \_\_\_)$

In **3–10**, use the Distributive Property to find each missing factor.

3. $4 \times 6 = (1 \times 6) + (\_\_\_ \times 6)$

4. $5 \times 8 = (\_\_\_ \times 8) + (2 \times 8)$

5. $4 \times 5 = (\_\_\_ \times 5) + (2 \times \_\_\_)$

6. $7 \times 6 = (3 \times \_\_\_) + (\_\_\_ \times \_\_\_)$

7. $3 \times 8 = (\_\_\_ \times 8) + (2 \times \_\_\_)$

8. $5 \times 7 = (2 \times \_\_\_) + (3 \times \_\_\_)$

9. $4 \times 7 = (\_\_\_ \times \_\_\_) + (2 \times \_\_\_)$

10. $5 \times 5 = (\_\_\_ \times 5) + (4 \times \_\_\_)$

11. Use Structure Tony broke a larger array into a 2×3 array and a 4×3 array. What did the larger array look like? Draw a picture. Write an equation to show the relationship between the larger array and the two smaller arrays.

12. Higher Order Thinking Rosa says she can break this array into 3 different sets of two smaller arrays. Is Rosa correct? Explain.

13. Algebra Marcus passed for 16 yards in the first half of a football game. He passed for a total of 49 yards in the entire game. What was Marcus's total passing yardage in the second half? Write equations to represent and solve the problem. Use ? for the unknown number.

49	
16	?

14. Lulu buys a dress for \$67, a hat for \$35, and shoes for \$49. How much does Lulu spend?

?		
\$67	\$35	\$49

Assessment Practice

15. Using the Distributive Property, which of the following expressions are equivalent to 7×6? Select all that apply.

- ☐ $(6 \times 7) + (6 \times 7)$
- ☐ $(5 \times 6) + (2 \times 6)$
- ☐ $(7 \times 6) + (1 \times 6)$
- ☐ $(7 \times 6) + (2 \times 6)$
- ☐ $(2 \times 6) + (5 \times 6)$

16. An equation is shown. Select all the ways you can use the Distributive Property to find the missing factors.

$7 \times 4 = (\square \times 4) + (\square \times 4)$

- ☐ $7 \times 4 = (5 \times 4) + (2 \times 4)$
- ☐ $7 \times 4 = (7 \times 4) + (1 \times 4)$
- ☐ $7 \times 4 = (1 \times 4) + (6 \times 4)$
- ☐ $7 \times 4 = (2 \times 4) + (5 \times 4)$
- ☐ $7 \times 4 = (6 \times 4) + (1 \times 4)$

Name ______________________

Additional Practice 3-2

Apply Properties: 3 and 4 as Factors

Another Look!

Find 2×3.

$2 \times 3 = 6$

Find 4×3.

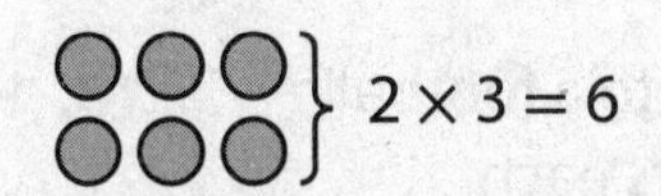

$2 \times 3 = 6$

$2 \times 3 = 6$

$6 + 6 = 12$

So, $4 \times 3 = 12$.

In **1–4**, use arrays or the Distributive Property to find each product.

1. $2 \times$ ___ $=$ ___

___ $\times 4 =$ ___

$8 +$ ___ $=$ ___

So, $3 \times 4 =$ ___.

2. Find 4×2.

___ $\times 2 =$ ___

$2 \times$ ___ $=$ ___

___ $+ 4 =$ ___

So, $4 \times 2 =$ ___.

3. Find 4×4.

$4 \times 4 = (4 \times$ ___$) + ($___ $\times 1)$

$4 \times 4 =$ ___ $+$ ___

$4 \times 4 =$ ___

4. Find 3×6.

$3 \times 6 = (2 \times 6) + ($___ $\times$ ___$)$

$3 \times 6 =$ ___ $+$ ___

$3 \times 6 =$ ___

In **5–14**, find each product.

5. $6 \times 3 =$ ___

6. $3 \times 7 =$ ___

7. $3 \times 3 =$ ___

8. $1 \times 4 =$ ___

9. $0 \times 4 =$ ___

10. $4 \times 9 =$ ___

11. 3×8

12. 5×4

13. 3×2

14. 10×4

15. Generalize How can you use 2s facts to find 4×8?

16. Maria said $7 \times 3 = 21$. Connie said $3 \times 7 = 21$. Who is correct? Explain.

17. Five people bought tickets to a football game. They bought 3 tickets each. How many tickets were bought? Draw an array.

18. Higher Order Thinking Mark is having a party. He invited 35 people. Mark sets up 8 tables with 4 chairs at each table. Does Mark have enough tables and chairs for all of his guests? Explain.

19. Barney divides a rectangle into fourths. Show two ways he could do this.

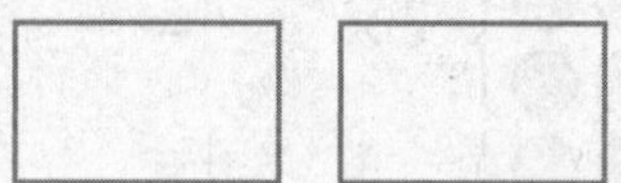

Assessment Practice

20. Jillian bought 3 boxes of crayons. Each box had the same number of crayons. Which equation can be used to find the number of crayons Jillian bought?

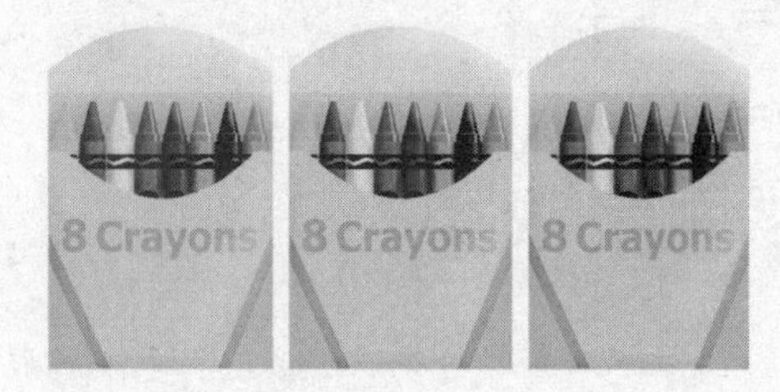

Ⓐ $(3 \times 8) + (3 \times 8) = ?$

Ⓑ $(3 \times 4) + (3 \times 4) = ?$

Ⓒ $(8 \times 8) + (3 \times 3) = ?$

Ⓓ $(3 \times 3) + (8 \times 8) = ?$

21. Which of the following is **NOT** a way to use the Distributive Property to find 4×7?

Ⓐ $(4 \times 3) + (4 \times 3)$

Ⓑ $(2 \times 7) + (2 \times 7)$

Ⓒ $(4 \times 3) + (4 \times 4)$

Ⓓ $(4 \times 2) + (4 \times 5)$

Name ______________________

Practice Video Tools Games

Additional Practice 3-3

Apply Properties: 6 and 7 as Factors

Another Look!

You can use multiplication facts you already know to find other multiplication facts.

Find 6×9. Use a 3s fact.

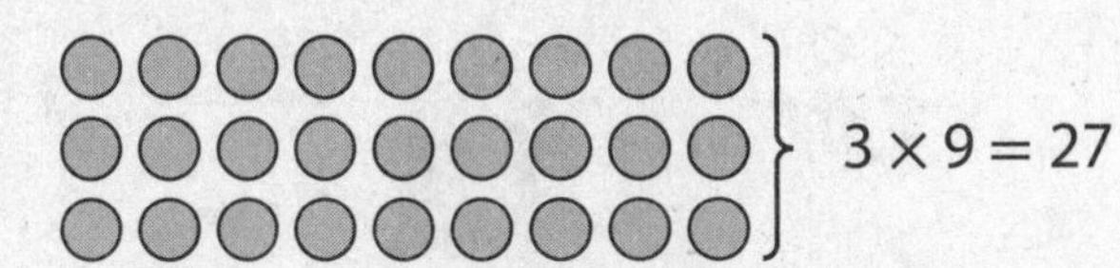

$3 \times 9 = 27$

$3 \times 9 = 27$

$27 + 27 = 54$

So, $6 \times 9 = 54$

Find 7×5. Use a 2s fact.

$2 \times 5 = 10$

$5 \times 5 = 25$

$10 + 25 = 35$

So, $7 \times 5 = 35$.

In **1** and **2**, use known facts to find each product.

1. $6 \times 4 = ?$

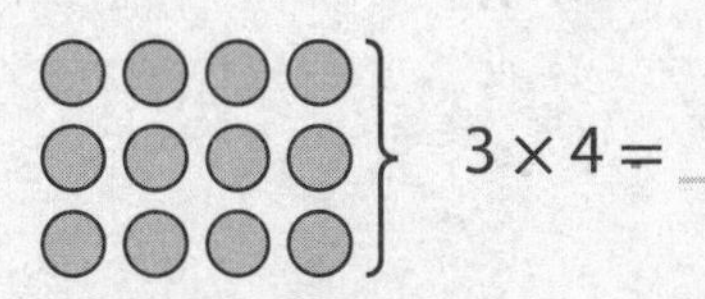

$3 \times 4 =$ ____

$3 \times 4 =$ ____

$12 +$ ____ $=$ ____

So, $6 \times 4 =$ ____.

2. $7 \times 4 = ?$

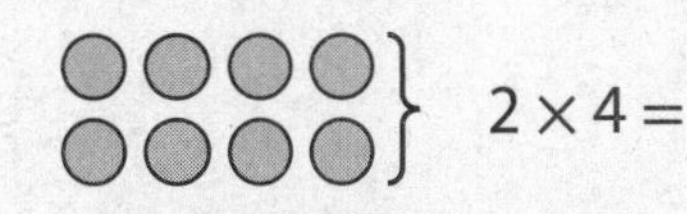

$2 \times 4 =$ ____

$5 \times 4 =$ ____

____ $+$ ____ $=$ ____

So, $7 \times 4 =$ ____.

In **3–11**, find each product.

3. $2 \times 7 =$ ____

4. $6 \times 7 =$ ____

5. $7 \times 9 =$ ____

6. $6 \times 4 =$ ____

7. $6 \times 8 =$ ____

8. $7 \times 7 =$ ____

9. $6 \times 2 =$ ____

10. $8 \times 7 =$ ____

11. $3 \times 7 =$ ____

12. Emmet buys 7 egg salad sandwiches at Sam's Café. How much money does Emmet spend?

13. Al buys 4 chicken salad sandwiches and 3 tuna salad sandwiches. How much money does Al spend? How did you find the answer?

Sandwiches	
Tuna Salad	$6
Egg Salad	$4
Chicken Salad	$7

14. **enVision® STEM** Raul's science class is studying chicken eggs. The eggs take 3 weeks to hatch. There are 7 days in each week. How many days does it take for the eggs to hatch?

15. **Number Sense** What multiplication fact can be found by using the arrays for 2×9 and 5×9?

16. **Use Appropriate Tools** Nan made an array to find $5 \times 3 = 15$. How can she use a tool to show 6×3?

17. **Higher Order Thinking** Harold says, "To find 6×8, I can use the facts for 5×4 and 1×4." Do you agree? Explain.

Assessment Practice

18. Select numbers to create a different expression that is equal to 8×7.

2 3 5 7 8 9

$8 \times 7 = (\square \times 7) + (\square \times 7)$

19. Select numbers to create a different expression that is equal to 7×9.

2 3 4 6 8 9

$7 \times 9 = (\square \times 9) + (\square \times \square)$

Name ______________________

Additional Practice 3-4

Apply Properties: 8 as a Factor

Another Look!

Find 8×6. Double a 4s fact.

$4 \times 6 = 24$

$4 \times 6 = 24$

$24 + 24 = 48$

So, $8 \times 6 = 48$.

DATA

4s Facts	
$4 \times 0 = 0$	$4 \times 5 = 20$
$4 \times 1 = 4$	$4 \times 6 = 24$
$4 \times 2 = 8$	$4 \times 7 = 28$
$4 \times 3 = 12$	$4 \times 8 = 32$
$4 \times 4 = 16$	$4 \times 9 = 36$

In **1** and **2**, double a 4s fact to find the product.

1. $8 \times 5 = ?$

$4 \times 5 =$ ____

$4 \times 5 =$ ____

$20 +$ ____ $=$ ____

So, $8 \times 5 =$ ____.

2. $8 \times 3 = ?$

$4 \times 3 =$ ____

$4 \times 3 =$ ____

____ $+$ ____ $=$ ____

So, $8 \times 3 =$ ____.

In **3–9**, find the products.

3. $2 \times 8 =$ ____

4. $4 \times 8 =$ ____

5. $8 \times 5 =$ ____

6. 7×8

7. 8×9

8. 1×8

9. 8×6

10. Luis made the arrays shown at the right to find 5×8. Explain how he could change the arrays to find 7×8. Add to Luis's drawing to show your solution.

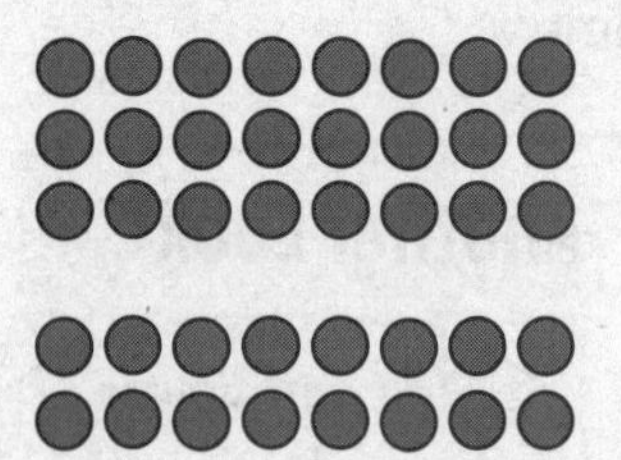

11. **enVision® STEM** An octopus has 8 arms. At the aquarium there are 3 octopuses in one tank. How many arms do the octopuses have all together? What are two strategies you can use to find the answer?

12. **Use Structure** During the California Gold Rush, miners sometimes paid \$10 for a glass of water. What was the total cost if 8 miners each bought one glass of water? How can you use a 4s fact to find the answer?

13. How many pints are in 5 gallons?

14. **Higher Order Thinking** Lila makes a chart that has 8 rows and 4 columns. How many spaces are in her chart? Explain why Lila can use 8s facts or 4s facts to solve.

Assessment Practice

15. Ted is stocking a shelf with packages of rolls. There are 8 rolls in each package. Select all the correct equations that could show how many rolls are on the shelf.

- ☐ $4 \times 8 = 32$
- ☐ $2 \times 8 = 16$
- ☐ $7 \times 8 = 65$
- ☐ $6 \times 8 = 44$
- ☐ $9 \times 8 = 72$

16. Select all the expressions that can be used to find 8×5.

- ☐ $(4 \times 5) + (4 \times 5)$
- ☐ $(4 \times 4) + (4 \times 1)$
- ☐ $(4 \times 3) + (4 \times 2)$
- ☐ $(8 \times 3) + (8 \times 2)$
- ☐ $(2 \times 5) + (2 \times 5) + (2 \times 5) + (2 \times 5)$

Name ______________________

 Practice  Video  Tools Games

Additional Practice 3-5
Practice Multiplication Facts

Another Look!

Find 8×4.

You can use a picture or known facts to find 8×4.

Picture

8×4 means 8 groups of 4.

?							
4	4	4	4	4	4	4	4

Combine equal groups to find the product.

So, $8 \times 4 = 32$.

Known Facts

Use 4s facts to help.

$4 \times 4 = 16$

$4 \times 4 = 16$

$16 + 16 = 32$

So, $8 \times 4 = 32$.

In **1** and **2**, use a picture and known facts to find the product.

1. $3 \times 6 = ?$

?		
6	6	____
6	12	____

$2 \times 6 =$ ____

$1 \times 6 =$ ____

$3 \times 6 =$ ____

$12 +$ ____ $=$ ____

2. $3 \times 3 = ?$

?		
3	3	____
3	6	____

$2 \times 3 =$ ____

$1 \times 3 =$ ____

$3 \times 3 =$ ____

$6 +$ ____ $=$ ____

In **3–8**, multiply.

3. $3 \times 2 =$ ____

4. $8 \times 3 =$ ____

5. $6 \times 7 =$ ____

6. $10 \times 7 =$ ____

7. $4 \times 0 =$ ____

8. $7 \times 2 =$ ____

9. Make Sense and Persevere The home team had 4 three-pointers, 10 two-pointers, and 6 free throws. The visiting team scored 5 three-pointers, 8 two-pointers, and 5 free throws. Which team scored more points? Explain.

Basketball Points

Type	Points
Three-Pointer	3 points
Two-Pointer	2 points
Free Throw	1 point

10. Higher Order Thinking Martina has 3 bags of tennis balls. There are 6 pink, 5 yellow, and 2 white balls in each bag. How many tennis balls does Martina have in all? Show how you found the answer.

11. Number Sense Without multiplying, how can you tell which product will be greater, 4×3 or 4×5? Explain.

12. Kristie has 4 rows of 9 stalls in her barn. If each stall has 1 horse, how many horses are in the barn?

13. Jeremy flew 8 times last week for work. If each flight was 2 hours long, how much time did Jeremy spend in the air?

Assessment Practice

14. Select the possible ways to display 30 counters in equal groups.

- ☐ 2 groups of 10
- ☐ 3 groups of 10
- ☐ 5 groups of 6
- ☐ 6 groups of 5
- ☐ 10 groups of 3

15. Select the possible ways to display 18 counters in an array.

- ☐ 3 rows of 6
- ☐ 9 rows of 2
- ☐ 6 rows of 3
- ☐ 8 rows of 3
- ☐ 2 rows of 9

Name ____________________

Practice Video Tools Games

Additional Practice 3-6

The Associative Property: Multiply with 3 Factors

Another Look!

Use the Associative Property of Multiplication to find the product of $4 \times 2 \times 5$.

The Associative Property of Multiplication states that the way the factors are grouped does not change the product.

One Way

$4 \times 2 \times 5$

$(4 \times 2) \times 5$

$8 \times 5 = 40$

Another Way

$4 \times 2 \times 5$

$4 \times (2 \times 5)$

$4 \times 10 = 40$

1. Find the product of $4 \times 2 \times 3$ two different ways.

$4 \times 2 \times 3$

$(4 \times 2) \times 3$

___ $\times 3 =$ ___

$4 \times 2 \times 3$

$4 \times (2 \times 3)$

$4 \times$ ___ $=$ ___

In **2–16**, find each product. You may draw a picture to help.

2. $3 \times 2 \times 1 =$ ___

3. $2 \times 3 \times 5 =$ ___

4. $4 \times 3 \times 2 =$ ___

5. $4 \times 2 \times 7 =$ ___

6. $3 \times 3 \times 2 =$ ___

7. $2 \times 4 \times 5 =$ ___

8. $2 \times 2 \times 6 =$ ___

9. $4 \times 1 \times 5 =$ ___

10. $5 \times 1 \times 3 =$ ___

11. $6 \times 1 \times 5 =$ ___

12. $3 \times 3 \times 4 =$ ___

13. $4 \times 2 \times 6 =$ ___

14. $5 \times 5 \times 2 =$ ___

15. $2 \times 2 \times 5 =$ ___

16. $3 \times 2 \times 2 =$ ___

17. Mrs. Stokes bought 3 packages of fruit juice. Each package has 2 rows with 6 boxes in each row. How many boxes of fruit juice did Mrs. Stokes buy? Use equations to solve.

18. **Higher Order Thinking** Write two different multiplication equations for the arrays shown and find the product.

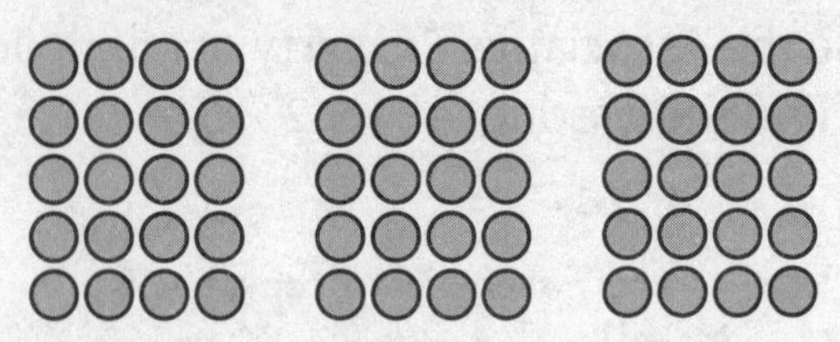

19. Matt has a block. He uses one of the flat surfaces of the block to trace a triangle. What type of solid figure is Matt's block?

20. **Vocabulary** Write an equation that has 20 as the *product* and 4 as a *factor*.

21. **Reasoning** Amy has 3 bags of marbles, and Ron has 2 bags of marbles. There are 6 marbles in each of their bags. How many marbles do they have in all? Show how you know.

22. Marco bought 6 sheets of stamps. On each sheet there are 3 rows of stamps with 3 stamps in each row. How many stamps did Marco buy?

Assessment Practice

23. Use properties of operations to select all the expressions that could be used to find $5 \times 2 \times 3$.

- ☐ $(2 \times 5) \times 3$
- ☐ $5 \times 2 \times 2$
- ☐ $5 \times (3 \times 2)$
- ☐ $(5 \times 2) \times 3$
- ☐ $5 \times (2 \times 3)$

24. An expression is shown. Select all the equivalent expressions.

$5 \times 1 \times 9$

- ☐ $(5 \times 1) \times 9$
- ☐ $(1 \times 5) \times 9$
- ☐ $(5 \times 1) \times 5$
- ☐ $5 \times (1 \times 9)$
- ☐ $(9 \times 9) \times 1$

Name ______________________

Practice Video Tools Games

Additional Practice 3-7
Repeated Reasoning

Another Look!

John used facts he knows to solve 6×7 and 6×5. He wrote these equations.

$6 \times 7 = (5 \times 7) + (1 \times 7) = 42$

$6 \times 5 = (5 \times 5) + (1 \times 5) = 30$

Tell how you can use repeated reasoning to find multiplication facts.

- I can look for repeated calculations.
- I can make generalizations about the repeated calculations.

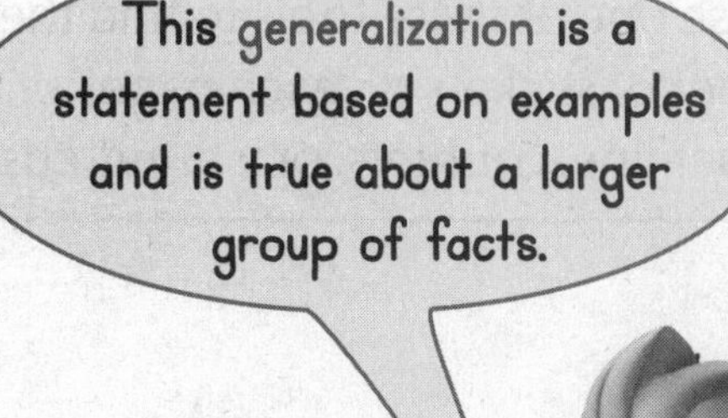

Make a generalization.
Test whether this is true for other facts.

I can break facts with 6 into 5s and 1s facts.

This is true for other facts with 6: $6 \times 9 = (5 \times 9) + (1 \times 9) = 54$

Generalize
Pam wrote the equations below.

1. Tell how you can use repeated reasoning to find multiplication facts.

2. Which factors did Pam use repeatedly? Make a generalization.

$7 \times 6 = (5 \times 6) + (2 \times 6) = 42$

$7 \times 9 = (5 \times 9) + (2 \times 9) = 63$

$7 \times 7 = (5 \times 7) + (2 \times 7) = 49$

3. Complete this equation to test whether your generalization is true for other facts. Explain.
$7 \times 8 = (\_ \times \_) + (\_ \times \_) = \_\_\_$

Performance Task

Julia puts her stickers into arrays in an album. Some of her stickers are animal stickers. There are a different number of stickers on each page. The table at the right shows information about the stickers in Julia's album.

DATA

Julia's Stickers

Page Number	Animal Stickers	Rows of Stickers	Columns of Stickers
1	7	4	7
2	4	4	6
3	9	8	9
4	9	8	6

4. **Use Appropriate Tools** Explain how you can use one of these tools to find the number of stickers on each page: a number line, counters, or a hundreds chart.

5. **Make Sense and Persevere** Julia multiplies to find the total number of stickers on each page. For each page, tell the factors that she multiplies.

6. **Use Structure** Look at the facts you wrote for Exercise **5**. Break these facts into 1s, 2s, 3s, and 5s facts to find the total number of stickers on each page.

Page 1
(___ × ___) = (___ × ___) + (___ × ___) = ___
Page 2
(___ × ___) = (___ × ___) + (___ × ___) = ___
Page 3
(___ × ___) = (___ × ___) + (___ × ___) = ___
Page 4
(___ × ___) = (___ × ___) + (___ × ___) = ___

7. **Generalize** Look at the 1s, 2s, 3s, and 5s facts above. What generalizations can you make? Test each generalization with another fact.

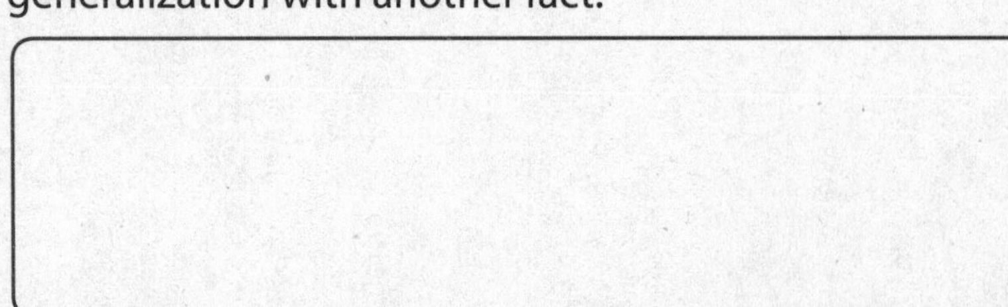

Name ________________________

Practice Video Tools Games

Additional Practice 4-1
Relate Multiplication and Division

Another Look!

Multiplication

6 rows of 4 glue sticks

$6 \times 4 = 24$

24 glue sticks

Division

24 glue sticks in 6 equal rows

$24 \div 6 = 4$

4 glue sticks in each row

Here is the fact family for 4, 6, and 24:

$4 \times 6 = 24$ $\quad$ $24 \div 4 = 6$

$6 \times 4 = 24$ $\quad$ $24 \div 6 = 4$

In **1** and **2**, use the relationship between multiplication and division to complete each equation.

1. $2 \times 7 = 14$

$14 \div 2 =$ ____

2. $81 \div 9 = 9$

$9 \times$ ____ $= 81$

In **3–6**, write the fact family.

3. Write the fact family for 4, 7, and 28.

4. Write the fact family for 2, 10, and 20.

5. Write the fact family for 2, 8, and 16.

6. Write the fact family for 7, 8, and 56.

7. Use the array to write a multiplication equation and a division equation.

8. **Higher Order Thinking** For every row of objects in an array there are 2 columns. The total number of objects in the array is 18. How many rows and columns does the array have?

9. **enVision® STEM** Julio's class was making bridges out of balsa wood to see which bridge could hold the most weight. Each of the 4 people in Julio's group made 2 bridges. What fact family represents the total bridges made by the group?

DATA

Name	Bridges Made
Julio	2
Rosa	2
Miguel	2
Clara	2

10. **Reasoning** There are 5 pairs of scissors in one package. Mrs. Hill bought 35 scissors for students in her art classes. How many packages did she buy?

11. Serena has a set of toy trains. She has 3 passenger cars. What is the total length of her passenger cars?

DATA

Serena's Train Cars

Type	Length in Inches
Engine	4
Tender	3
Passenger Car	9
Caboose	7

Assessment Practice

12. Select numbers to create a multiplication equation that could be used to solve $14 \div 2 = \square$.

2 3 4 7 14 20

$\square \times 2 = \square$

13. Select numbers to create a multiplication equation that could be used to solve $42 \div 7 = \square$.

2 3 6 7 24 42

$\square \times 7 = \square$

Name ______________________

Practice Video Tools Games

Additional Practice 4-2

Use Multiplication to Divide with 2, 3, 4, and 5

Another Look!

You can think multiplication to find division facts.

Find $16 \div 2$.

What You Think	What You Write
$2 \times ? = 16$ ↑ 2 times what number equals 16? $2 \times 8 = 16$	$16 \div 2 = 8$

Find $12 \div 3$.

What You Think	What You Write
$3 \times ? = 12$ ↑ 3 times what number equals 12? $3 \times 4 = 12$	$12 \div 3 = 4$

Find $24 \div 4$.

What You Think	What You Write
$4 \times ? = 24$ ↑ 4 times what number equals 24? $4 \times 6 = 24$	$24 \div 4 = 6$

Find $40 \div 5$.

What You Think	What You Write
$5 \times ? = 40$ ↑ 5 times what number equals 40? $5 \times 8 = 40$	$40 \div 5 = 8$

In **1–16**, find each quotient.

1. $14 \div 2 =$ ____

2. $35 \div 5 =$ ____

3. $15 \div 3 =$ ____

4. $32 \div 4 =$ ____

5. $9 \div 3 =$ ____

6. $18 \div 2 =$ ____

7. $16 \div 2 =$ ____

8. $21 \div 3 =$ ____

9. $2\overline{)12}$

10. $3\overline{)27}$

11. $5\overline{)25}$

12. $4\overline{)20}$

13. $5\overline{)30}$

14. $5\overline{)45}$

15. $2\overline{)10}$

16. $4\overline{)28}$

17. Be Precise You have 18 erasers and use 3 erasers each month. How many months will your erasers last? Identify the quotient, dividend, and divisor.

18. Write a fact family using the numbers 5, 6, and 30.

19. Paul drew two different polygons. One shape has 4 sides. The other shape has fewer than 4 sides. What could be the two shapes Paul drew?

20. Megan arranges 25 chairs into 5 equal rows. Write and solve an equation to find how many chairs are in each row.

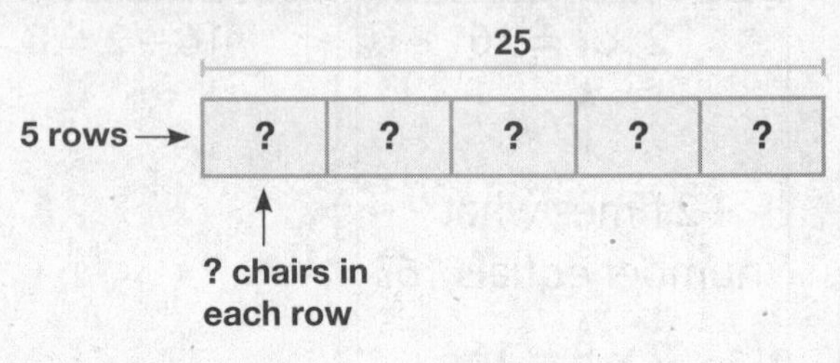

21. Higher Order Thinking Carl has 16 rubber balls to share with his 2 brothers and 1 sister. If Carl and his brothers and sister each get the same number of rubber balls, how many rubber balls will each of them get?

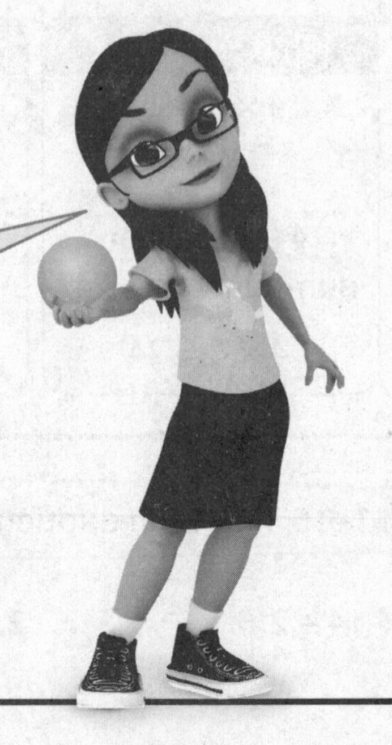

Assessment Practice

22. Which expression can help you divide $40 \div 5$?

Ⓐ 5×8
Ⓑ 5×7
Ⓒ 5×6
Ⓓ 5×5

23. Which expression can help you divide $16 \div 4$?

Ⓐ 4×3
Ⓑ 4×4
Ⓒ 4×5
Ⓓ 4×6

Name ______________________

Practice Video Tools Games

Additional Practice 4-3

Use Multiplication to Divide with 6 and 7

Another Look!

Martha has 42 pine trees to plant on a plot of land. If Martha plants the trees in 6 equal rows, how many trees will be in each row? If she plants 7 equals rows, how many trees will be in each row?

You can divide to find how many trees are in each row.

Find $42 \div 6$.

What You Think	What You Write
What number times 6 is 42?	$42 \div 6 = 7$
$7 \times 6 = 42$	There will be 7 trees in each row.

Find $42 \div 7$.

What You Think	What You Write
What number times 7 is 42?	$42 \div 7 = 6$
$6 \times 7 = 42$	There will be 6 trees in each row.

In **1** and **2**, draw a bar diagram to find the quotient.

1. Find $56 \div 7$.

2. Find $36 \div 6$.

In **3–13**, find the quotient.

3. $30 \div 6 =$ ____

4. $28 \div 7 =$ ____

5. $42 \div 6 =$ ____

6. $54 \div 6 =$ ____

7. $6\overline{)48}$

8. $7\overline{)56}$

9. $7\overline{)70}$

10. $7\overline{)49}$

11. Divide 60 by 6.

12. Divide 7 by 7.

13. Find 21 divided by 7.

In **14** and **15**, use the picture at the right.

There are 7 sides on the birdhouse.

14. Each side of the birdhouse will need 9 nails. How many nails are needed for the whole birdhouse?

15. If only 7 nails are used on each side, how will the total number of nails needed change?

16. Twenty-four students are going to the zoo. They are going in 4 equal groups. Write and solve an equation to find how many students are in each group.

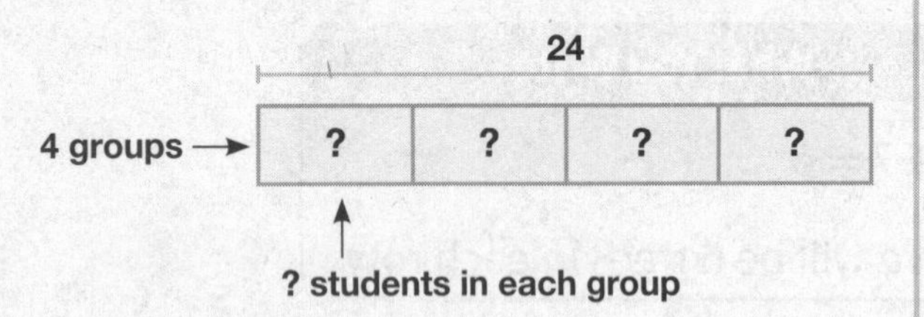

17. Make Sense and Persevere There are 42 roses in the garden. Diane picks 7 roses for each bouquet of flowers. How many bouquets can she make? How many more bouquets can Diane make if she uses 6 roses in each bouquet?

18. Higher Order Thinking Juanita read 48 pages. She read more than 5 chapters, but less than 10 chapters. All chapters are the same length. How many chapters could Juanita have read? How many pages are in those chapters?

19. Manny has 28 chapters in a book to read. He reads 7 chapters each week. How many weeks will it take for Manny to read the book?

Assessment Practice

20. Which multiplication fact can you use to help find the value of the unknown number in the equation $49 \div 7 = \square$?

Ⓐ 5×7

Ⓑ 6×7

Ⓒ 7×7

Ⓓ 8×7

21. Which multiplication fact can you use to help find the value of the unknown number in the equation $48 \div 6 = \square$?

Ⓐ 5×6

Ⓑ 6×6

Ⓒ 7×6

Ⓓ 8×6

Name ______________________

 Practice  Video  Tools  Games

Additional Practice 4-4

Use Multiplication to Divide with 8 and 9

Another Look!

Multiplication facts can help you to find division facts when 8 or 9 is the divisor.

There are 32 counters. There are 8 rows of counters. How many counters are in each row?

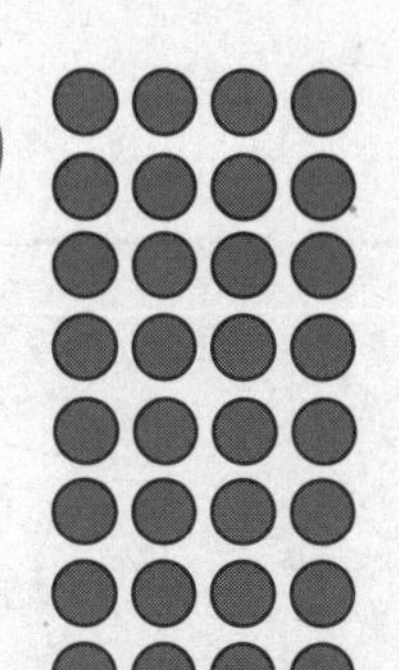

Find $32 \div 8$.

What You Think	What You Write
8 times what number equals 32? $8 \times 4 = 32$	$32 \div 8 = 4$ There are 4 counters in each row.

There are 45 counters. There are 9 equal groups. How many counters are in each group?

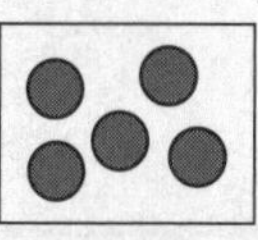 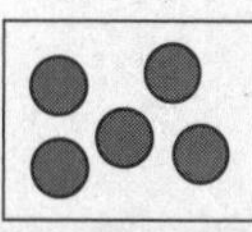 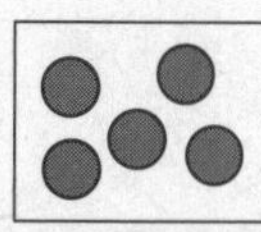

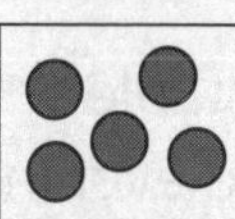 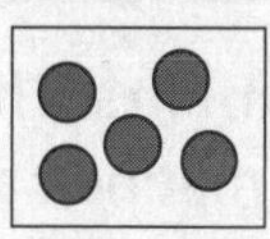 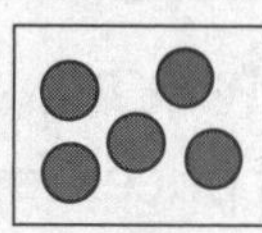

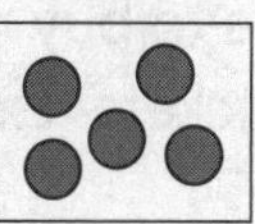 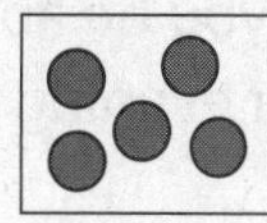 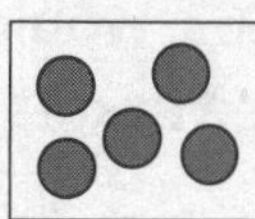

Find $45 \div 9$.

What You Think	What You Write
9 times what number equals 45? $9 \times 5 = 45$	$45 \div 9 = 5$ There are 5 counters in each group.

In **1–3**, use the multiplication equation to help find each quotient.

1. $54 \div 9 = ?$
$9 \times$ ____ $= 54$
So, $54 \div 9 =$ ____.

2. $24 \div 8 = ?$
$8 \times$ ____ $= 24$
So, $24 \div 8 =$ ____.

3. $56 \div 8 = ?$
$8 \times$ ____ $= 56$
So, $56 \div 8 =$ ____.

In **4–12**, find each quotient.

4. $36 \div 9 =$ ____

5. $63 \div 9 =$ ____

6. $80 \div 8 =$ ____

7. $9\overline{)72}$

8. $8\overline{)48}$

9. $9\overline{)81}$

10. $8\overline{)8}$

11. $9\overline{)90}$

12. $9\overline{)27}$

13. Maluwa has 9 identical tiles. When she counts the total number of sides on the tiles, she gets 72. Draw a picture of what her tile could look like, and name that shape.

14. Each month Bailey deposits money in her savings account. Over 8 months, she has added \$48. If Bailey deposited the same amount every month, how much is one deposit?

15. **Construct Arguments** The table at the right shows prices for matinee and evening movies. With \$63, would you be able to buy more matinee tickets or evening tickets? Explain.

DATA

Movie Prices	
Matinee	\$7
Evening Movie	\$9

16. Teri scored 64 points in the first 8 basketball games she played in. She scored the same number of points in each game. Write and solve an equation to find the number of points Teri scored in each game.

17. **Higher Order Thinking** Adam made 19 paper cranes on Monday and 8 more on Tuesday. He gave all the cranes away to 9 friends so that each friend had the same number of cranes. How many cranes did each friend receive? Explain your answer.

Assessment Practice

18. Find $72 \div 8$ by selecting numbers to complete the following equations. Numbers may be selected more than once.

2 3 6 8 9

$8 \times \square = 72$

$72 \div 8 = \square$

19. Find $27 \div 9$ by selecting numbers to complete the following equations. Numbers may be selected more than once.

2 3 4 8 9

$9 \times \square = 27$

$27 \div 9 = \square$

Name ______________________

Additional Practice 4-5
Multiplication Patterns: Even and Odd Numbers

Another Look!

Even numbers have 0, 2, 4, 6, or 8 in the ones place. Odd numbers have 1, 3, 5, 7, or 9 in the ones place.

Think about the numbers 0, 2, 4, 6, and 8. When you divide these numbers by 2, nothing is left over.
These numbers are even.

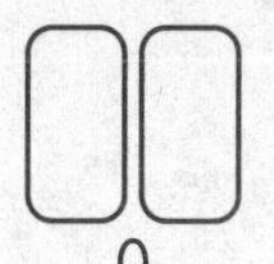
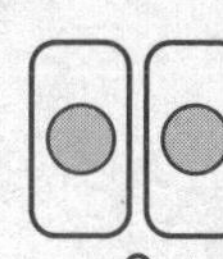
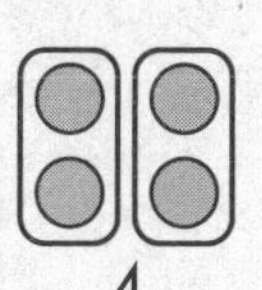

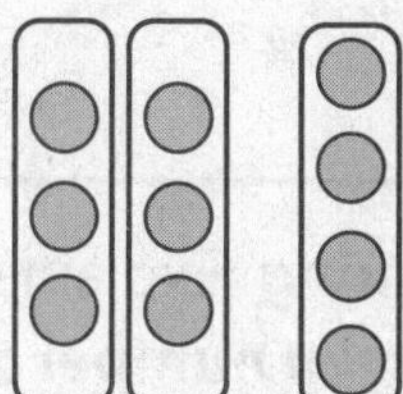
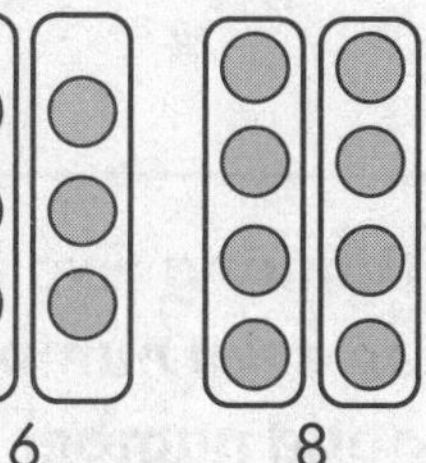

All even numbers can be shown as two equal groups. When multiplying, if at least one factor is even, the product will be even.

$4 \times 5 = (2 \times 2) \times 5$
$4 \times 5 = 2 \times (2 \times 5)$.

So, $4 \times 5 = 2 \times 10$.
The product is 2 equal groups of 10.

Think about the numbers 1, 3, 5, 7, and 9. When you divide these numbers by 2, there is 1 left over.
These numbers are odd.

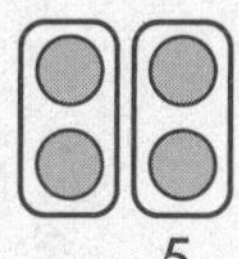

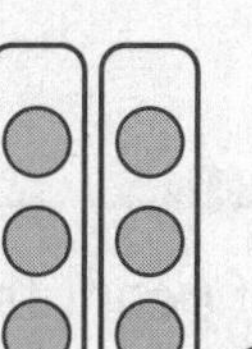

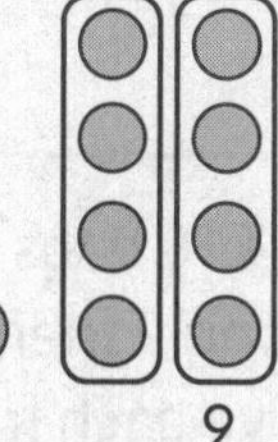

You cannot think of odd numbers as 2 equal groups with none left over. When multiplying, if both factors are odd, the product will be odd.

$7 \times 5 = 35$
$1 \times 9 = 9$

In **1–4**, circle the digit in the ones place. Then write *even* or *odd*.

1. 36 is ______.   **2.** 18 is ______.   **3.** 83 is ______.   **4.** 40 is ______.

In **5–7**, circle the factors that can be divided by 2.
Then write *even* or *odd* to describe the product and solve.

5. $7 \times 4 = ?$

7×4 is ______.

$7 \times 4 = 28$

6. $6 \times 6 = ?$

6×6 is ______.

$6 \times 6 = 36$

7. $5 \times 9 = ?$

5×9 is ______.

$5 \times 9 = 45$

8. Ted bought 1 box of whistles, 1 box of streamers, and 1 box of stickers. How many party favors did he buy in all? Show your work.

DATA

Party Favors

Item	Number per Box
Whistles	12
Hats	24
Streamers	48
Stickers	36

9. Don says that 9×9 is even. Is he correct? Explain.

10. Generalize Explain why the product of 2 times any number is an even number.

11. Sandra has 18 bags of peanuts to equally share among 9 friends. How many bags can she give each friend? Draw a bar diagram to help solve.

12. Higher Order Thinking Explain whether the product of an **even number** × **odd number** × **odd number** is even or odd.

Assessment Practice

13. Select all of the equations where you can use properties of operations to show that the product will be even.

- ☐ $1 \times 3 = ?$
- ☐ $3 \times 5 = ?$
- ☐ $7 \times 1 = ?$
- ☐ $8 \times 2 = ?$
- ☐ $6 \times 6 = ?$

14. Select all of the equations that do **NOT** have even products.

- ☐ $7 \times 3 = ?$
- ☐ $6 \times 2 = ?$
- ☐ $1 \times 3 = ?$
- ☐ $5 \times 7 = ?$
- ☐ $9 \times 6 = ?$

Name ______________________

Additional Practice 4-6

Division Involving 0 and 1

Another Look!

Rule	Example	What You Think	What You Write
When any number is divided by 1, the quotient is that number.	$7 \div 1 = ?$	1 times what number is 7? $1 \times 7 = 7$ So, $7 \div 1 = 7$.	$7 \div 1 = 7$ or $1\overline{)7}$ with quotient 7
When any number (except 0) is divided by itself, the quotient is 1.	$8 \div 8 = ?$	8 times what number is 8? $8 \times 1 = 8$ So, $8 \div 8 = 1$.	$8 \div 8 = 1$ or $8\overline{)8}$ with quotient 1
When zero is divided by a number (except 0), the quotient is 0.	$0 \div 5 = ?$	5 times what number is 0? $5 \times 0 = 0$ So, $0 \div 5 = 0$.	$0 \div 5 = 0$ or $5\overline{)0}$ with quotient 0
You cannot divide a number by 0.	$9 \div 0 = ?$	0 times what number is 9? There is no number that works, so $9 \div 0$ cannot be done.	$9 \div 0$ cannot be done.

In **1–8**, write the quotient.

1. $5 \div 1 =$ ____ **2.** $9 \div 9 =$ ____ **3.** $0 \div 8 =$ ____ **4.** $6 \div 6 =$ ____

5. $4 \div 1 =$ ____ **6.** $1\overline{)7}$ **7.** $8\overline{)8}$ **8.** $7\overline{)0}$

In **9** and **10**, use the sign at the right.

9. Be Precise Aiden has $20. He spends all of his money on ride tickets. How many ride tickets does Aiden buy?

10. Tanji spends $8 on ride tickets and gives an equal number of tickets to each of 8 friends. How many tickets does each friend get?

11. Which of these has the greatest quotient: $6 \div 6$, $5 \div 1$, $0 \div 3$, or $8 \div 8$? Explain.

12. Number Sense Place the numbers 0, 1, 3, and 3 in the blanks so that the number sentence is true.

$\_\_\_\_ \div \_\_\_\_ > \_\_\_\_ \div \_\_\_\_$

13. The number of students at Netherwood Elementary School is an odd number between 280 and 300. List all the possible numbers of students there could be.

14. Higher Order Thinking Write and solve a story problem that goes with $6 \div 6$.

Assessment Practice

15. Use division properties to match each equation to its quotient.

	0	1
$9 \div 9 = ?$	☐	☐
$0 \div 6 = ?$	☐	☐
$2 \div 2 = ?$	☐	☐

16. Use division properties to match each equation to its quotient.

	0	1
$7 \div 7 = ?$	☐	☐
$0 \div 1 = ?$	☐	☐
$0 \div 4 = ?$	☐	☐

Name ____________________

Additional Practice 4-7
Practice Multiplication and Division Facts

Another Look!

A class made popcorn for a carnival. Ten students each made 3 cups of popcorn. The students put the popcorn in bags that hold 6 cups each. Find the total number of cups. Then find how many bags of popcorn the students made.

You can solve the problems using multiplication and division.

Multiplication

How many total cups of popcorn did they make?

$10 \times 3 = ?$

Number of students → 10; Cups each student made → 3; Total number of cups → ?

$10 \times 3 = 30$

The students made a total of 30 cups of popcorn.

Division

How many groups of 6 are in 30?

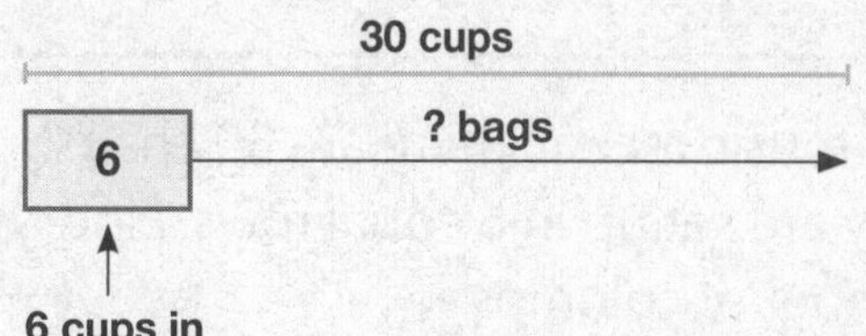

6 cups in each bag

Divide the total number of cups by the number of cups in each bag:

$30 \div 6 = 5$ ← Number of bags

The students made 5 bags of popcorn.

In **1–9**, use multiplication and division to complete the fact family.

1. $21 \div 3 =$ ____
$3 \times$ ____ $= 21$
$21 \div$ ____ $= 3$
____ $\times 3 = 21$

2. ____ $= 36 \div 6$
$36 = 6 \times$ ____

3. $2 =$ ____ $\div 9$
____ $= 2 \times 9$
$9 =$ ____ $\div 2$
____ $= 9 \times 2$

4. ____ $= 54 \div 9$
$54 = 9 \times$ ____
$9 = 54 \div$ ____
$54 =$ ____ $\times 9$

5. $18 \div 6 =$ ____
$6 \times$ ____ $= 18$
$18 \div$ ____ $= 6$
____ $\times 6 = 18$

6. $40 \div 5 =$ ____
$5 \times$ ____ $= 40$
$40 \div$ ____ $= 5$
____ $\times 5 = 40$

7. $14 \div 2 =$ ____
$2 \times$ ____ $= 14$
$14 \div$ ____ $= 2$
____ $\times 2 = 14$

8. $25 \div 5 =$ ____
$5 \times$ ____ $= 25$

9. ____ $= 32 \div 4$
$32 = 4 \times$ ____
$4 = 32 \div$ ____
$32 =$ ____ $\times 4$

In **10** and **11**, use the chart at the right.

10. Make Sense and Persevere Ellis asked some classmates to name their favorite color. He recorded the information in this chart. How many classmates answered the question?

11. Suppose Ellis asked more classmates to name their favorite color. If 4 more classmates named blue this time, how many classmates named blue in all?

12. At a music recital, there are 30 chairs. They are set up in 6 equal rows. Find the number of columns.

13. A music teacher has 4 drum kits. Each kit has 2 drumsticks. Each drumstick costs \$3. How many drumsticks does she have? What is the cost to replace them all?

14. Higher Order Thinking A chessboard has 8 rows of squares with 8 squares in each row. Two players each put 16 chess pieces on the board, with each piece on its own square. How many squares are empty now? Explain your answer.

Assessment Practice

15. Use the relationship between multiplication and division to find the value of each unknown.

Equation	Value of Unknown
$24 \div 4 = ?$	☐
$4 \times ? = 24$	☐
$8 = 56 \div ?$	☐
$8 \times ? = 56$	☐

16. Use properties of operations to find the value of each unknown.

Equation	Value of Unknown
$7 \div 1 = ?$	☐
$? = 3 \div 3$	☐
$? = 9 \times 1$	☐
$4 \times 0 = ?$	☐

Name ____________________

Practice Video Tools Games

Additional Practice 4-8

Solve Multiplication and Division Equations

Another Look!

Remember that an equation uses an equal sign (=) to show the value on the left is the same as the value on the right.

Equations have unknown numbers. These numbers may be represented by question marks.

$10 = 40 \div ?$

This equation means 10 is equal to 40 divided by some number. You know $40 \div 4 = 10$, so $? = 4$.

You can write equations to represent math problems.

1. Frankie has some nickels. His nickels have a value of 45 cents. How many nickels does Frankie have? Complete the table to write an equation to represent the problem.

Use a ? to represent the number of nickels Frankie has.	?
Nickels are worth 5 cents. You can multiply the number of nickels by 5 to find the total value of the coins.	? × ____
Frankie's nickels are worth 45 cents.	? × 5 = ____

To solve the problem, find the value of ? that makes the equation true: ____ × 5 = 45. Frankie has ____ nickels.

In **2–5**, find the value of ? that makes the equation true.

2. $? \div 5 = 6$

3. $36 = 6 \times ?$

4. $14 = ? \times 2$

5. $81 \div ? = 9$

In **6** and **7**, write and solve an equation for each problem.

6. A restaurant has 24 chairs and some tables. There are 4 chairs at each table. How many tables are there?

7. Suzanne buys 6 paint sets. Each set contains the same number of brushes. She has 18 brushes. How many brushes are in each paint set?

8. Carlos has a string that is 24 inches long. He wants to divide it into 3 equal parts. Write an equation to find how long each part will be. Use a ? to represent the unknown number. Then solve your equation.

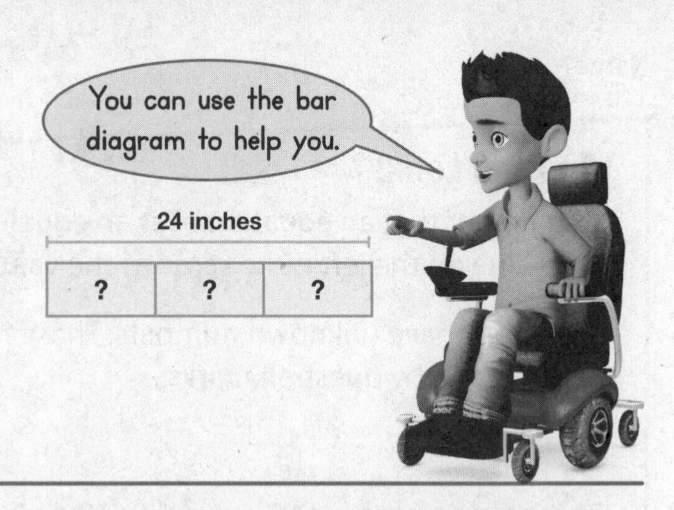

9. Higher Order Thinking Hector spent from Sunday to the following Saturday at the beach. Each day he found an equal number of shells. If Hector found 63 shells, how many shells did he find on Tuesday? Explain your answer.

10. Make Sense and Persevere Ella solves the equation $32 \div ? = 8$. She says the value of ? is 4. Does Ella's answer make sense? Explain.

11. Reasoning Do points *A* and *B* represent the same number, or do they represent different numbers? Explain.

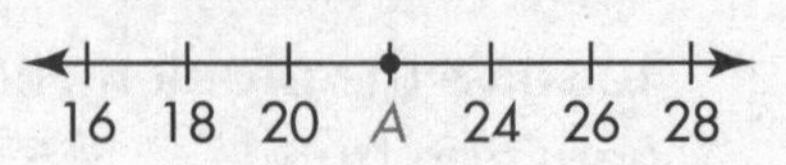

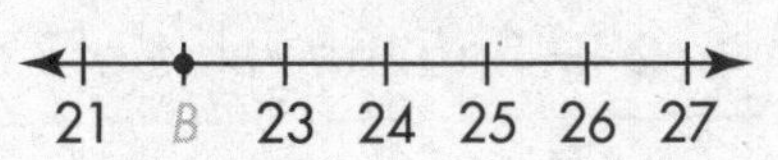

Assessment Practice

12. What is the value of the unknown in the equation $32 \div ? = 4$?

Ⓐ 6

Ⓑ 7

Ⓒ 8

Ⓓ 9

13. What is the value of the unknown in the equation $10 \times ? = 80$?

Ⓐ 5

Ⓑ 6

Ⓒ 7

Ⓓ 8

Name ____________________

Practice Video Tools Games

Additional Practice 4-9
Make Sense and Persevere

Another Look!

To solve a two-step problem, you may need to find the answer to a hidden question first. Then you can use that answer to solve the problem.

Sandra has $22 to spend on school supplies. She buys a backpack and spends the rest of her money on notebooks. How many notebooks does Sandra buy?

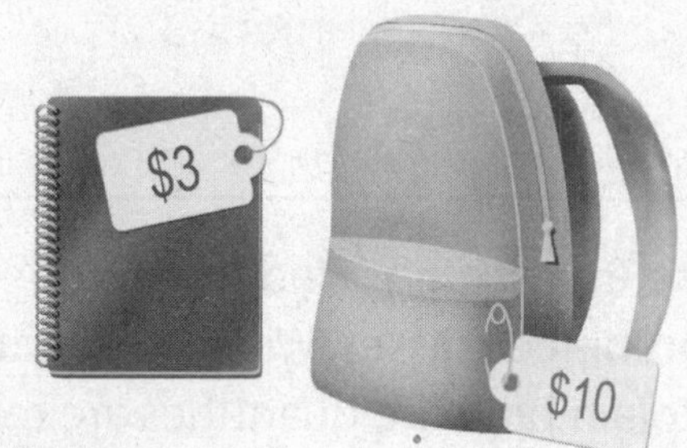

Tell how to make sense of the problem.

- I can identify what is known from the problem.
- I can look for and answer any hidden questions.
- I can make a plan to solve the problem.

Tell which operations you will use. Then solve the problem.

I will use subtraction and division.

A backpack costs $10. $22 – $10 = $12.

Sandra now has $12 to spend on notebooks. Each notebook costs $3.

$12 ÷ $3 = 4. Sandra can buy 4 notebooks.

If you are stuck, you can persevere by trying a different strategy.

Make Sense and Persevere

There are 5 players on a basketball team. In a game, 4 players scored 6 points each. The team scored a total of 34 points. How many points did the other player score?

1. Tell how to make sense of the problem.

2. Tell the quantities you know. Then explain what you need to find first to solve the problem.

3. Tell which operations you will use. Then solve the problem.

Performance Task

Zoo Field Trip

The third-grade class at Thomas Elementary School goes on a trip to the zoo. Students are in groups of 6. Mr. Bell's and Ms. Ridley's classes are combined.

DATA

Classroom Teacher	Number of Students
Mr. Bell	18
Ms. Ridley	24
Ms. Holtz	17

4. **Make Sense and Persevere** The teachers want to know how many groups will be in the combined classes. What do you need to know to solve?

5. **Use Reasoning** Find the number of groups in the combined classes. Write an equation for each step. Explain how the quantities are related.

Make sense of the information in the problem by identifying the quantities. Think: Is there a hidden question I need to solve first?

6. **Critique Reasoning** Ryan solved the problem above. He says there are 6 groups of 6 students and 1 group of 5 students. What did Ryan do wrong?

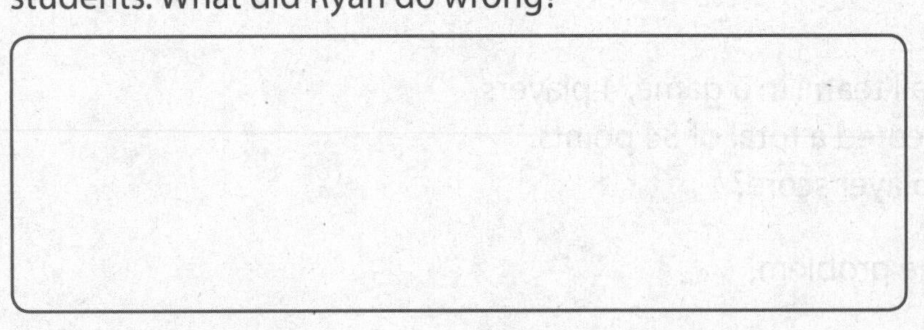

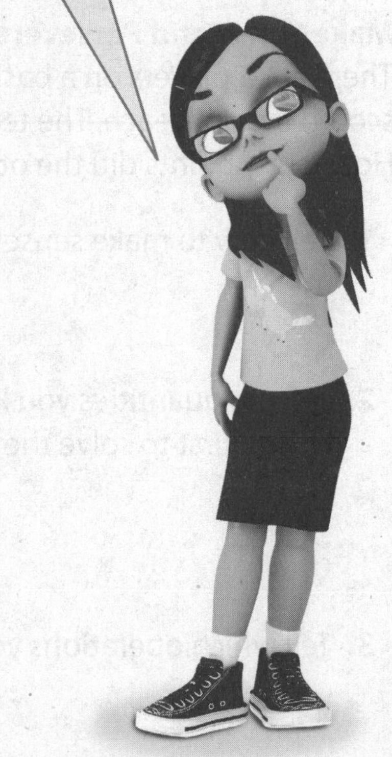

7. **Generalize** If you wanted to find the number of groups of 6 students if Mr. Bell's and Ms. Holtz's classes were combined, could you use the same strategy you used in Exercise **5**? Explain.

Name ______________________

Practice Video Tools Games

Additional Practice 5-1
Patterns for Multiplication Facts

Another Look!

You can find and explain multiplication patterns.

×	1	2	3	4	5	6	7	8	9
6	6	12	18	24	30	36	42	48	54

You can see that the products of 6 increase by 6 as the other factor increases.

So, you know that 4 groups of 6 is the same as 3 groups of 6 plus 1 more group of 6. You can use the Distributive Property to explain.

$4 \times 6 = (3 + 1) \times 6$

$= (3 \times 6) + (1 \times 6)$

$= 18 + 6$

$= 24$

In **1–5**, use the multiplication table shown at the right.

×	1	2	3	4	5	6	7	8	9
1	1	2	3	4	5	6	7	8	9
2	2	4	6	8	10	12	14	16	18
3	3	6	9	12	15	18	21	24	27
4	4	8	12	16	20	24	28	32	36
5	5	10	15	20	25	30	35	40	45
6	6	12	18	24	30	36	42	48	54
7	7	14	21	28	35	42	49	56	63
8	8	16	24	32	40	48	56	64	72
9	9	18	27	36	45	54	63	72	81

1. Find the column which has products that are the sum of the shaded numbers in each row. Shade this column.

2. Show 3 examples of the pattern that relates the shaded columns.

3. Explain why this pattern is true.

4. Find a similar pattern using different products. Shade the columns on the multiplication table.

5. Explain how you choose which columns to shade.

6. Teresa bought 3 boxes of chocolate. Each box has 9 pieces of chocolate inside. Teresa gave away 15 pieces of chocolate. How many pieces of chocolate does she have left?

7. **Vocabulary** Margie divided 24 by 3. The *dividend* is ______. The *quotient* is ______.

8. **Look for Relationships** Look at the multiples of 2. What pattern do you see?

×	1	2	3	4	5	6	7	8	9	10
2	2	4	6	8	10	12	14	16	18	20

9. Look at the table used in Exercises **1–5** on the previous page. Does this table have more even products or more odd products? Explain.

10. **Higher Order Thinking** Chris needs to find the product of two numbers. One of the numbers is 11. The answer also needs to be 11. How will Chris solve this problem? Explain.

Assessment Practice

11. Look at the shaded products in the multiplication table shown below.

×	1	2	3	4	5	6	7	8	9
1	1	2	3	4	5	6	7	8	9
2	2	4	6	8	10	12	14	16	18
3	3	6	9	12	15	18	21	24	27
4	4	8	12	16	20	24	28	32	36
5	5	10	15	20	25	30	35	40	45
6	6	12	18	24	30	36	42	48	54
7	7	14	21	28	35	42	49	56	63
8	8	16	24	32	40	48	56	64	72
9	9	18	27	36	45	54	63	72	81

What pattern and property of operations is shown in the shaded row and column?

Ⓐ The products in the row and the column are the same; The Identity Property of Multiplication

Ⓑ The products in the row and the column are the same. Changing the order of the factors does not change the product; The Commutative Property of Multiplication

Ⓒ The products in the row and the column are the same; The Distributive Property

Ⓓ There are no patterns or properties.

Name ____________________

Practice Video Tools Games

Additional Practice 5-2

Use a Table to Multiply and Divide

Another Look!

Find $24 \div 6$.

You can think of a division problem as a multiplication fact that is missing a factor.

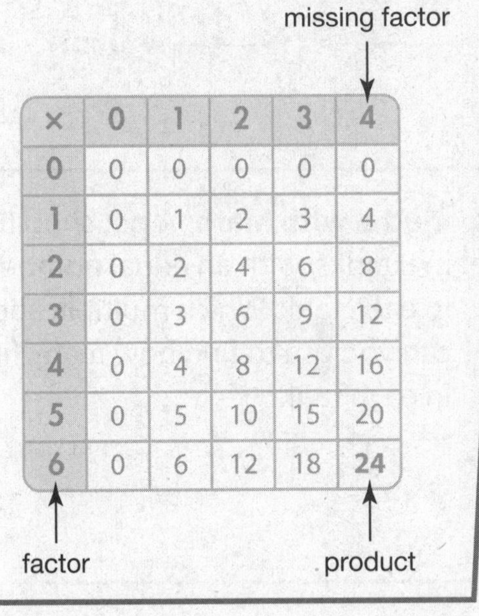

×	0	1	2	3	4
0	0	0	0	0	0
1	0	1	2	3	4
2	0	2	4	6	8
3	0	3	6	9	12
4	0	4	8	12	16
5	0	5	10	15	20
6	0	6	12	18	**24**

A. Find the factor you already know in the first column of the table. In **6** × ? = 24, that factor is **6**.

B. Go across the row until you get to the product. In 6 × ? = **24**, the product is **24**.

C. Go straight to the top of that column. The number at the top of the column is 4. So, the missing factor is 4 and $24 \div 6 = 4$.

In **1–3**, find the value that makes the equations correct. Use a multiplication table to help.

1. ____ = 8 ÷ 2

2 × ____ = 8

2. 12 ÷ 4 = ____

4 × ____ = 12

3. 16 ÷ 8 = ____

16 = 8 × ____

In **4** and **5**, find the missing factors and products.

4.

×	☐	6	☐
0			
☐		30	
9	45		63
☐		42	

5.

×	☐	☐	9
2	8		
☐			81
3		9	
☐			72

6. Christina has these two tiles. Draw a new shape she can create with both tiles. Then name the shape and tell how many sides the new shape has.

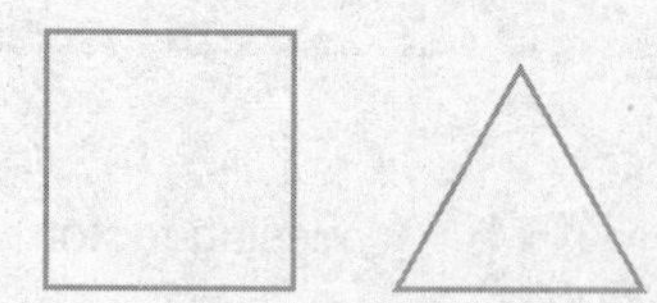

7. There are 3 drawers in Mona's dresser. Each drawer has the same number of shirts. Mona has 27 shirts. How many shirts are in each drawer?

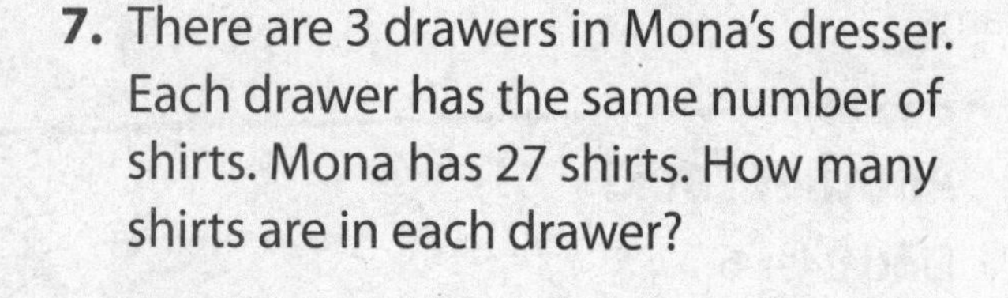

8. **Model with Math** A pet shop has 24 fish in 8 tanks, with an equal number of fish in each tank. Which multiplication fact can you use to find how many fish are in each tank?

9. **Algebra** Ethan went to the farmers' market and bought 57 pieces of fruit. He bought 15 pears, 22 apples, and some peaches. Write an equation to find how many peaches Ethan bought. Use an unknown to represent the number of peaches.

10. **enVision® STEM** There are 18 solar panels on a house. The solar panels are arranged in 3 equal columns. How many rows of solar panels are on this house? Explain how to solve the problem.

11. **Higher Order Thinking** Mike says he can use a multiplication table to find $5 \div 0$. Is he correct? Explain.

Assessment Practice

12. Use the relationship between multiplication and division to find the missing number in $63 \div 7 = \square$.

Ⓐ 70

Ⓑ 56

Ⓒ 9

Ⓓ 8

×	0	1	2	3	4	5	6	7	8	9
0	0	0	0	0	0	0	0	0	0	0
1	0	1	2	3	4	5	6	7	8	9
2	0	2	4	6	8	10	12	14	16	18
3	0	3	6	9	12	15	18	21	24	27
4	0	4	8	12	16	20	24	28	32	36
5	0	5	10	15	20	25	30	35	40	45
6	0	6	12	18	24	30	36	42	48	54
7	0	7	14	21	28	35	42	49	56	63
8	0	8	16	24	32	40	48	56	64	72
9	0	9	18	27	36	45	54	63	72	81

Name ______________________

Additional Practice 5-3
Use Strategies to Multiply

Another Look!

Find 6×4.

One Way

Draw a bar diagram and use skip counting.

6×4 means 6 groups of 4.

Each section of the bar diagram is 1 group of 4.

?

4	4	4	4	4	4
4	8	12	16	20	24

Skip count by 4s to solve.

So, $6 \times 4 = 24$.

Another Way

Using the Distributive Property is another way to solve this problem. Use 3s facts to help.

$3 \times 4 = 12$

$3 \times 4 = 12$

$12 + 12 = 24$

So, $6 \times 4 = 24$.

In **1** and **2**, show two different ways to find the product.

1. $3 \times 5 = ?$

?

5	5	___
5	10	___

$2 \times 5 =$ ___

$1 \times 5 =$ ___

$3 \times 5 =$ ___ $10 +$ ___ $=$ ___

2. $3 \times 4 = ?$

?

4	4	___
4	8	___

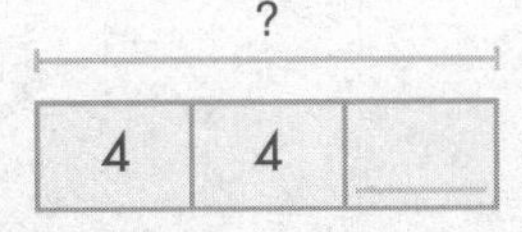

$2 \times 4 =$ ___

$1 \times 4 =$ ___

$3 \times 4 =$ ___ $8 +$ ___ $=$ ___

In **3–8**, multiply.

3. $7 \times 2 =$ ___

4. ___ $= 8 \times 5$

5. $6 \times 8 =$ ___

6. $9 \times 7 =$ ___

7. $4 \times 8 =$ ___

8. ___ $= 7 \times 3$

9. Make Sense and Persevere The home team scored 3 touchdowns. The visiting team scored 4 field goals. Which team scored more points? Show your strategy.

DATA

Football Points

Type	Points
Touchdown	6 points
Field Goal	3 points
Safety	2 points

10. Rick says, "To find 2×5, I can skip count by 5s: 5, 10, 15, 20, 25. The product is 25." Explain what Rick did wrong.

11. Algebra Write the symbols to make the equations correct.

$81 = 9 \square 9$

$9 \square 6 = 54$

$9 = 72 \square 8$

12. Higher Order Thinking Jill has 4 bags of marbles. There are 3 red, 5 green, 2 yellow, and 6 black marbles in each bag. How many marbles does Jill have? Show how you found the answer.

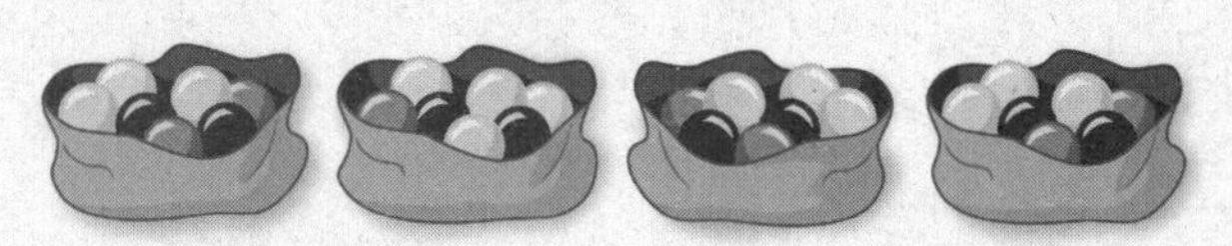

13. Mr. Roberts plans to drive a total of 56 miles. He has 29 more miles to go. How many miles has he driven so far?

56 miles

?	29 miles

Assessment Practice

14. Which shows one way you could use properties of operations to find 5×2?

Ⓐ $(5 \times 2) \times 2$

Ⓑ $5 \times (2 \times 2)$

Ⓒ $(3 \times 2) + (2 \times 2)$

Ⓓ $(5 + 2) + (5 + 2)$

15. Which multiplication equation could you use to help find $32 \div 8 = \square$?

Ⓐ $8 \times 8 = 64$

Ⓑ $4 \times 8 = 32$

Ⓒ $1 \times 8 = 8$

Ⓓ $4 \times 4 = 16$

Name ______________________

Practice Video Tools Games

Additional Practice 5-4
Solve Word Problems: Multiplication and Division Facts

Another Look!

Rico has 32 pine cones. He uses 8 pine cones to make a sculpture in art class. If Rico makes more sculptures with 8 pine cones for each, how many total sculptures can he make?

Draw a bar diagram to represent the problem.

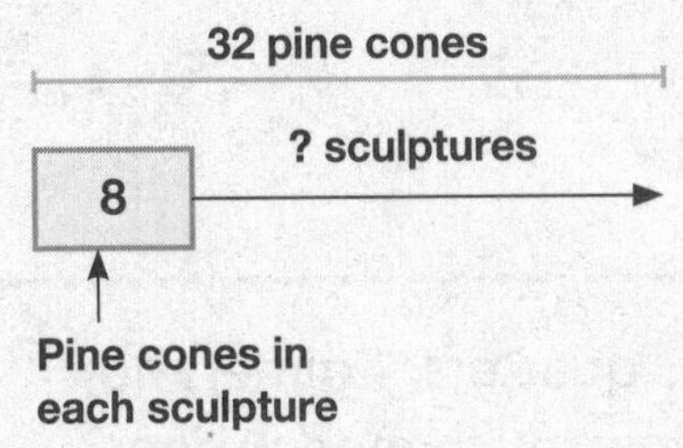

Multiply or divide to solve: $4 \times 8 = 32$ or $32 \div 8 = 4$.

So, Rico can make 4 sculptures.

A bar diagram can help you see there is more than one way to think about this problem.

In **1** and **2**, draw a bar diagram to represent the problem. Then solve.

1. Victor buys some six-packs of soda for a party. He buys 42 cans in all. How many six-packs of soda did Victor buy?

2. Lester listens to 8 songs every time he does his exercise routine. He did his exercise routine 3 times this week. How many songs did Lester listen to while exercising this week?

In **3** and **4**, write an equation with an unknown to represent the problem. Then solve.

3. There are 9 players on a baseball team. A club has 9 baseball teams. How many baseball players are in the club?

4. Megan earned $4 for an hour of babysitting. On Saturday, she earned $16. How many hours did she babysit?

5. Andre is setting up folding chairs for a school assembly. He sets up 4 rows of chairs. Each row has 7 chairs. How many chairs does Andre set up? Complete the bar diagram and write an equation to solve.

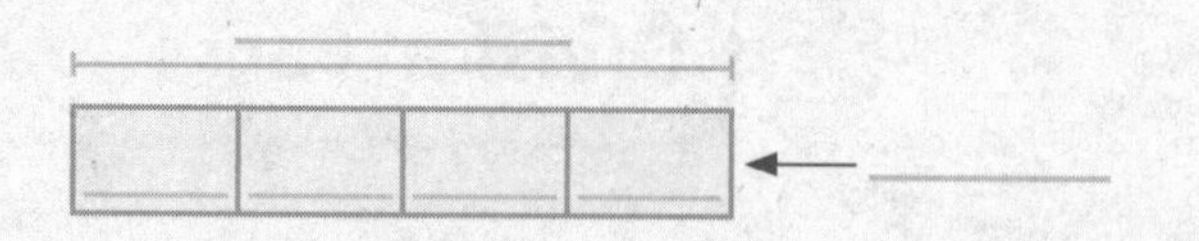

6. Higher Order Thinking Thirty-six students ride a school bus home. The same number of students get off at each stop. Harriet knows how many students got off at one stop. How could she find how many stops the bus made?

7. Mr. Ameda has 4 children. He gives each of them 2 cookies. He spends $40 on the cookies. How much did each cookie cost?

8. Yogesh has 3 quarters, 1 dime, and 2 pennies. How much money does Yogesh have?

9. Critique Reasoning Neville and Anthony are solving this problem: Barbara bought 3 packages of pencils with 6 pencils in each package. How many pencils did she buy in all?

Neville says, "I add because of the words *in all*. The answer is 9 pencils." Anthony says, "I multiply because there are equal groups. The answer is 18 pencils." Who is correct? Explain.

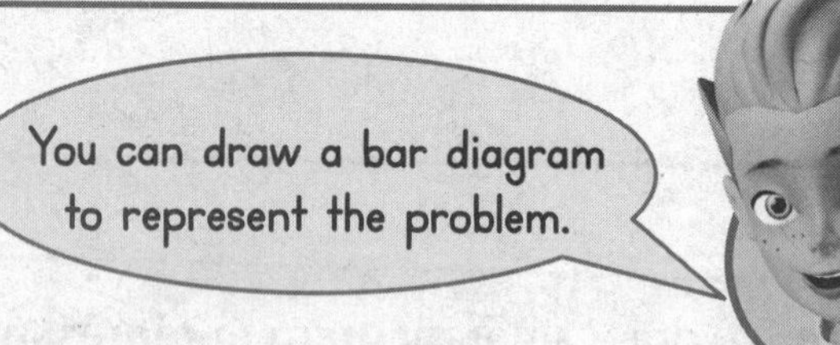

Assessment Practice

10. Garrett uses 5 apples to bake an apple pie. On Sunday, he bakes 2 pies. How many apples does Garrett need on Sunday?

Select numbers and an operation to complete an equation that could be used to answer the problem. Then solve the equation.

2	3	5	8	+
9	10	25	52	×

? = ☐☐☐

? = ☐ apples

11. Ella has 27 apples. If Ella uses 3 apples to make each tart, how many tarts can Ella make?

Select numbers and an operation to complete an equation that could be used to answer the problem. Then solve the equation.

3	6	9	10	÷
20	27	33	72	×

? = ☐☐☐

? = ☐ tarts

Name ____________________

Practice Video Tools Games

Additional Practice 5-5
Write Multiplication and Division Math Stories

Another Look!

Write a story for 4×9.

Josephine had 4 friends over for a snack. She gave each friend 9 cherries. How many cherries did Josephine give in all?

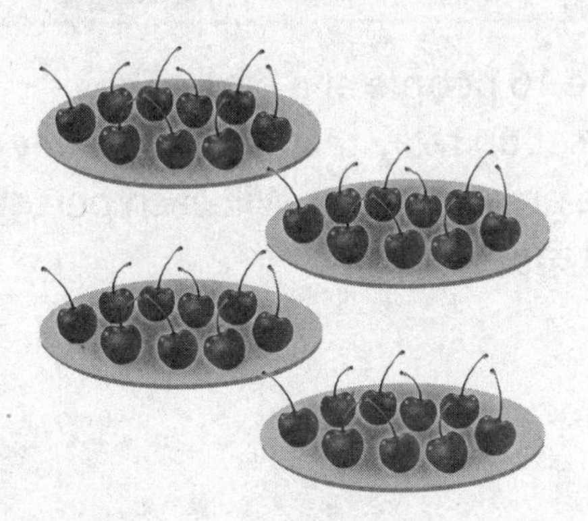

Write a story for $12 \div 4$.

Cami has 12 crayons and some cans. She put 4 crayons in each can. How many cans did Cami use?

In **1** and **2**, write a multiplication story for each equation. Then find the product. You can draw a picture to help.

1. $4 \times 3 =$ ____

2. $5 \times 2 =$ ____

In **3** and **4**, write a division story for each equation. Use counters or draw a picture to solve.

3. $48 \div 6 =$ ____

4. $56 \div$ ____ $= 8$

5. Reasoning Write a multiplication story about these tennis balls. Write an equation for your story.

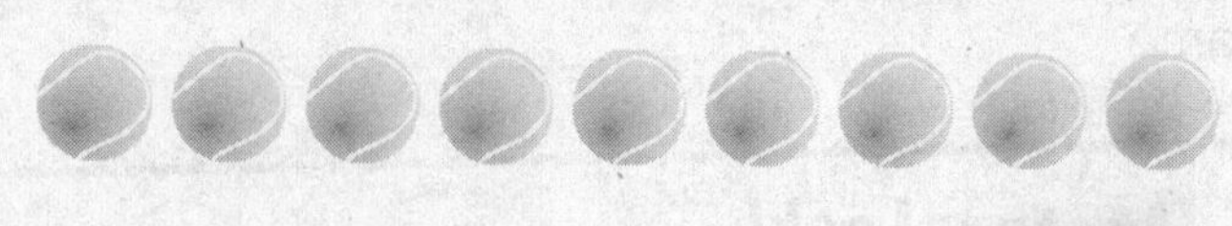

6. Draw a bar diagram that shows 6×7. How many sections does your bar diagram have? Explain. Then find the product.

7. There are 16 people at a party. They want to set up relay teams with exactly 3 people on each team. Will each person be on a team? Explain.

8. Higher Order Thinking Complete the sentences with numbers that make sense. Do not use the number 1. Then write the division equation that matches the story, and draw a picture to solve.

"There are 35 rabbits at the fair. The rabbits are kept in ____ hutches with ____ rabbits in each hutch."

Assessment Practice

9. Judy writes the following story for $24 \div 4 = ?$.
There are 24 dogs at daycare. Four dogs are walked in each group. How many groups are there?
Select the correct answer for Judy's story.

Ⓐ 4

Ⓑ 6

Ⓒ 12

Ⓓ 24

4 dogs in each group

Name ______________________

Additional Practice 5-6

Look For and Use Structure

Another Look!

How can you tell without computing which of the symbols >, <, or = should be placed in the circle below?

$4 \times 6 \times 2$ ◯ $6 \times 2 \times 4$

Tell how you can use the structure of mathematics to complete the task.

- I can think about properties I know.
- I can look for patterns and use them as needed.

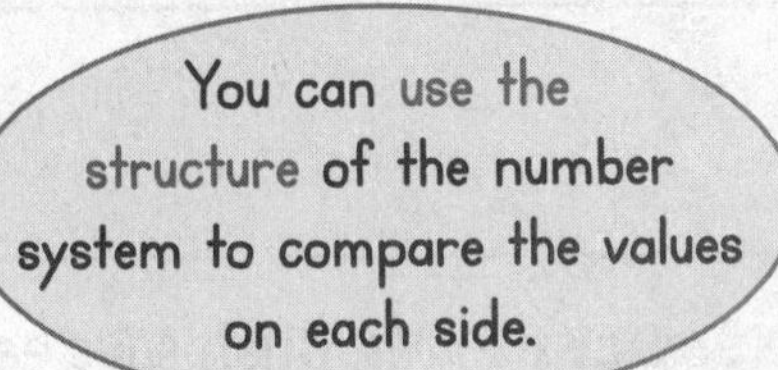

Look at the expressions. Explain how you can use the factors you see to compare without computing.

The same 3 factors are on each side of the circle. I know that the same factors grouped in a different way have the same product. So, the expressions are equal.

$4 \times (6 \times 2)$ (=) $(6 \times 2) \times 4$

Use Structure

Maria wrote the expression at the left of the circle below. Riaz wrote the expression at the right of the circle below. Find without computing which of the symbols >, <, or = should be placed in the circle.

Maria **Riaz**

$4 \times 8 \times 3$ ◯ $2 \times 3 \times 8$

1. Tell how you can use the structure of mathematics to complete the task.

2. Look at the expressions. Explain how you can use the factors you see to compare without computing.

3. Whose expression has the greater value? Write the correct symbol >, <, or = in the circle above.

Performance Task

Baseball League

Ms. Bush manages a baseball league. She buys the bucket of baseballs shown to share among the teams. She wants to use all the baseballs. The league will have either 6 or 9 teams. There are 14 players on each team. Ms. Bush is trying to decide whether to charge \$3 or \$4 for each baseball.

4. Make Sense and Persevere What information do you know from the problem?

5. Use Structure Ms. Bush says each team will get more baseballs if there are 6 teams in the league. Mr. Rosin says each team will get more baseballs if there are 9 teams in the league. Who is correct?

Compare by writing the symbol >, <, or =. Tell how to decide without computing.

$36 \div 6 \bigcirc 36 \div 9$

6. Use Structure Suppose Ms. Bush charges \$4 per baseball. Would each team pay more if there are 6 teams or 9 teams?

Compare by writing the symbol >, <, or =. Tell how to decide without computing.

$(36 \div 6) \times \$4 \bigcirc (36 \div 9) \times \$4$

7. Construct Arguments Ms. Bush wants to set up the league so that each team pays the least amount. Should there be 6 or 9 teams? Should each baseball cost \$3 or \$4? Explain.

Name ____________________

Additional Practice 6-1
Cover Regions

Another Look!

You can find the area of the rectangle below by counting the number of unit squares that cover it.

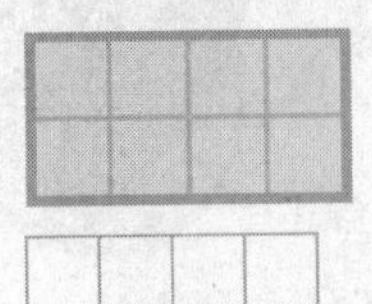

Eight unit squares cover the rectangle.

So, the area of the rectangle is 8 square units.

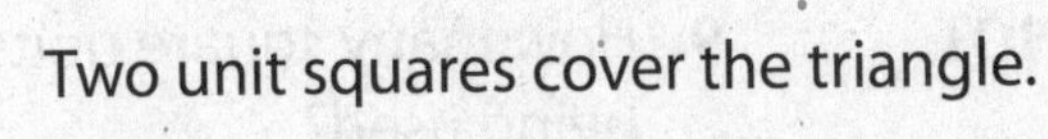

Two unit squares cover the triangle.

So, the area of the triangle is 2 square units.

Sometimes you need to estimate area. You can combine partially filled squares to approximate full squares.

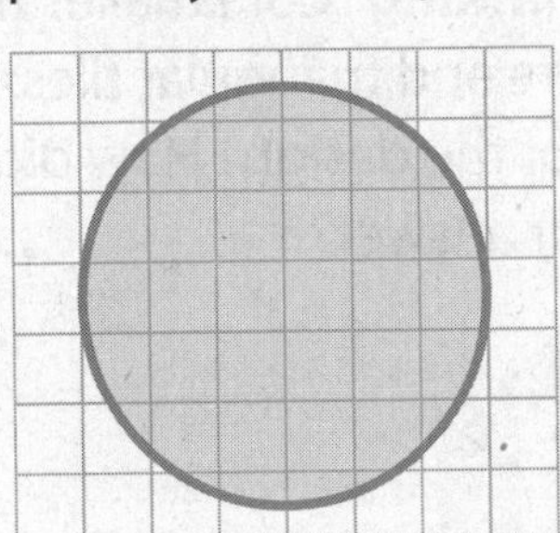

About 28 unit squares cover the circle.

So, the area of the circle is about 28 square units.

Area is the number of unit squares used to cover a region with no gaps or overlaps.

In **1–6**, count to find the area of the shapes. Tell if the area is an estimate.

1.

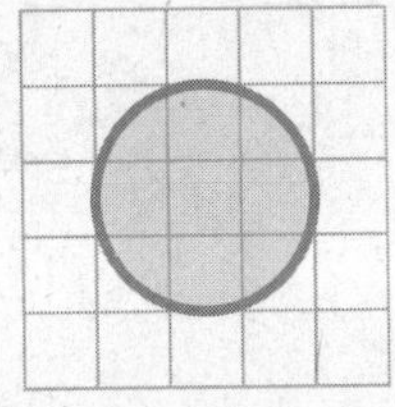

2.

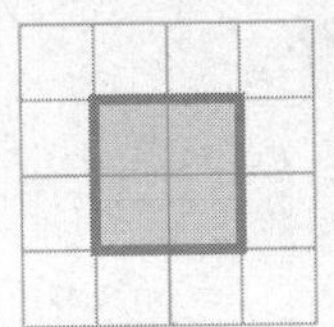

3.

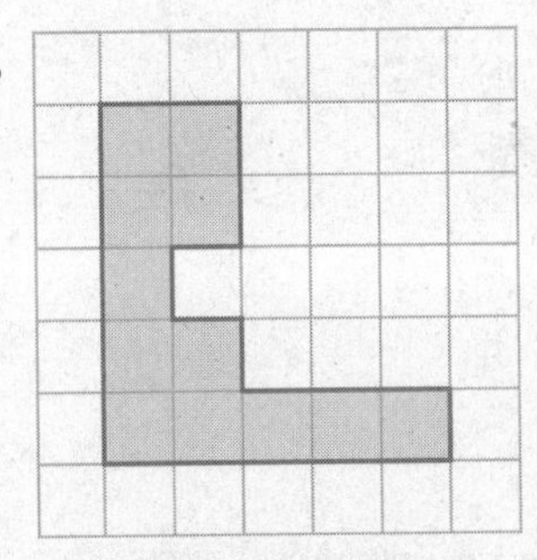

4.

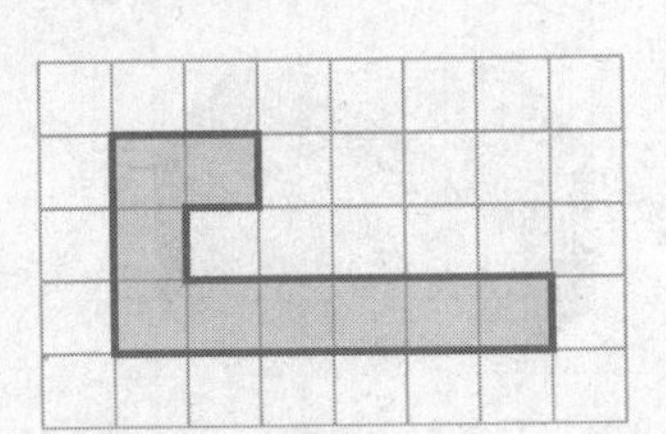

5.

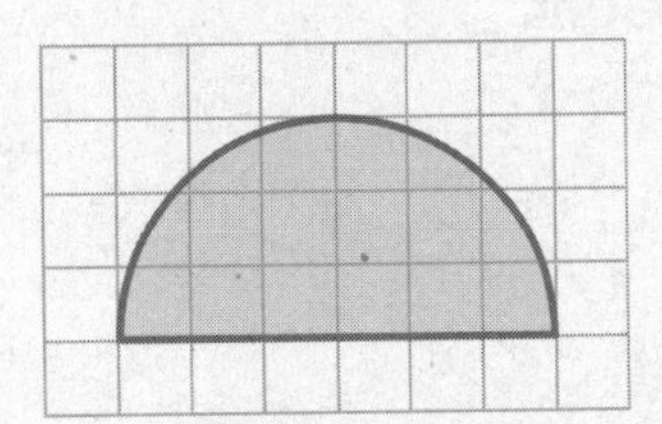

6.

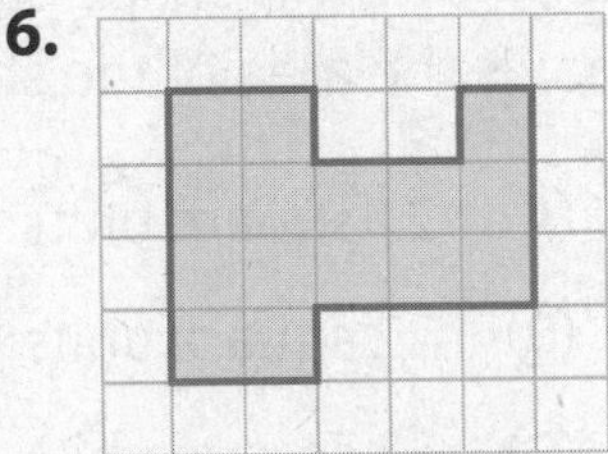

In **7–9**, use the diagram at the right.

7. What is the area of the soccer section of the field?

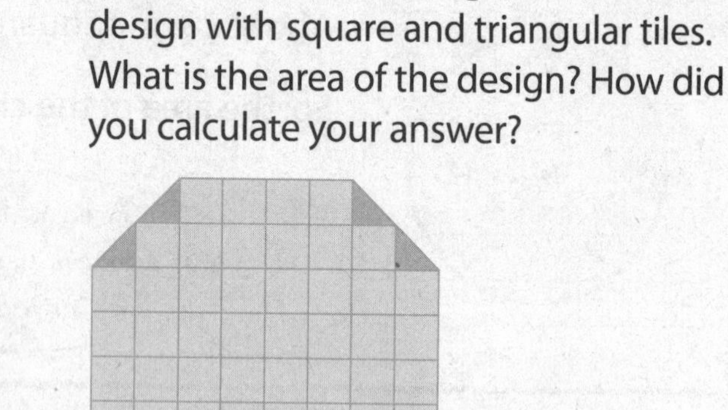

8. What is the area of the field that is **NOT** being used?

9. How many square units of the field are being used?

10. Reasoning A bookstore has a sale. When customers pay for 2 books, they get another book free. If Pat pays for a box of 16 books, how many books does he get for free? How many books does Pat now have? Write division and addition equations to show how the quantities are related.

11. Higher Order Thinking Cora makes this design with square and triangular tiles. What is the area of the design? How did you calculate your answer?

Assessment Practice

12. Tyler draws this shape on grid paper. What is the area of the shape?

Ⓐ 21 square units

Ⓑ 22 square units

Ⓒ 23 square units

Ⓓ 24 square units

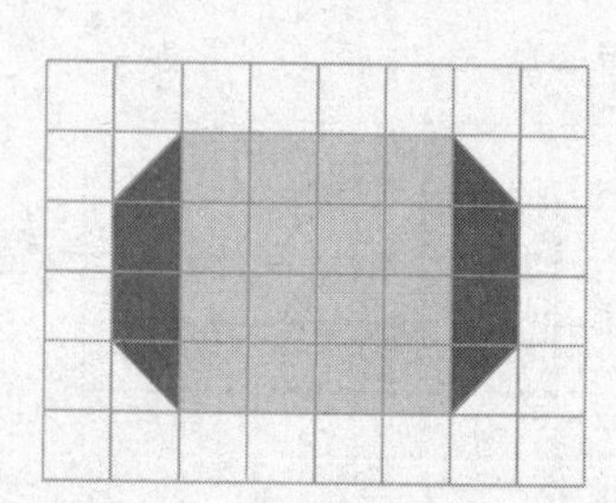

Name ____________________

Practice Video Tools Games

Additional Practice 6-2

Area: Non-Standard Units

Another Look!

A unit square is a square with sides that are each 1 unit long.

Unit squares can be different sizes. The size of the unit square you use determines the area of a figure.

= 1 square unit

There are 12 unit squares.

The area of this figure is 12 square units.

= 1 square unit

There are 48 unit squares.

The area of this figure is 48 square units.

In **1** and **2**, draw unit squares to cover the figures and find the area. Use the unit squares shown.

1.

= 1 square unit

= 1 square unit

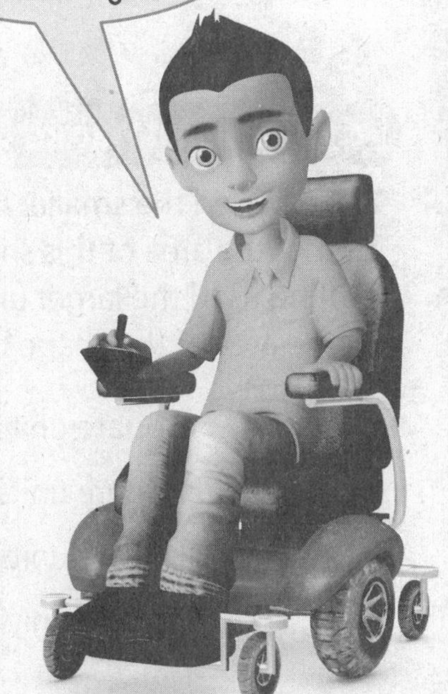

2.

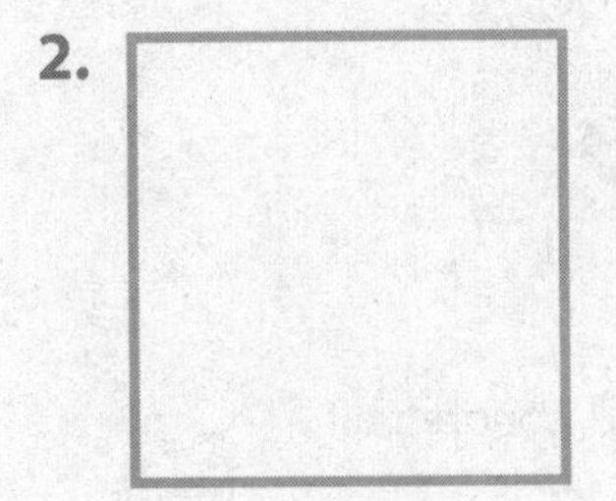

= 1 square unit

= 1 square unit

3. Be Precise Inez finds that the area of this figure is 9 square units. Draw unit squares to cover this figure.

4. Vocabulary Fill in the blanks: Yasmeen can cover a figure with 7 rows of 8 ____________ to find the figure's ____________.

5. Number Sense Paula is making gift bags for each of her 5 friends. Each bag will have 6 markers. How many markers will Paula need? Skip count by 6s to find the answer. Then write a multiplication equation to represent the problem.

6. Higher Order Thinking Helen makes the rectangle on the right from tiles. Each tile is 1 unit square. Helen says the white tiles cover more area than the black tiles. Do you agree? Explain.

Assessment Practice

7. Rick used the smaller unit square and found that the area of this shape is 16 square units. If he used the larger unit square, what would the area of the shape be?

Ⓐ 1 square unit

Ⓑ 2 square units

Ⓒ 3 square units

Ⓓ 4 square units

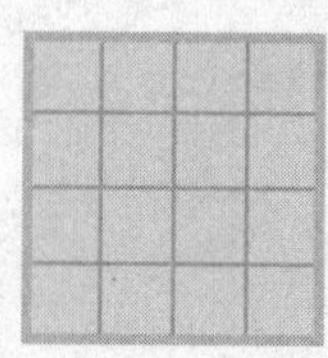

□ = 1 square unit

□ = 1 square unit

Name ______________________

Practice Video Tools Games

Additional Practice 6-3
Area: Standard Units

Another Look!

Count how many unit squares cover this figure.

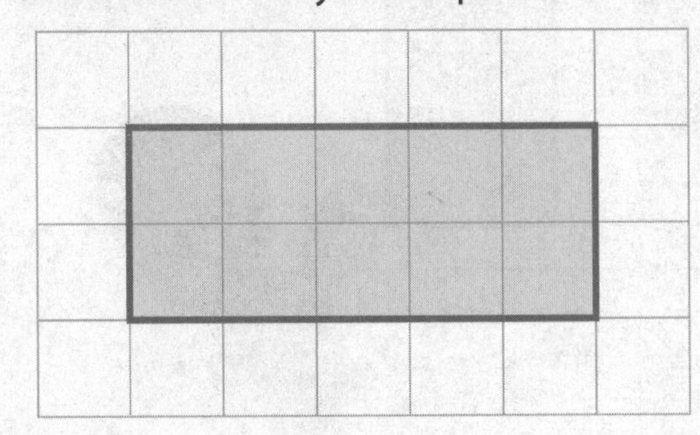

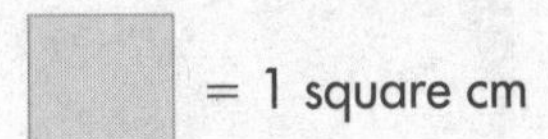
= 1 square cm

- 10 unit squares cover the figure.
- Each unit square equals 1 square centimeter.

The area of the figure is 10 square centimeters.

In **1–6**, each unit square represents a standard unit. Count the shaded unit squares. Then write the area.

1.

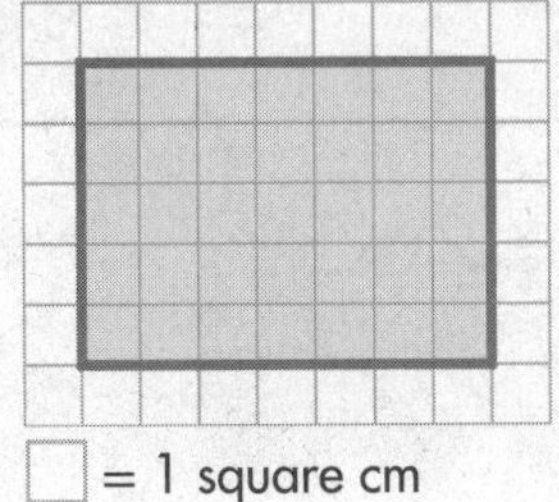
= 1 square cm

2.

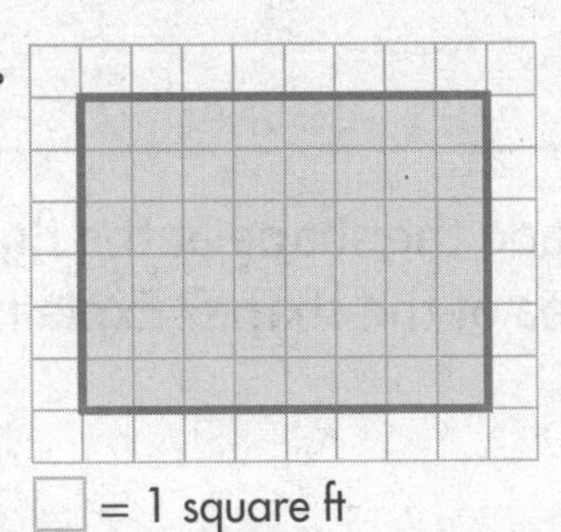
= 1 square ft

3.

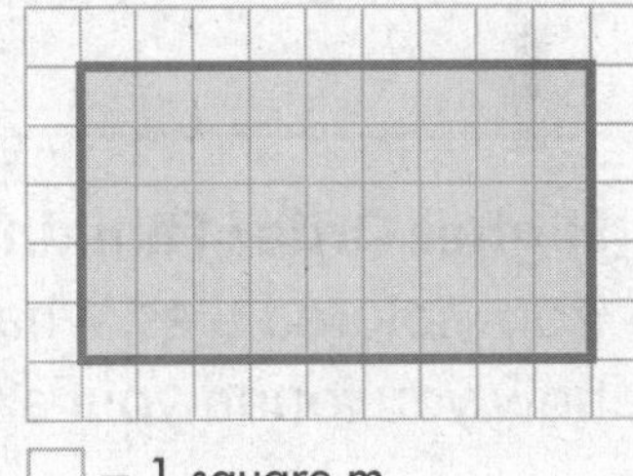
= 1 square m

4.

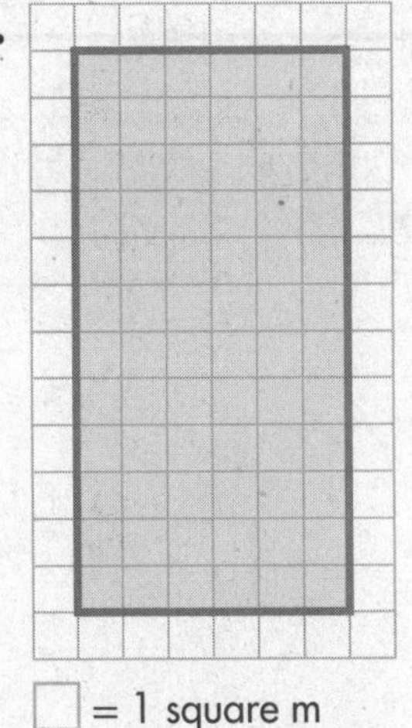
= 1 square m

5.

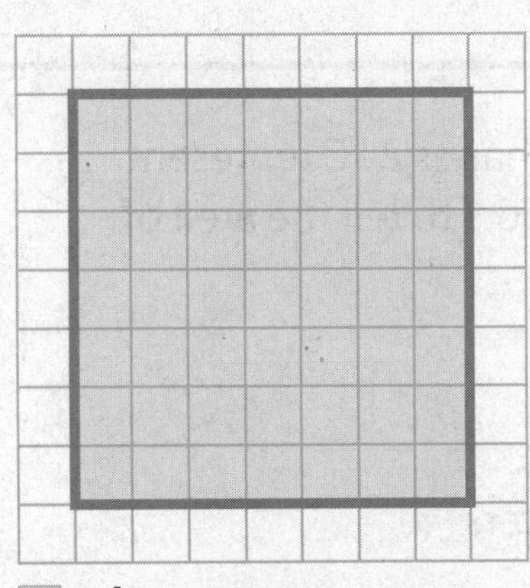
= 1 square cm

6.

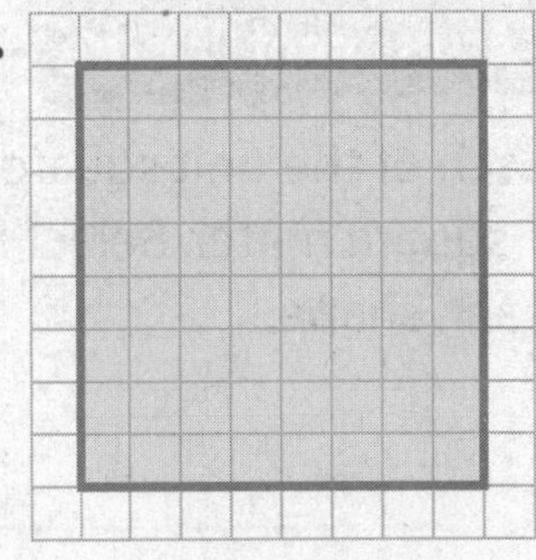
= 1 square in.

In **7** and **8**, use the diagram at the right.

7. Be Precise What is the area of Tom's photo? Explain how you know which units to use.

8. What is the area in square inches of all the photos combined? Explain.

9. Is the area of a desk more likely to be 8 square feet or 8 square inches? Explain.

10. Michele has 5 coins worth $0.75 in all. What coins does she have?

11. Higher Order Thinking Sam made the shape at the right from colored tiles. What is the area of the shape? Explain how you found your answer.

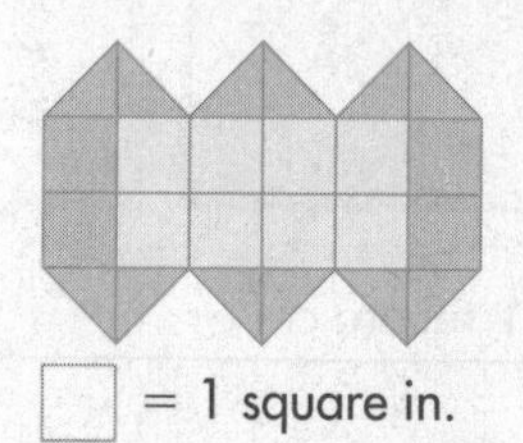

12. Each of the unit squares in Shapes A–C represent 1 square meter. Select numbers to tell the area of each shape.

1 2 4 6 7 8

Shape A ☐☐ square meters

Shape B ☐☐ square meters

Shape C ☐☐ square meters

A
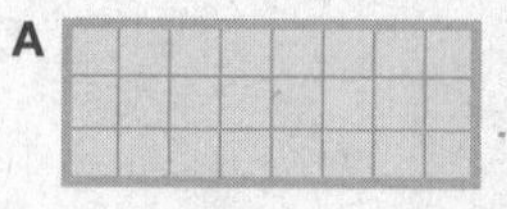

B
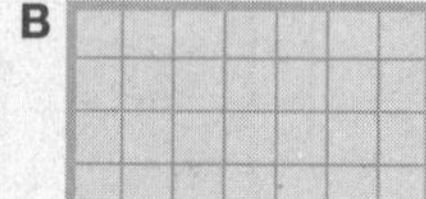

C

Name ____________________

Practice Video Tools Games

Additional Practice 6-4
Area of Squares and Rectangles

Another Look!

What is the area of Rectangle A? What is the length of Rectangle B?

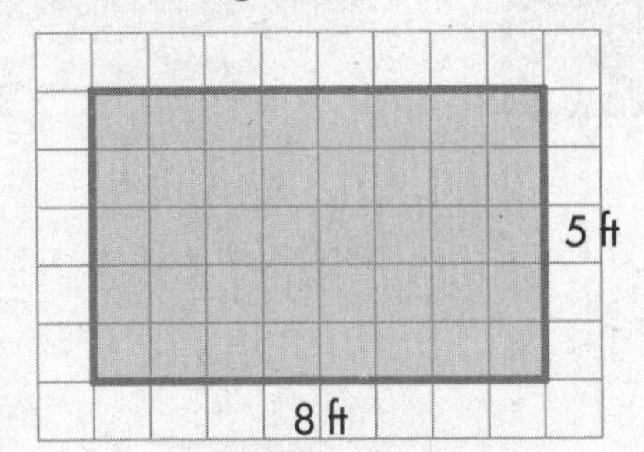

Rectangle A

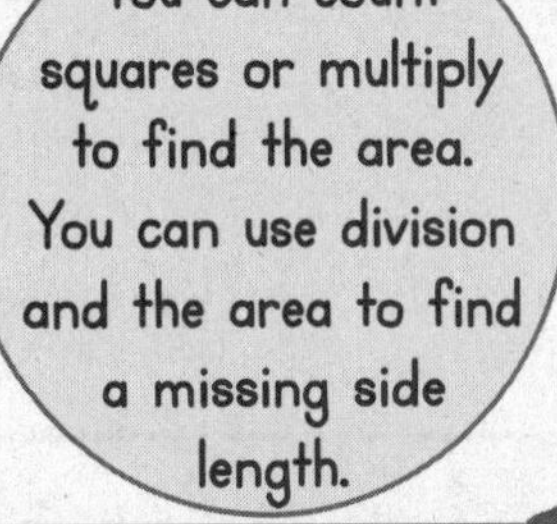

Rectangle B

A. You can count the number of unit squares in Rectangle A to find its area. There are 40 unit squares. Each unit square is 1 square foot.

You also can count the number of rows and multiply that number by the number of squares in each row.

$5 \times 8 = 40$ square feet

B. The area of Rectangle B is 20 square feet, and the width is 5 feet.

$20 = 5 \times ?$

You can use division to find the length of Rectangle B.

$20 \div 5 = 4$ feet

In **1–3**, find the area.

1. 2 m, 9 m

2. 6 in., 4 in.

3. 3 cm, 8 cm

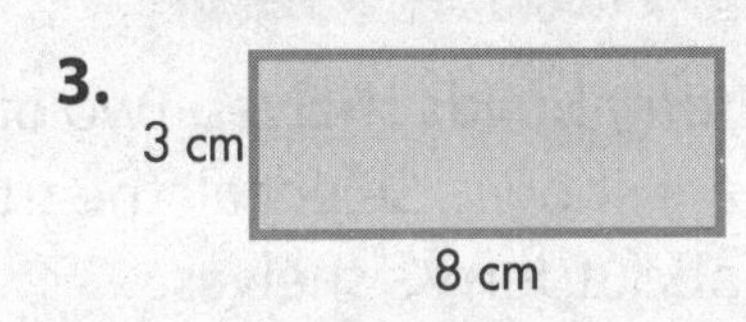

In **4–6**, find the missing length of one side. Use grid paper to help.

4. 9 ft, ? ft, 54 square ft

5. 8 cm, ? cm, 64 square cm

6. ? m, 6 m, 42 square m

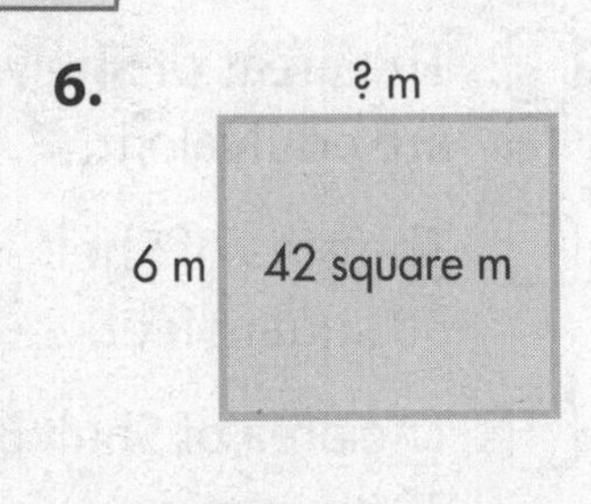

7. **Number Sense** Rachel's family went on a car trip. They traveled 68 miles the first day. They traveled 10 fewer miles the second day. They traveled 85 miles the third day. How many miles did they travel?

8. **Critique Reasoning** Diane says that the area of this shape is 32 square inches, because $4 \times 8 = 32$. Do you agree? Explain.

8 in.

4 in.

9. **Higher Order Thinking** Rubin drew this diagram of his garden. How can you divide the shape to find the area? What is the area of the garden?

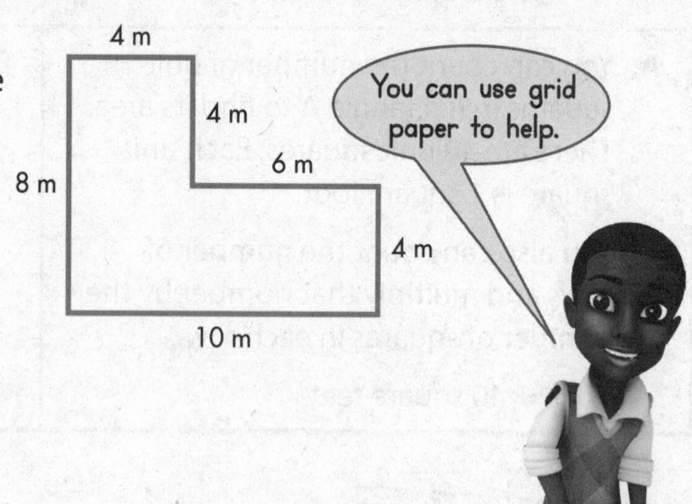

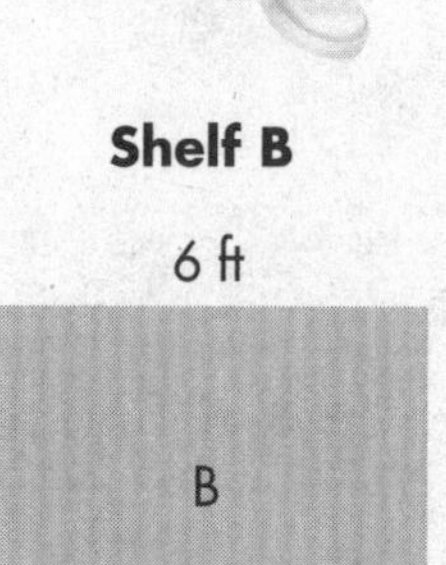

10. Jerry builds shelves. Two of his shelves are shown. Select all the true statements about Jerry's shelves.

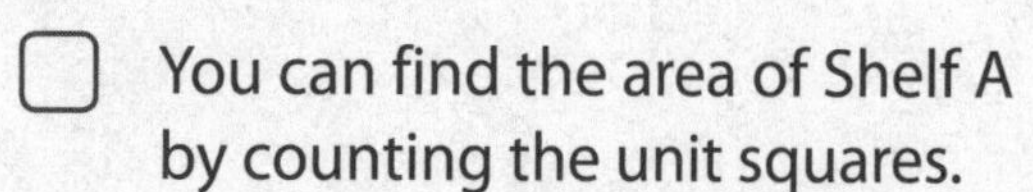
☐ You can find the area of Shelf A by counting the unit squares.

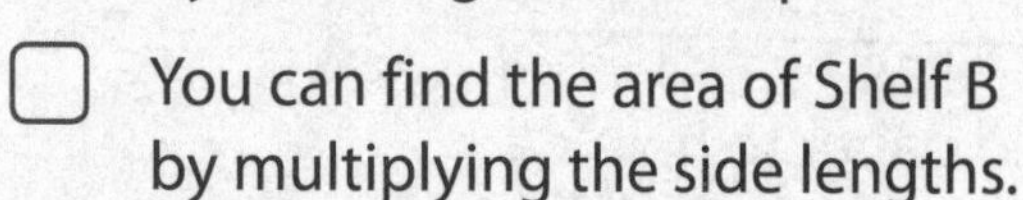
☐ You can find the area of Shelf B by multiplying the side lengths.

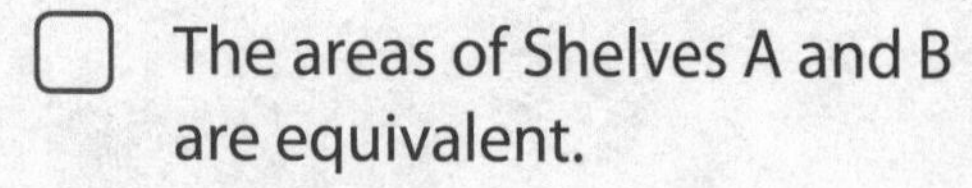
☐ The areas of Shelves A and B are equivalent.

☐ The area of Shelf A is 30 square feet.

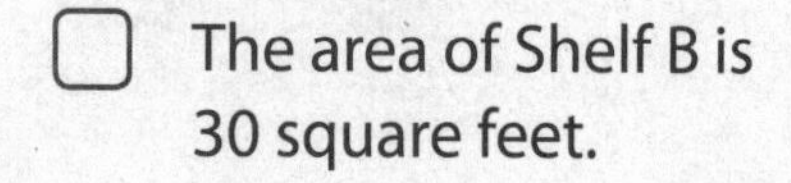
☐ The area of Shelf B is 30 square feet.

Shelf A

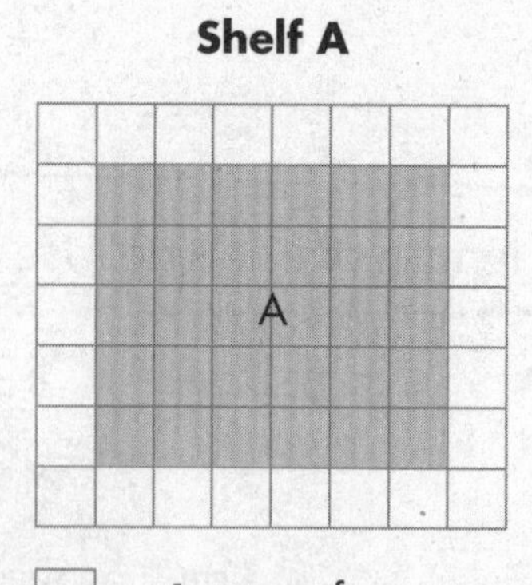

Shelf B

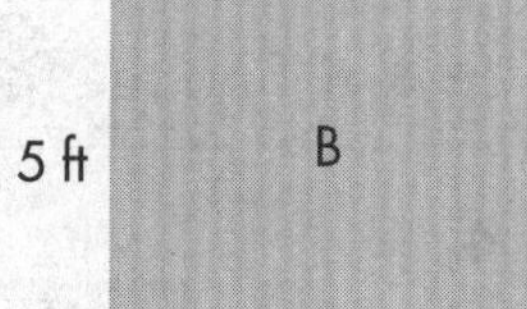

Name ____________________

Practice | Video | Tools | Games

Additional Practice 6-5

Apply Properties: Area and the Distributive Property

Another Look!

You can use the Distributive Property to break an area into smaller rectangles to find more familiar facts to multiply.

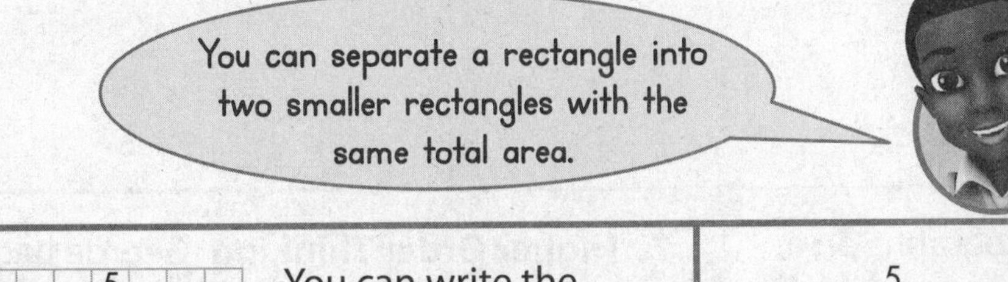

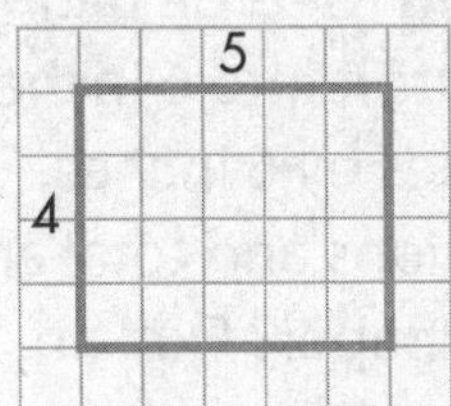

You can write the multiplication fact that represents the area of the large rectangle.

$4 \times 5 = 20$

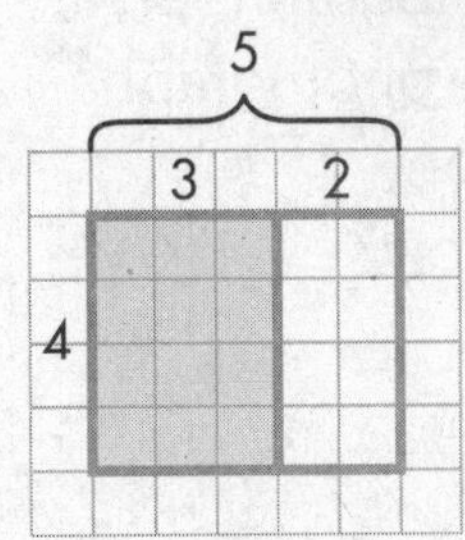

You can write the multiplication facts that represent the area of each of the smaller rectangles.

$4 \times 5 = 4 \times (3 + 2)$

$4 \times 5 = (4 \times 3) + (4 \times 2)$

$4 \times 5 = 12 + 8 = 20$

In **1–4**, complete the equations that represent the picture.

The areas of the large rectangles are equal to the sum of the areas of the smaller rectangles.

1.

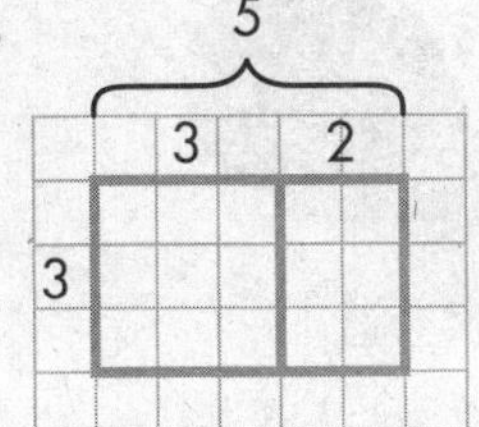

$3 \times \square = \square \times (3 + \square)$

$3 \times \square = (3 \times \square) + (\square \times 2)$

$3 \times \square = \square + \square = 15$

2.

$\square \times 7 = \square \times (\square + 4)$

$\square \times 7 = (\square \times 3) + (4 \times \square)$

$\square \times 7 = \square + \square = 28$

3.

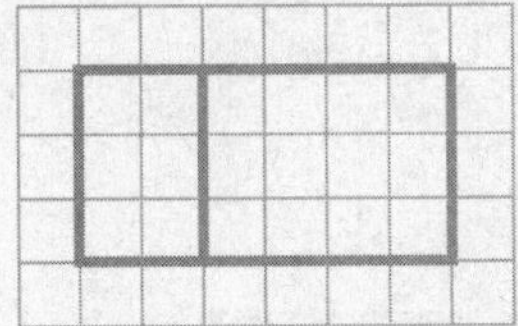

$3 \times \square = \square \times (2 + \square)$

$3 \times \square = (3 \times \square) + (\square \times 4)$

$3 \times \square = \square + \square = 18$

4.

$\square \times 6 = \square \times (\square + 3)$

$\square \times 6 = (\square \times 3) + (5 \times \square)$

$\square \times 6 = \square + \square = 30$

5. Tina divided the rectangle at the right into two smaller parts. Show another way to divide the rectangle into two smaller parts. Write the equation you could use to find the area of the two smaller rectangles.

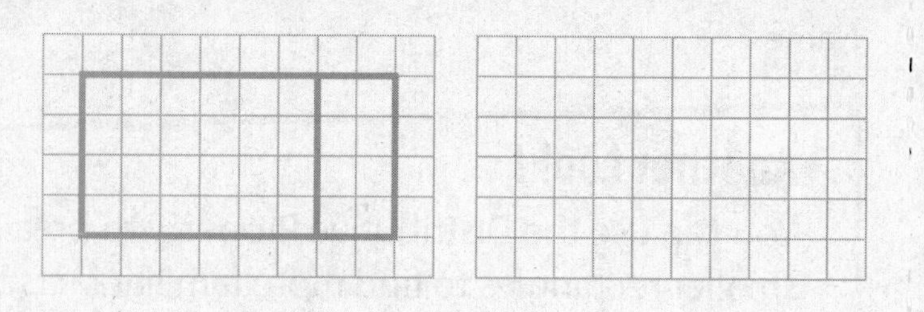

6. Lee wants to place 48 photographs on a wall at school. He puts the photographs into 8 equal rows. How many photographs are in each row?

7. **Higher Order Thinking** George had 1 sheet of paper. He cuts it into 6 inches by 5 inches, and 3 inches by 6 inches. What were the dimensions and total area of his original sheet of paper? Explain.

8. **Use Structure** Darren has a piece of wood that is 7 inches by 8 inches. Explain how he could divide this large rectangle into two smaller rectangles.

Assessment Practice

9. Which equation represents the total area of the shapes?

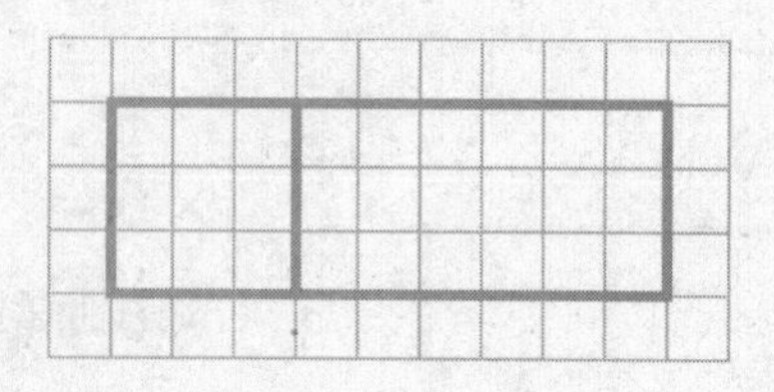

Ⓐ $3 \times 10 = 3 \times (3 + 6) = (3 \times 3) + (3 \times 6)$

Ⓑ $3 \times 9 = 3 \times (4 + 5) = (3 \times 4) + (3 \times 5)$

Ⓒ $3 \times 9 = 3 \times (3 + 6) = (3 \times 3) + (3 \times 6)$

Ⓓ $3 \times 9 = 3 \times (2 + 7) = (3 \times 2) + (3 \times 7)$

Name

Additional Practice 6-6

Apply Properties: Area of Irregular Shapes

Another Look!

How can you find the area of the irregular shape below?

You can count unit squares, or divide the shape into rectangles.

Place the shape on grid paper. Then you can count unit squares.

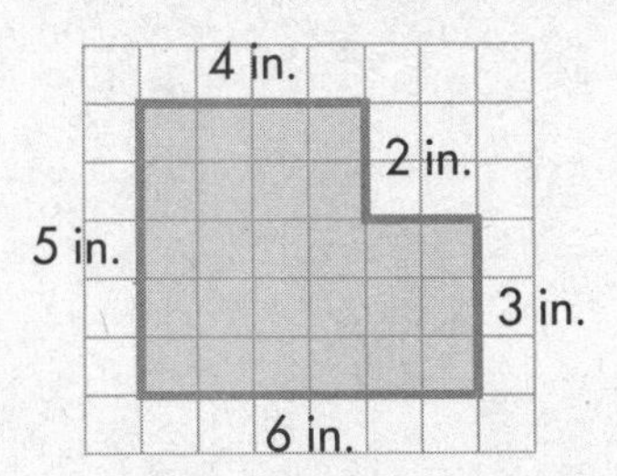

The area of the irregular shape is 26 square inches.

You can divide the shape into rectangles. Find the area of each rectangle. Then add the areas.

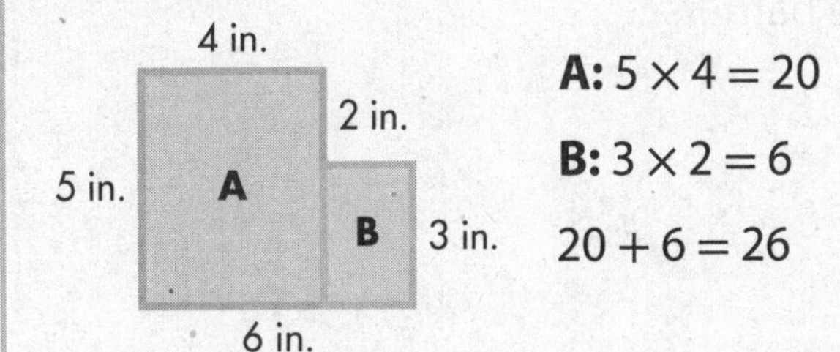

A: $5 \times 4 = 20$

B: $3 \times 2 = 6$

$20 + 6 = 26$

The area of the irregular shape is 26 square inches.

In **1–4**, find the area of each irregular shape. Use grid paper to help.

1.

2 in. 2 in. 6 in. 2 in. 5 in.

2.

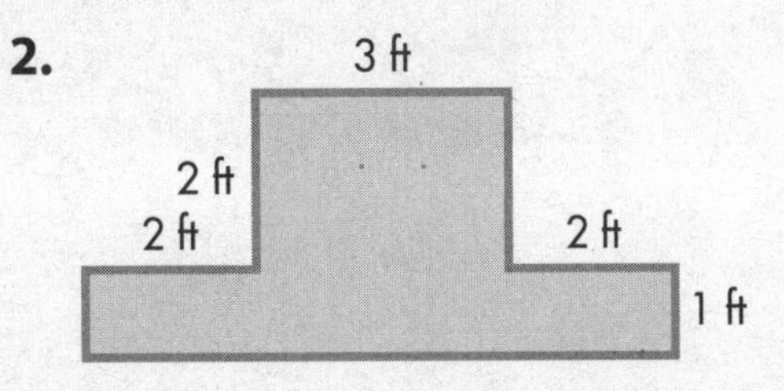

3.

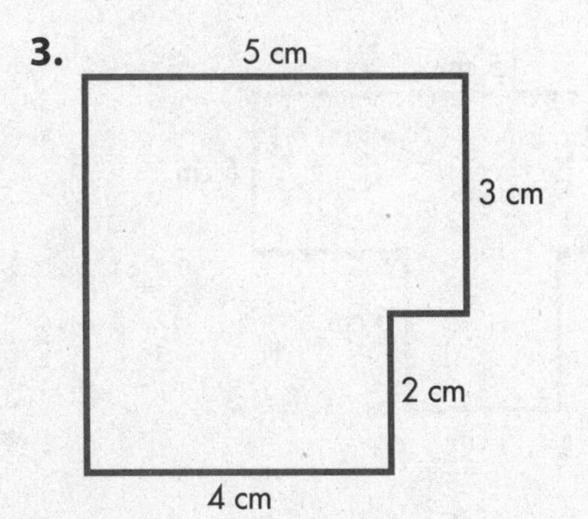

4.

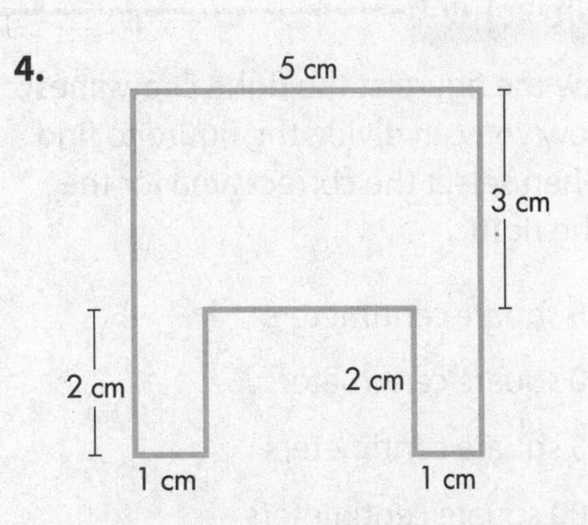

5. **Reasoning** Tony made this diagram of his vegetable garden. What is the total area? Explain your reasoning.

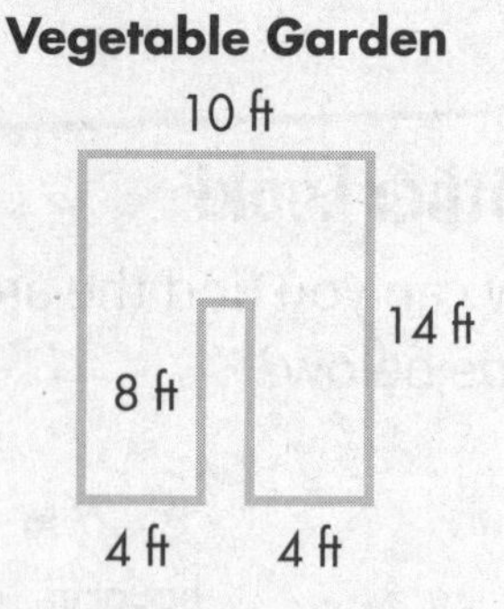

6. **enVision® STEM** Mr. Thomson wants to protect his garage by installing a flood barrier. He connects 2 barriers side by side. Each barrier is 9 feet long by 2 feet high. What is the combined area of the barriers?

7. **Number Sense** Hadori made this solid figure by paper folding. What is the name of the figure she made? How many faces, edges, and vertices does it have?

8. **Higher Order Thinking** Jordan made this design from three pieces of square-shaped cloth. What is the total area of the design Jordan made? Explain how you found your answer.

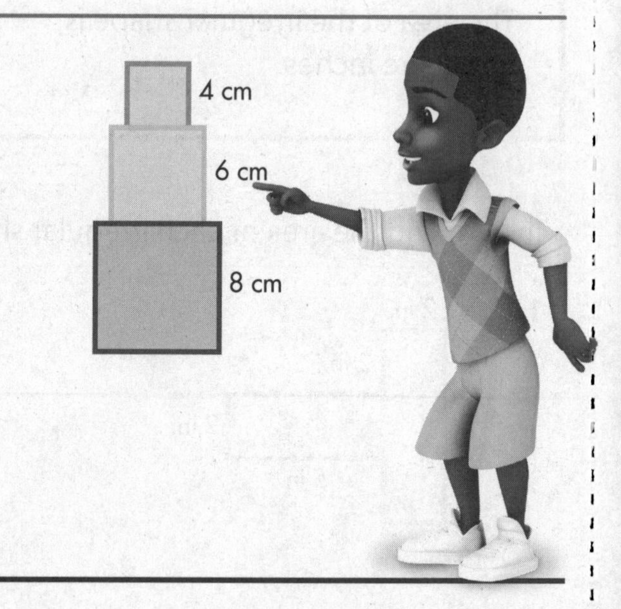

Assessment Practice

9. Daniel drew the figure at the right. Draw lines to show how you can divide the figure to find the area. Then select the correct area for the figure at the right.

   Ⓐ 25 square centimeters

   Ⓑ 50 square centimeters

   Ⓒ 75 square centimeters

   Ⓓ 100 square centimeters

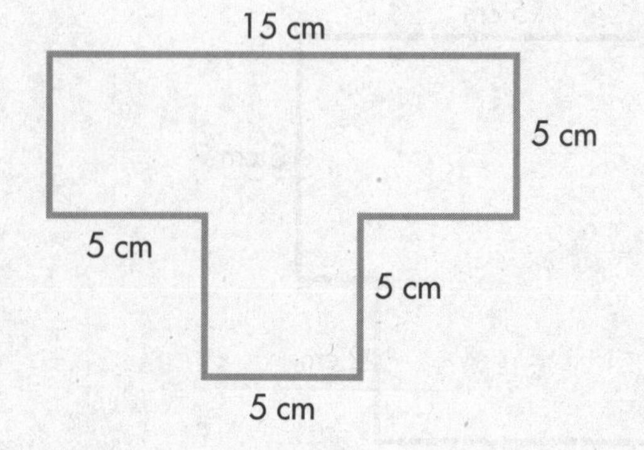

Name

Additional Practice 6-7
Look For and Use Structure

Another Look!

How can you find the area of the shaded part of the figure at the right?

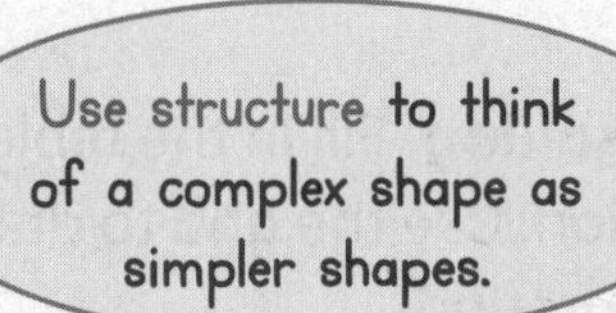

Tell how you can use structure to solve the problem.

- I can break the problem into simpler parts.
- I can find equivalent expressions.

Solve the problem.

The shaded area equals the total area minus the non-shaded area.

Find the area of the large rectangle. $5 \times 8 = 40$ square cm

Find the area of the small rectangle. $2 \times 3 = 6$ square cm

Subtract to find the area of the shaded part. $40 - 6 = 34$ square cm

The area of the shaded part is 34 square centimeters.

Use Structure

A tablet computer has a 1-inch border of plastic around the screen. What is the area of the plastic border?

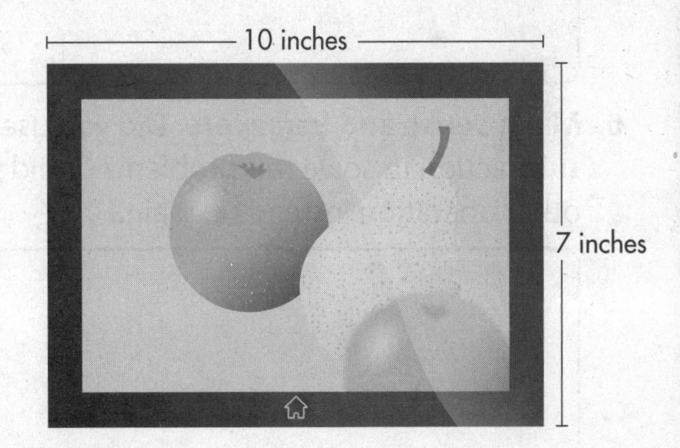

1. Tell how you can use structure to solve the problem.

2. Find two different ways to express the area of the screen.

3. Use these equivalent expressions to solve the problem.

Performance Task

Playground

Mr. Velasquez built a playground. It has one section with a slide and another section with a swing set. A pathway connects the two areas. The slide is 2 meters high. The areas and the pathway are covered in asphalt. Mr. Velasquez wants to know how much of the playground is covered in asphalt.

Section	Length (meters)	Width (meters)	Area
Swing set	8	3	
Slide	8	2	
Pathway	5	1	

4. Reasoning Fill in the table above to show the area of each section. Use the grid to draw a possible diagram of the playground.

5. Construct Arguments Find the total area covered in asphalt. Explain your reasoning using math.

6. Make Sense and Persevere Did you use addition or subtraction to solve this problem? Could you have used the other operation instead? Explain.

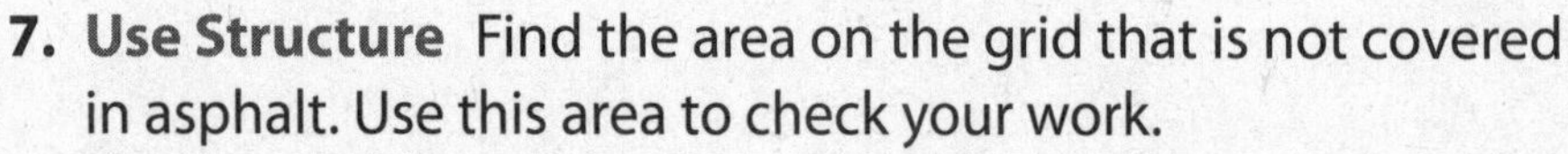

7. Use Structure Find the area on the grid that is not covered in asphalt. Use this area to check your work.

Name ______________________

Practice Video Tools Games

Additional Practice 7-1
Read Picture Graphs and Bar Graphs

Another Look!

You can use a picture graph or a bar graph to represent and interpret data.

Picture graphs use pictures or parts of pictures to represent data.

Gold Medals Won at 2010 Vancouver Winter Olympics

Country	Gold Medals
Sweden	◎ ◎ ◎ ◎ ◎
France	◎ ◎
Switzerland	◎ ◎ ◎ ◎ ◎ ◎
Russia	◎ ◎ ◎

Each ◎ = 1 gold medal.

Picture graphs have keys to explain the scale being used and what each picture represents.

Bar graphs use bars to represent data.

Bar graphs have scales that show the units used.

Each line in this bar graph represents 2 medals.

In **1–4**, use the picture graph at the right.

1. How many houses were built in City B and City F combined?

2. How many more houses were built in City D than in City E in 1 year?

3. What does the half of a house represent in the data for City A?

4. How many more houses were built in City A than in City C?

Number of Houses Built in 1 Year

City	Houses
City A	⌂ ⌂ ⌂ ⌂ ◿
City B	⌂ ⌂ ⌂ ⌂
City C	⌂ ⌂ ⌂
City D	⌂ ⌂ ⌂ ⌂ ⌂ ⌂ ⌂
City E	⌂ ⌂ ⌂ ⌂ ⌂
City F	⌂ ⌂ ⌂ ⌂ ⌂ ⌂

Each ⌂ = 10 houses. Each ◿ = 5 houses.

In **5–8**, use the picture graph at the right.

5. Compare the number of books Tamika read to the number of books Anders and Miguel combined read. Use the symbol >, <, or =.

6. **Reasoning** Which students read at least double the number of books that Anders read?

Books Read

Nancy	📖📖📖📖📖▯
Tamika	📖📖📖📖📖📖📖
Jamal	📖📖📖📖
Phil	📖📖📖📖▯
Anders	📖📖▯
Miguel	📖📖

Each 📖 = 4 books. Each ▯ = 2 books.

7. Which students read fewer than 12 books?

8. **Higher Order Thinking** How many more books did Tamika and Jamal read combined than Nancy and Anders combined?

Assessment Practice

In **9** and **10**, use the bar graph at the right.

9. How many fewer votes did soccer receive than baseball?

Ⓐ 1 vote

Ⓑ 2 votes

Ⓒ 3 votes

Ⓓ 4 votes

10. How many more votes did football and baseball receive than soccer and basketball?

Ⓐ 1 vote

Ⓑ 2 votes

Ⓒ 3 votes

Ⓓ 4 votes

Name ______________________

Practice

Video

Tools

Games

Additional Practice 7-2

Make Picture Graphs

Another Look!

The frequency table shows items that were ordered for lunch. Follow the steps below to learn how to make a scaled picture graph.

Data in a table can be shown in a picture graph.

DATA

Items Ordered

Food	Tally	Number
Pasta	𝍸 /	6
Salad	////	4
Casserole	𝍸 𝍸	10
Fish	𝍸 ////	9

Items Ordered

Pasta	3 whole symbols
Salad	2 whole symbols
Casserole	5 whole symbols
Fish	4 whole symbols, 1 half symbol

Each (whole symbol) = 2 meals.
Each (half symbol) = 1 meal.

Step 1	**Step 2**	**Step 3**
Write a title that explains what the picture graph shows.	Choose a symbol and a scale.	Draw in the graph the number of symbols that are needed for each item.

1. Complete the frequency table to show how Ms. Hashimoto's class voted for their favorite type of movie.

DATA

Favorite Type of Movie

Type	Tally	Number
Action	𝍸 ///	
Comedy	///	
Drama	𝍸 /	
Animated	𝍸 𝍸	

What was the difference in votes between the most popular movie type and the least popular movie type?

2. Use the table in Exercise 1 to complete the picture graph.

____

Action	
Comedy	
Drama	
Animated	

Each (whole circle) = _____ votes.
Each (half circle) = _____ vote.

How did you choose the number that each symbol represents?

3. enVision® STEM There are 61 days in March and April. Mrs. Dorsey recorded 18 sunny days in March and 12 sunny days in April. How many days were not sunny?

4. Vocabulary A ____________ can also be used to represent and compare the same data set using bars instead of pictures or symbols.

In **5–7**, use the picture graph at the right.

5. Pamela made this picture graph showing 14 students' favorite drinks. She drew 3 glasses to represent the 6 students who chose chocolate milk. Is her picture graph correct? Explain.

Favorite Drink	
Chocolate milk	🥛🥛🥛
Orange juice	🥛🥛🥛🥛
Each 🥛 = 2 students.	

6. Higher Order Thinking How would Pamela's picture graph change if 12 students chose grape juice as their favorite drink?

7. Make Sense and Persevere How could the scale change if her picture graph showed the favorite drinks of 70 students?

Assessment Practice

8. April counted cars painted 4 different colors. She made a frequency table to record the total number of cars for each color. Complete the picture graph to represent her data. Write the scale you used in the key.

Color of Cars	
Red	
Green	
Silver	
Black	

DATA

Color of Cars		
Color	**Tally**	**Number**
Red	𝍸 𝍸 𝍸 /	16
Green	𝍸 𝍸 𝍸 𝍸	20
Silver	𝍸 𝍸 𝍸 𝍸 ////	24
Black	𝍸 𝍸 ////	14

Name ____________________

Additional Practice 7-3
Make Bar Graphs

Another Look!

The table below shows the number of birds that visited a bird feeder.

Bird Feeder Visits

Day	Number of Birds
Monday	12
Tuesday	8
Wednesday	14
Thursday	10
Friday	5

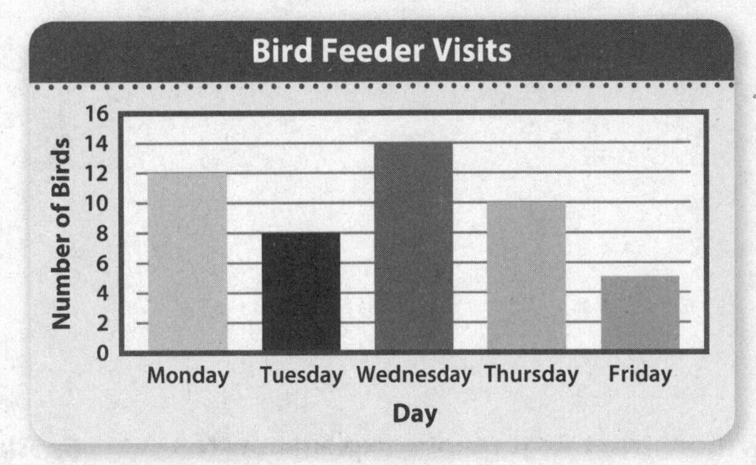

Follow the steps below to learn how to make the bar graph at the right.

Step 1	Step 2	Step 3	Step 4
Write each of the days and label the bottom of the graph "Day."	Choose a scale. Number the scale. Label the scale "Number of Birds."	Draw a bar for each day. Check that the bar lengths match the number in the table and the widths are the same.	Give the graph a title.

For **1–3**, use the table at the right.

1. Complete the bar graph to show the data. Remember to add a title.

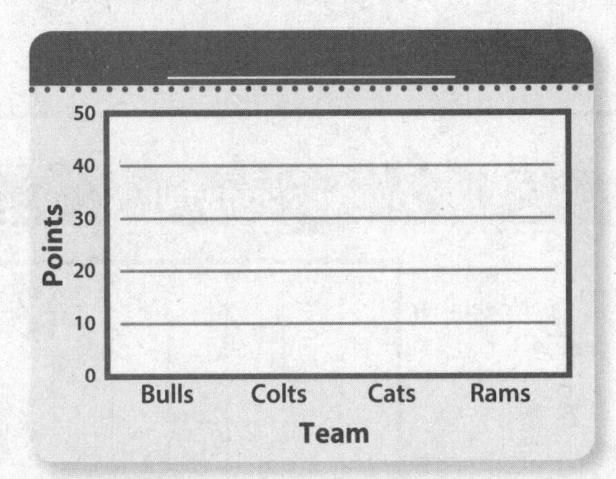

Field Day Results

Team	Points
Bulls	45
Colts	30
Cats	25
Rams	40

2. Explain how to use your bar graph to find the team with the most points.

3. If the Rams score 5 more points, which team's score will they match?

In **4–6**, use the table at the right.

4. Make a bar graph to show the data.

Favorite States to Visit	
State	**Number of Votes**
New York	25
Florida	35
California	30
Hawaii	20

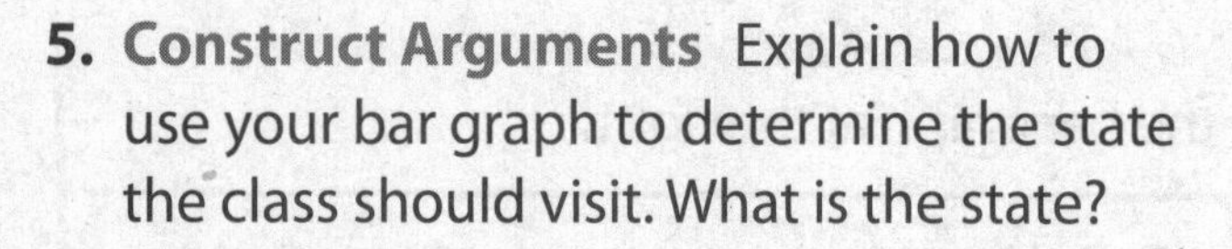

5. Construct Arguments Explain how to use your bar graph to determine the state the class should visit. What is the state?

6. Algebra The total number of votes for two states can be represented by the equation $35 + ? = 65$. Which state's number of votes makes this statement true?

7. enVision® STEM Dawn made a paper airplane and measured the distance it flew in feet for 30 tosses. The longest distance she measured was 45 feet. The shortest distance was 28 feet. How many more feet is the longest distance than the shortest distance?

8. Higher Order Thinking Kim makes a bar graph to record votes for the choice of a class pet. Each grid line represents 4 votes. Fish got 8 votes. The bar for hamster is 3 grid lines higher than the bar for fish. How many votes did hamster get?

Assessment Practice

9. Mr. Walker collected data on the average monthly snowfall in his town. Use the data to complete the bar graph.

Average Snowfall	
Month	**Snowfall (Inches)**
November	2
December	8
January	12

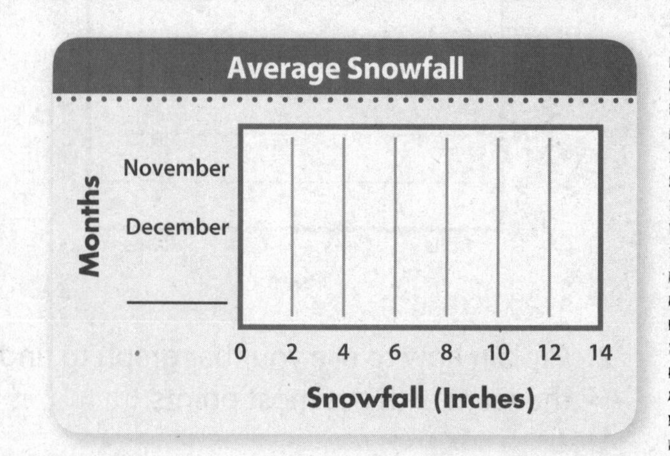

Name ____________________

Additional Practice 7-4
Solve Word Problems Using Information in Graphs

Another Look!

Students were asked to name their favorite type of dog. The picture graph shows the results of the survey.

Students' Favorite Dogs

Dog	Number Counted
Beagle	
Collie	
Shepherd	
Poodle	
Dalmatian	

Each [dog] = 2 votes. Each [half dog] = 1 vote.

You can use graphs to compare data and draw conclusions.

Some conclusions you can draw from the picture graph include:

- Shepherd was chosen by exactly 5 students.
- 2 fewer students chose dalmatian than chose beagle.
- 4 more students chose collie than chose beagle.

In **1–4**, use the bar graph at the right.

1. How many more votes did punch get than water?

2. How many fewer votes did milk get than juice and water combined?

3. How many more votes did juice get than punch and water combined?

4. What is the difference between the number of votes for juice and the number of votes for water and milk combined?

Make sure to look at the scale when reading the data in each graph.

In **5** and **6**, use the picture graph at the right.

5. Generalize Which type of shoe was sold least at Just Shoes? How do you know?

6. How many more pairs of boots than slippers were sold at Just Shoes? How did you find your answer?

In **7** and **8**, use the bar graph at the right.

7. Higher Order Thinking Jared, Alicia, Lydia, and Trey are cousins. Jared is 8 years older than Alicia. Lydia is 4 years younger than Trey. Trey is 18 years younger than Jared. Alicia is 22. Complete the graph to show their ages.

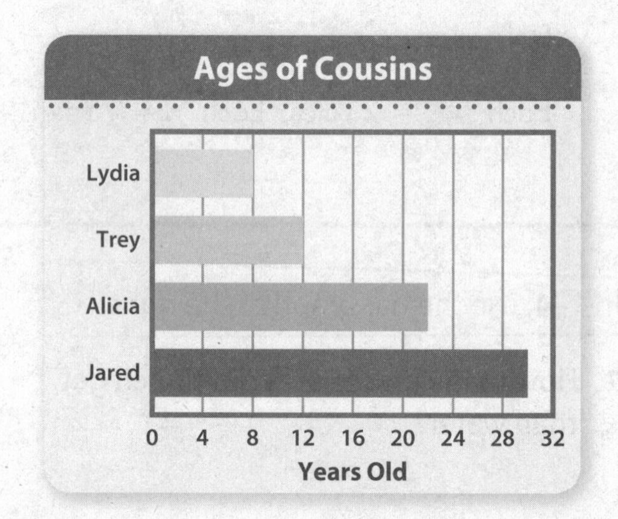

8. How many years older is Jared than Lydia?

Assessment Practice

9. Students at King Elementary School washed cars to raise money for a school trip.

How many more cars did the 4th graders and the 6th graders combined wash than the 5th graders?

Ⓐ 5 cars

Ⓑ 4 cars

Ⓒ 3 cars

Ⓓ 2 cars

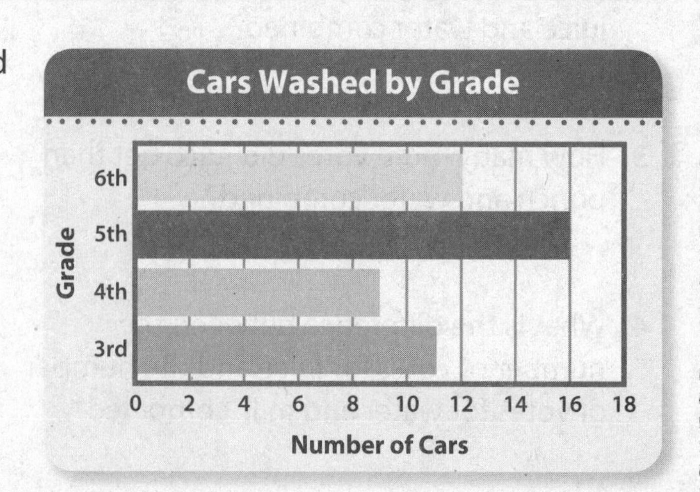

Name ____________________

Additional Practice 7-5
Precision

Another Look!

Wynton made a picture graph to record the music he would like to download. He has $35 to spend on music. He wants to buy at least 1 of each type of item. He wants to buy more singles than albums. What is one way Wynton can spend $35 on music?

When you are precise, you use math symbols and language correctly.

Tell how you can be precise when solving this problem.

- I can correctly use the information given.
- I can make sure my calculations are accurate.

Solve. Use math words and symbols to explain your thinking.

5 singles × $2 = $10   35 − 10 = $25 left

3 albums × $6 = $18   25 − 18 = $7 left

1 collection × $7 = $7   7 − 7 = $0 left

Wynton has spent exactly $35.
He has bought more singles than albums.

Music Available to Download	
Singles ($2 each)	♩ ♩ ♩ ♩
Albums ($6 each)	♩ ♩ ♩
Collections ($7 each)	♩ ♩
Each ♩ = 3 items.	

Be Precise

Casie made a picture graph to record the points that third-grade students scored on a test. Mrs. Wilson's group scored 40 points in all. There are 11 students in Mrs. Wilson's group. What is one way Mrs. Wilson's group may have scored 40 points?

1. Tell how you can be precise when solving this problem.

2. Solve. Use math words and symbols to explain your thinking.

Test Scores

Points	Number of Students
2 points	☺ ☺ ☺ ☺
4 points	☺ ☺ ☺
6 points	☺ ☺ ☺
Each ☺ = 3 students.	

Performance Task

Pizza Party!
Ms. Chavez is planning a class party. There are 28 students at the party. She wants to get at least 1 of each type of pizza and have enough pizza so each student gets 2 slices. Delivery takes 20 minutes. Ms. Chavez has $55 to spend.

Ready To Go Pizza Delivery

Pizza Type	Number of Pizzas Available
Cheese ($6 each)	🍕🍕🍕
Pepperoni ($8 each)	🍕🍕🍕🍕
Supreme ($10 each)	🍕🍕

Each 🍕 = 8 slices.

3. **Reasoning** How many slices of cheese pizza are available? How do you know?

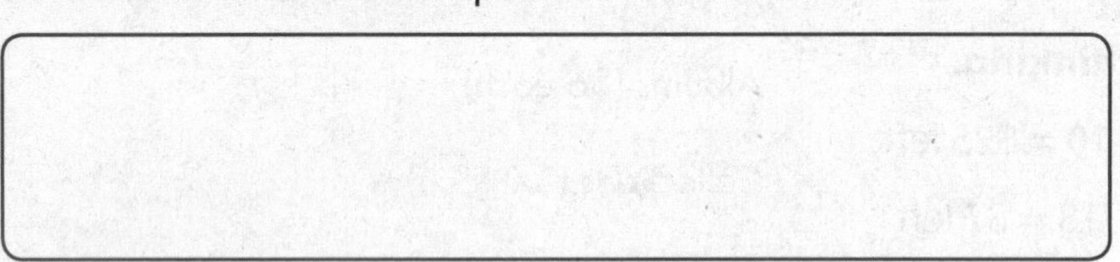

4. **Make Sense and Persevere** How many slices of pizza does Ms. Chavez need? Explain.

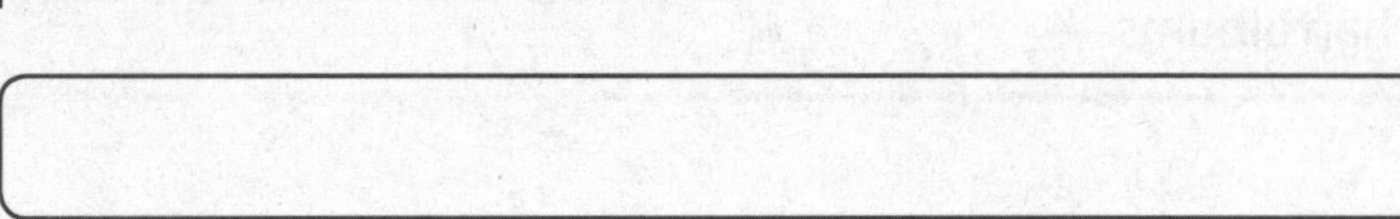

5. **Model with Math** Show how to find the number of pizzas Ms. Chavez should order.

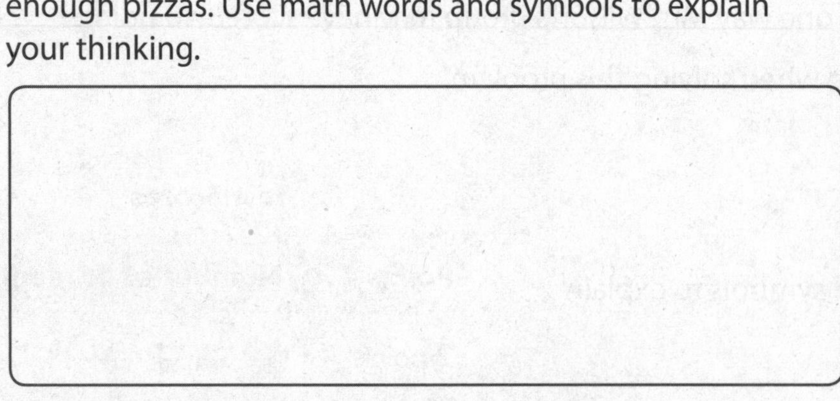

6. **Be Precise** Show one way Ms. Chavez can order enough pizzas. Use math words and symbols to explain your thinking.

7. **Make Sense and Persevere** Which information did you not need to help you solve the problem?

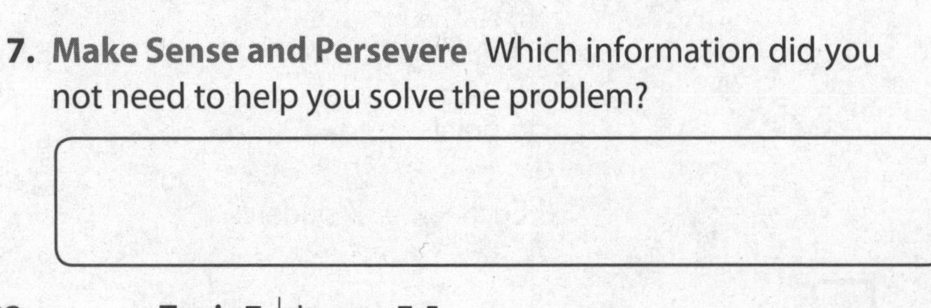

Name ____________

Practice Video Tools Games

Additional Practice 8-1
Addition Properties

Another Look!

Commutative (Order) Property of Addition
You can add numbers in any order and the sum will be the same.

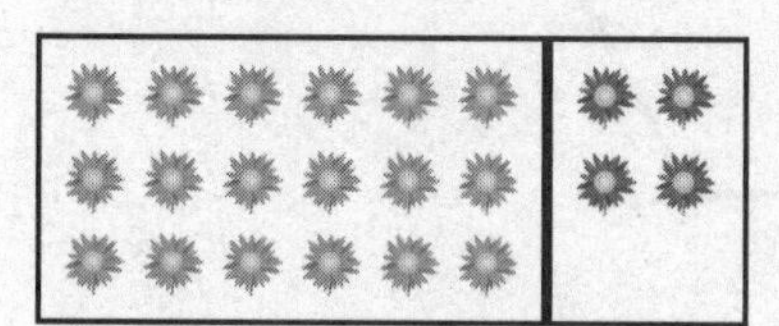

18 + 4 = 22

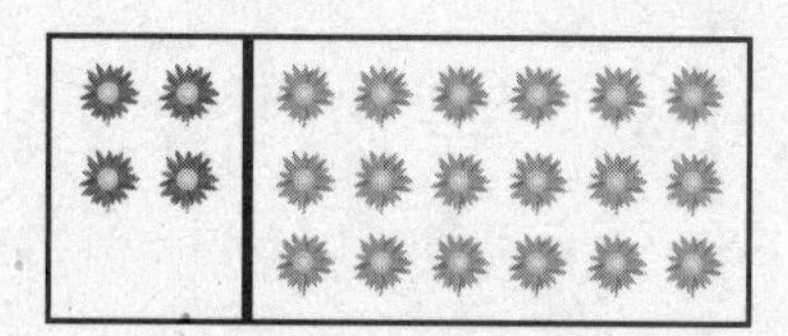

4 + 18 = 22

Associative (Grouping) Property of Addition
You can group numbers in any way and the sum will be the same.

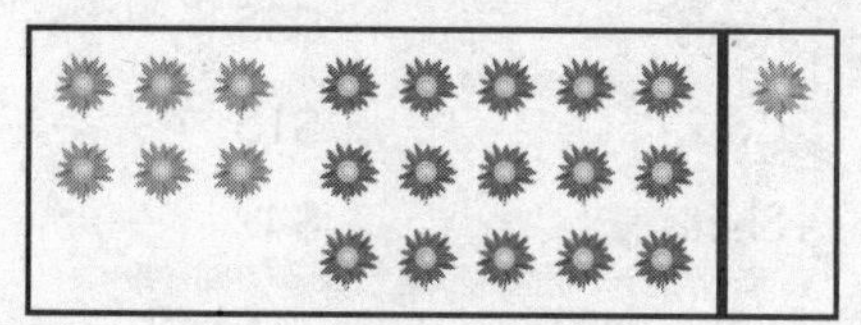

(6 + 15) + 1 = 22

6 + (15 + 1) = 22

Identity (Zero) Property of Addition
The sum of any number and zero equals that same number.

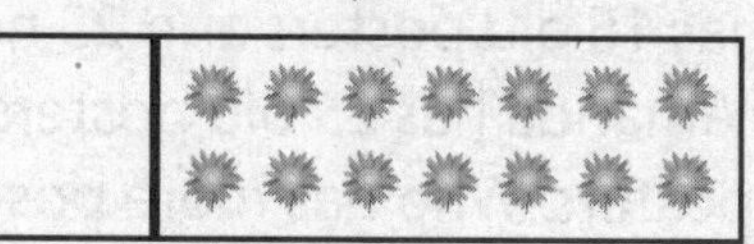

0 + 14 = 14

Addition properties make it easier to add numbers.

In **1–7**, write each missing number.

1. (____ + 15) + ____ = 29   ____ + (____ + ____) = ____

2. 30 + 40 = 40 + ____

3. ____ + 32 = 32

4. (48 + 27) + 3 = ____ + (27 + 3)

5. 29 + (22 + 27) = (29 + 22) + ____

6. 89 + ____ = 89

7. 35 + 49 = ____ + 35

8. Jake says adding 0 to an addend does not change a sum. Is he correct? Explain. Include an equation in your explanation.

9. Draw lines onto the hexagon below to show how you can cut it into new shapes. What are the shapes you made?

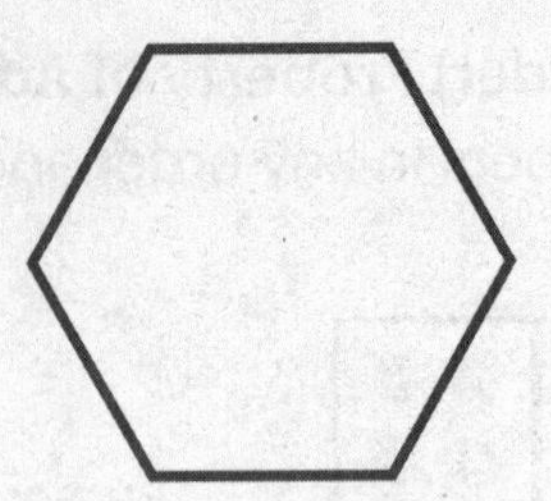

10. Use Structure Troy wants to buy pants, shoes, and a cap. Use the Associative Property of Addition to show two ways he can add the prices to find the total cost. Then find the total.

DATA

Clothing Sale	
Pants	$35
Cap	$15
Shoes	$49

11. Higher Order Thinking Does $65 - (45 - 20) = (65 - 45) - 20$? How do you know?

12. Minnie has 16 old posters and 25 new posters. Amanda has 25 old posters and 16 new posters. Who has more posters? Explain.

Assessment Practice

13. Use place value to find the sum of $16 + 14 + 17$.

Ⓐ 44

Ⓑ 45

Ⓒ 46

Ⓓ 47

14. Use properties of operations to find the sum of $31 + 20 + 19$.

Ⓐ 80

Ⓑ 70

Ⓒ 60

Ⓓ 50

Name ______________________

Practice Video Tools Games

Additional Practice 8-2

Algebra: Addition Patterns

Another Look!

The sums of the addends in the diagonal corners of the outlined box are equal. They form a pattern.

+	20	21	22	23	24
10	30	31	32	33	34
11	31	32	33	34	35
12	32	33	34	35	36
13	33	34	35	36	37
14	34	35	36	37	38

Use the Associative Property.

$32 + 36 = 32 + (2 + 34)$
$= (32 + 2) + 34$
$= 34 + 34$

So, $32 + 36 = 34 + 34$.

Use the Commutative and Associative Properties.

$32 + 36 = (11 + 21) + (13 + 23)$
$34 + 34 = (11 + 23) + (13 + 21)$

$(11 + 21) + (13 + 23) = (11 + 21) + (13 + 23)$
$68 = 68$

+	20	21	22	23	24	25	26	27
10	30	31	32	33	34	35	36	37
11	31	32	33	34	35	36	37	38
12	32	33	34	35	36	37	38	39
13	33	34	35	36	37	38	39	40
14	34	35	36	37	38	39	40	41
15	35	36	37	38	39	40	41	42
16	36	37	38	39	40	41	42	43
17	37	38	39	40	41	42	43	44

1. Describe a pattern shown by the shaded sums. Explain why the pattern is true.

2. Describe a pattern shown by the outlined sums. Explain why the pattern is true.

3. Draw circles around sums in the table to show a pattern you see. Describe your pattern. Explain why it is true.

4. Look for Relationships Ryan found a pattern on the addition table. He shaded two diagonal lines that show his pattern. What is his pattern?

+	36	37	38	39	40	41	42
22	58	59	60	61	62	63	64
23	59	60	61	62	63	64	65
24	60	61	62	63	64	65	66
25	61	62	63	64	65	66	67
26	62	63	64	65	66	67	68
27	63	64	65	66	67	68	69
28	64	65	66	67	68	69	70

5. Ryan wrote the equations to the right for one of his diagonals. Write equations for the other diagonal.

6. Look at Ryan's equations and your equations. What do you notice about them? Explain why.

$24 + 36 = 60$ ____ + ____ = ____

$25 + 37 = 62$ ____ + ____ = ____

$26 + 38 = 64$ ____ + ____ = ____

$27 + 39 = 66$ ____ + ____ = ____

$28 + 40 = 68$ ____ + ____ = ____

7. Higher Order Thinking Tomas made an addition table using 2-digit numbers. Write down a pattern that you used in another problem. Does that pattern work for Tomas's table? Find an example and explain why it does or does not work.

+	67	68	69	70	71	72
67	134	135	136	137	138	139
68	135	136	137	138	139	140
69	136	137	138	139	140	141
70	137	138	139	140	141	142
71	138	139	140	141	142	143
72	139	140	141	142	143	144

Assessment Practice

8. Look at the shaded cells in the addition table below.

+	10	11	12	13	14	15	16
10	20	21	22	23	24	25	26
11	21	22	23	24	25	26	27
12	22	23	24	25	26	27	28
13	23	24	25	26	27	28	29
14	24	25	26	27	28	29	30
15	25	26	27	28	29	30	31
16	26	27	28	29	30	31	32

Which pattern and property of operations are shown in the shaded cells?

Ⓐ Each sum has the same addends; The Commutative Property of Addition

Ⓑ Each sum has the same addends; The Identity Property of Addition

Ⓒ Each sum has the same addends; The Associative Property of Addition

Ⓓ There are no patterns or properties.

Name ______________________

 Practice  Video  Tools  Games

Additional Practice 8-3
Mental Math: Addition

Another Look!

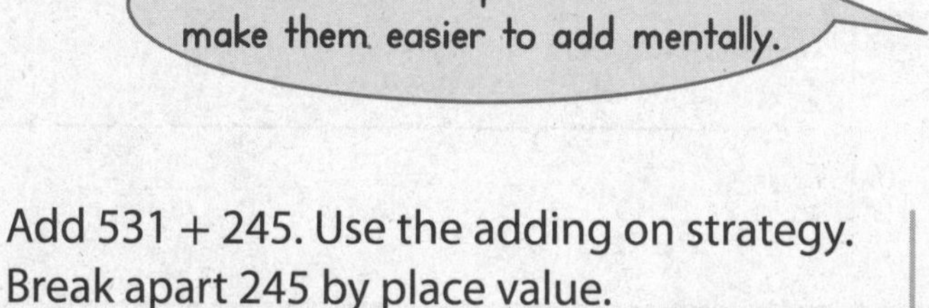

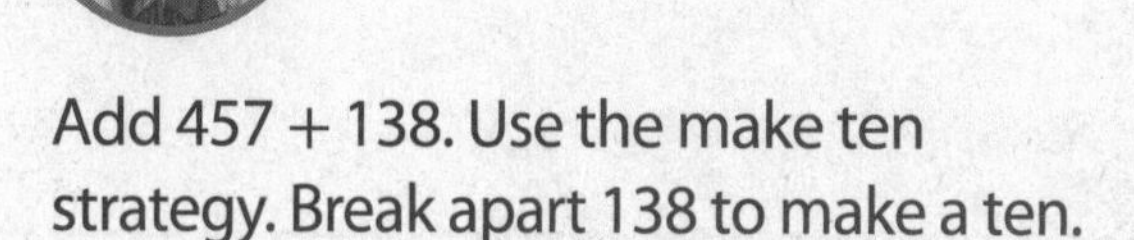

Add 531 + 245. Use the adding on strategy. Break apart 245 by place value.

	hundreds		tens		ones
245 =	200	+	40	+	5

Add 200 to 531: 531 + 200 = 731.

Add 40 to 731: 731 + 40 = 771.

Add 5 to 771: 771 + 5 = 776.

So, 531 + 245 = 776.

Add 457 + 138. Use the make ten strategy. Break apart 138 to make a ten.

Break 138 into 100 + 35 + 3.

Add 3 to 457 to make a ten.
457 + 3 = 460

Add 100 to 460.
460 + 100 = 560

Add 35 to 560.
560 + 35 = 595

So, 457 + 138 = 595.

In **1** and **2**, find each sum.

1. 624 + 171 = ____

171 = 100 + 70 + ____

Add 100 to 624: 624 + 100 = ____.

Add 70 to 724: 724 + 70 = ____.

Add 1 to 794: 794 + 1 = ____.

2. 628 + 237 = ____

Break 237 into 200 + 35 + ____.

628 + 2 = ____

630 + 200 = ____

830 + 35 = ____

In **3–14**, use mental math to add.

3. 136 + 43 **4.** 29 + 636 **5.** 218 + 274 **6.** 325 + 437

7. 358 + 373 **8.** 691 + 264 **9.** 167 + 244 **10.** 482 + 488

11. 395 + 427 **12.** 138 + 248 **13.** 103 + 541 **14.** 675 + 237

15. In November, Juanita saves $242. In December, she saves $80 less than in November. How much does she save in all? Use an equation to represent the problem.

16. Todd wants to find 352 + 116. Break apart 116 by place value and use the open number line and the adding on strategy to find the sum.

17. Explain how you can break apart one of the addends and use the make a ten strategy to find the total number of points Jeannie and Kevin scored.

18. **Use Appropriate Tools** What tool could you use to show how to break apart 286 into hundreds, tens, and ones? Explain how you would use this tool.

19. **Higher Order Thinking** Find 301 + 173 + 427 using mental math and the Associative Property of Addition. Show how you can use the property to group two of the addends.

Assessment Practice

20. Find 173 + 123. Break apart 123 by place value, and then use the adding on strategy. Select numbers to complete the equations.

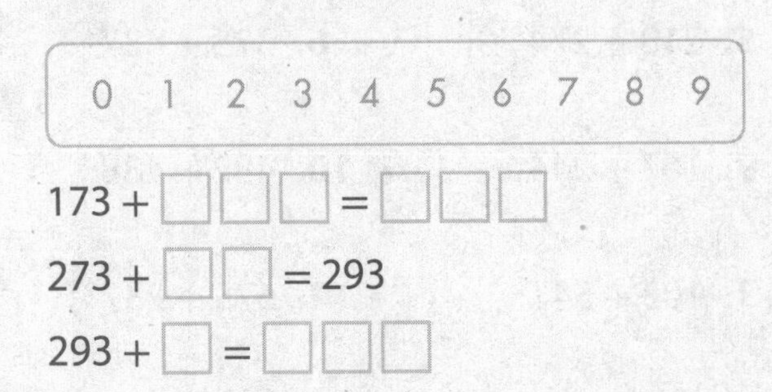

0 1 2 3 4 5 6 7 8 9

173 + □□□ = □□□

273 + □□ = 293

293 + □ = □□□

21. Find 323 + 156. Break apart 156 by place value, and then use the adding on strategy. Select numbers to complete the equations.

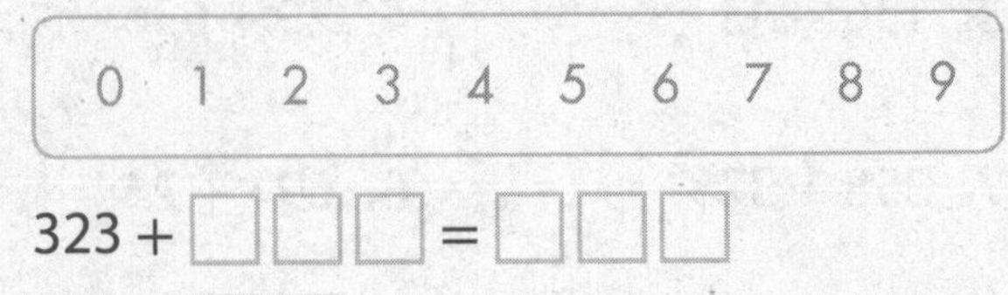

0 1 2 3 4 5 6 7 8 9

323 + □□□ = □□□

423 + □□ = 473

473 + □ = □□□

Name ________________

Additional Practice 8-4

Mental Math: Subtraction

Another Look!

Megan had 372 buttons. She used 14 buttons to make a collage. How many buttons does Megan have now?

Count back.

Start at 372.

$372 - 300 = 72$

$72 - 50 = 22$

$22 - 8 = 14$

$300 + 50 + 8 = 358$

Count up.

Start at 14.

$14 + 300 = 314$

$314 + 50 = 364$

$364 + 8 = 372$

$300 + 50 + 8 = 358$

Use properties.

You can add 6 to both 372 and 14.

$$\begin{array}{r} 372 + 6 \rightarrow 378 \\ \underline{-14 + 6 \rightarrow \quad 20} \\ 358 \end{array}$$

Adding the same amount to each number does not change the difference.

In **1–20**, find each difference using mental math.

1. 232 − 117

$232 + 3 \rightarrow 235$

$-117 + 3 \rightarrow$ ____

2. 940 − 109

$940 + 1 \rightarrow$ ____

$-109 + 1 \rightarrow 110$

3. 281 − 112

$281 + 8 \rightarrow 289$

$-112 + 8 \rightarrow$ ____

4. 309 − 195

$309 + 5 \rightarrow$ ____

$-195 + 5 \rightarrow 200$

5. 656 − 127

6. 781 − 536

7. 228 − 119

8. 647 − 355

9. 153 − 37

10. 777 − 135

11. 841 − 281

12. 976 − 918

13. 959 − 415

14. 604 − 406

15. 543 − 132

16. 975 − 242

17. 490 − 255

18. 460 − 212

19. 800 − 325

20. 769 − 428

21. enVision® STEM Julie recorded the heights of three different trees in this table. Use mental math to find how much taller the redwood tree is than the sequoia tree.

DATA

Tree Heights

Tree	Height (ft)
Sequoia	173
Tanbark	75
Redwood	237

22. Generalize Cassie has 20 bracelets. How many can she give to her sister if she wants to keep 11 or more bracelets? What repeats in the possibilities?

23. Gillian started to find 888 – 291. This is what she did.

$$888 - 291 = ?$$
$$888 - 300 = 588$$

What should Gillian do next?

24. Higher Order Thinking How many more total raffle tickets did Ms. Hudson's and Mr. Nealy's classes sell than Mrs. Robertson's class? Explain.

DATA

Raffle Tickets Sold

Class	Number of Tickets
Ms. Hudson	352
Mr. Nealy	236
Mrs. Robertson	429

Assessment Practice

25. Use the relationship between addition and subtraction to find 255 – 132. Select numbers from the box to complete the work on the open number line and the equations.

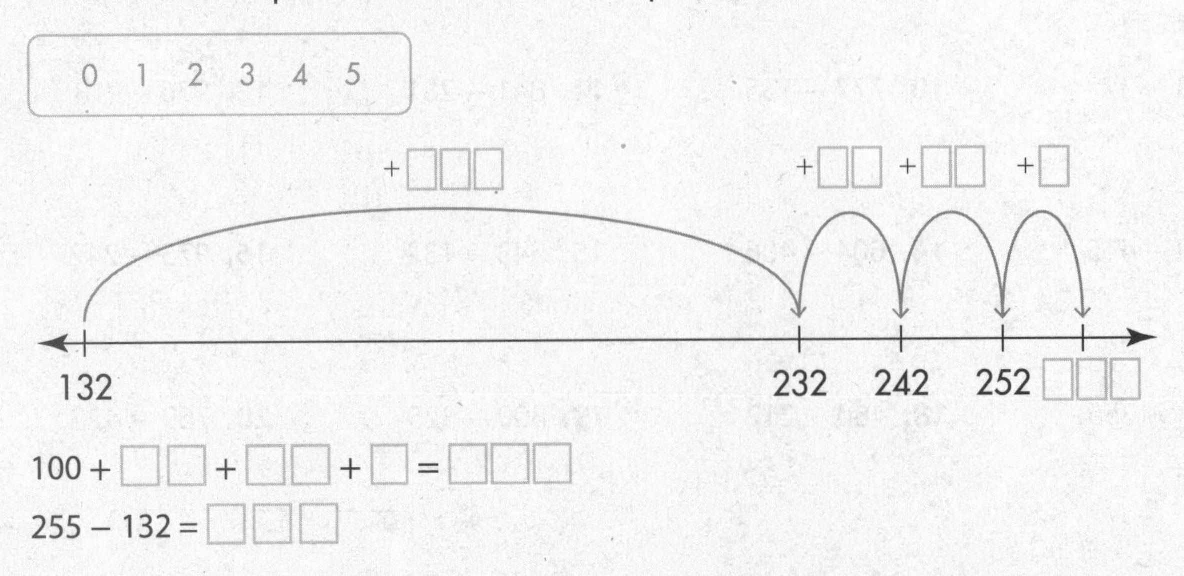

Name

Tools

Additional Practice 8-5

Round Whole Numbers

Another Look!

You can use number lines and what you know about place value to help round numbers.

If a number is halfway between, round to the greater number.

Round 483 to the nearest ten.

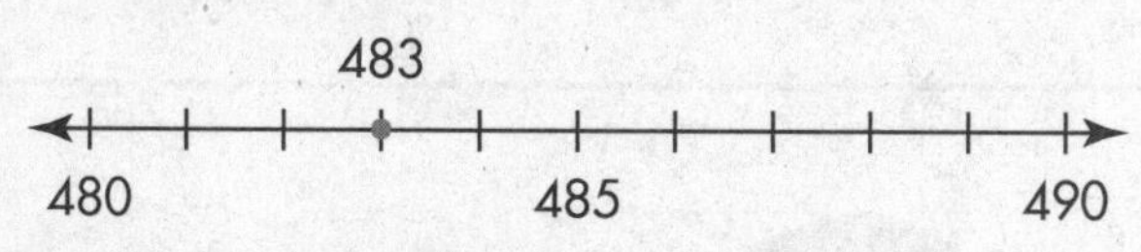

483 is closer to 480 than 490, so 483 rounds to 480.

Round 483 to the nearest 100.

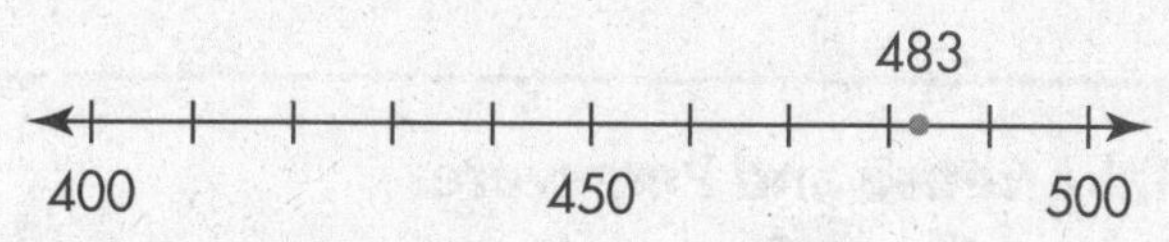

483 is closer to 500 than 400, so 483 rounds to 500.

1. Round 328 to the nearest ten.

2. Round 630 to the nearest hundred.

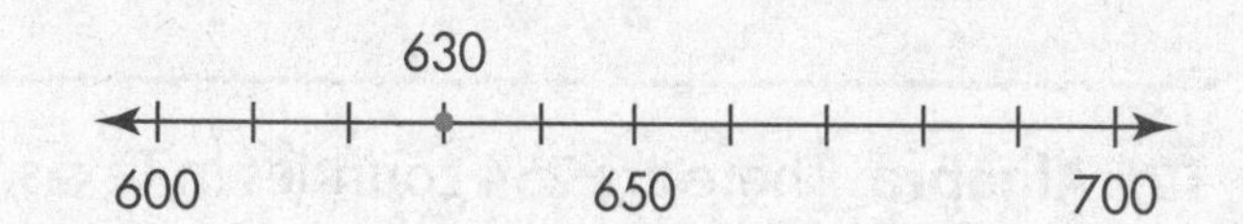

3. Round 649 to the nearest hundred.

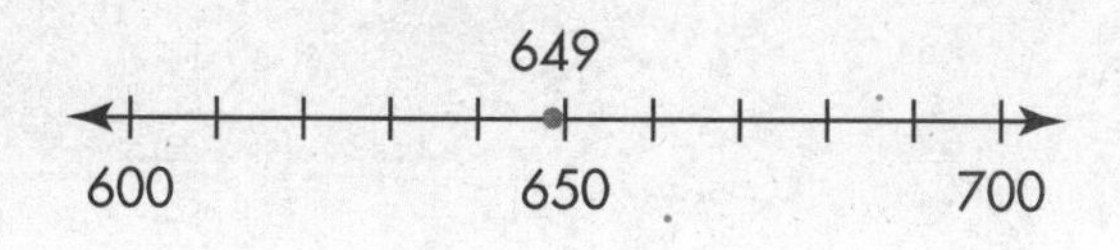

4. Round 155 to the nearest ten.

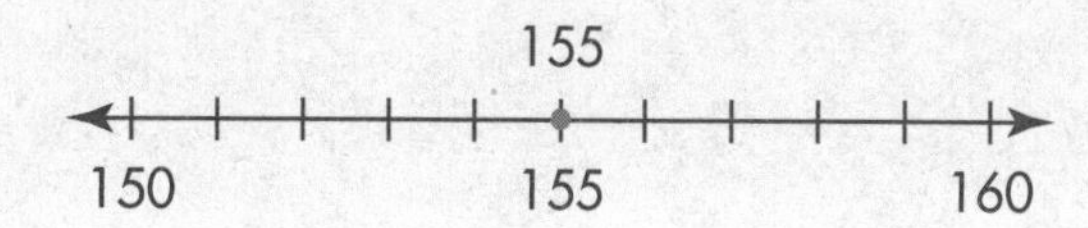

5. Round 262 to the nearest ten.

6. Round 753 to the nearest hundred.

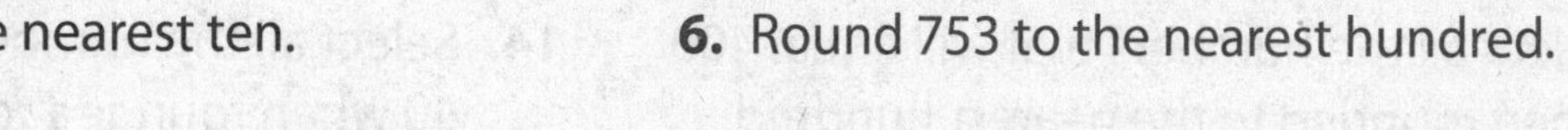

7. Round 429 to the nearest ten and hundred.

8. Round 234 to the nearest ten and hundred.

9. Use the number line to show a number that rounds to 170 when it is rounded to the nearest ten.

10. Higher Order Thinking When this 3-digit number is rounded to the nearest hundred, it rounds to 900. The digit in the ones place is the fifth odd number you count beginning with 1. The sum of the digits is 22. What is the number?

11. Make Sense and Persevere
I have 1 flat surface. I have 1 vertex. You can trace my flat surface to make a circle. Which shape am I? Circle the correct solid figure.

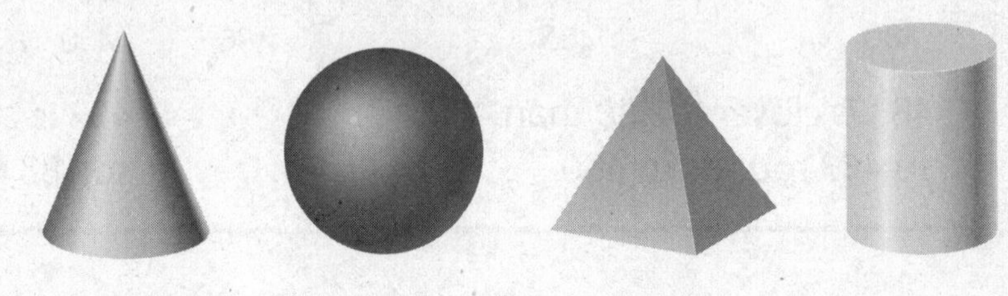

12. Algebra There are 254 counties in Texas. Zane rounds the number of counties to the nearest ten. What is the difference between the actual number of counties and Zane's rounded number? Solve this problem using an equation and an unknown.

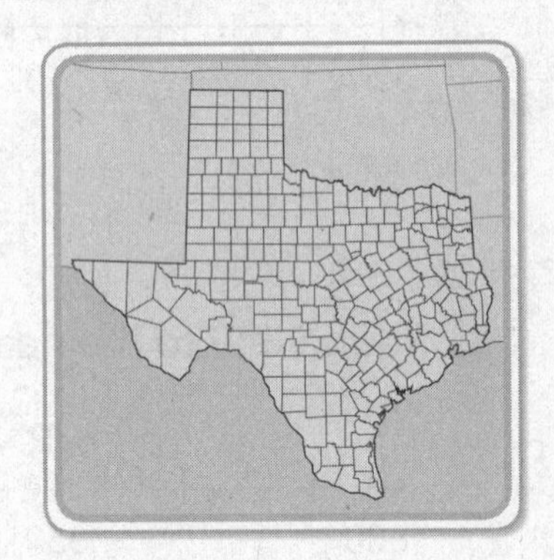

Assessment Practice

13. Select all the numbers that will equal 400 when rounded to the nearest hundred.

- ☐ 351
- ☐ 369
- ☐ 401
- ☐ 413
- ☐ 448

14. Select all the numbers that will equal 40 when rounded to the nearest ten.

- ☐ 39
- ☐ 42
- ☐ 45
- ☐ 50
- ☐ 51

Name ____________________

Practice Video Tools Games

Additional Practice 8-6
Estimate Sums

Another Look!

There is more than one way you can estimate.

The students at Silver School are saving cereal box tops.

About how many box tops have the students saved? When you find *about* how many, you estimate.

Estimate by rounding each addend. Then, add the rounded numbers.

Round to the nearest ten.

$$\begin{array}{r} 136 \rightarrow 140 \\ +\ 178 \rightarrow 180 \\ \hline 320 \end{array}$$

The students have saved about 320 box tops.

Round to the nearest hundred.

$$\begin{array}{r} 136 \rightarrow 100 \\ +\ 178 \rightarrow 200 \\ \hline 300 \end{array}$$

The students have saved about 300 box tops.

In **1–4**, round to the nearest ten to estimate.

1. $144 \rightarrow$ ____ $+\ 298 \rightarrow$ ____ ____

2. $271 \rightarrow$ ____ $+\ 487 \rightarrow$ ____ ____

3. $225 \rightarrow$ ____ $+\ 294 \rightarrow$ ____ ____

4. $359 \rightarrow$ ____ $+\ 107 \rightarrow$ ____ ____

In **5–8**, round to the nearest hundred to estimate.

5. 291 + 268

6. 378 + 136

7. 436 + 309

8. 365 + 487

9. **Critique Reasoning** Sun-Yi estimated 270 + 146 and got 320. Is her estimate reasonable? Explain.

10. **Vocabulary** Miguel has 334 baseball cards and 278 football cards. He says, "I have 612 cards in all." Is that reasonable? Explain using the words *round* and *estimate*.

11. Paige and her friend Karla planted 4 types of rosebushes for the Dundee Community Center. The bar graph at the right shows the color and number of each bush the girls planted. How many more red and pink rosebushes were planted than yellow and white rosebushes?

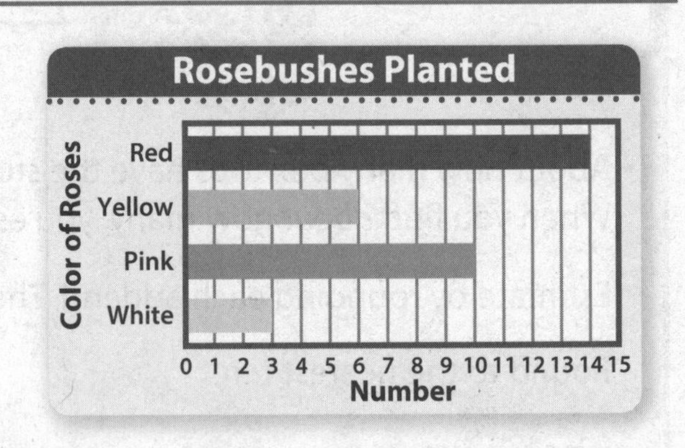

12. **Higher Order Thinking** On Monday, Cheryl drove from Austin to Fort Worth and back to Austin. On Tuesday, she drove from Austin to Jackson. Find about how far Cheryl drove to the nearest ten miles and to the nearest hundred miles.

DATA

Distances from Austin, TX

City	Miles Away
Memphis, TN	643
Fort Worth, TX	189
Jackson, MS	548

Assessment Practice

13. Round to the nearest 10 to estimate the sums.

	Estimate
355 + 198 is about	
342 + 221 is about	
131 + 422 is about	

14. Round to the nearest 100 to estimate the sums.

	Estimate
573 + 65 is about	
355 + 398 is about	
184 + 475 is about	

Name ____________________

Practice Video Tools Games

Additional Practice 8-7
Estimate Differences

Another Look!

Members of the Biology Club caught 288 butterflies and 136 grasshoppers in their nets. About how many more butterflies than grasshoppers did the club catch?

When you find *about* how many, you estimate. You can estimate by rounding.

Round to the nearest hundred.

288 → 300
− 136 → 100
200

There were about 200 more butterflies than grasshoppers caught.

Round to the nearest ten.

288 → 290
− 136 → 140
150

There were about 150 more butterflies than grasshoppers caught.

In **1–8**, round to the nearest hundred to estimate.

1. 584 → ___
− 347 → ___

2. 274 → ___
− 147 → ___

3. 615 → ___
− 523 → ___

4. 831 → ___
− 143 → ___

5. 422 − 142

6. 725 − 278

7. 682 − 224

8. 363 − 187

In **9–16**, round to the nearest ten to estimate.

9. 146 → ___
− 118 → ___

10. 428 → ___
− 332 → ___

11. 588 → ___
− 491 → ___

12. 351 → ___
− 106 → ___

13. 654 − 585

14. 355 − 186

15. 274 − 207

16. 522 − 330

17. Number Sense Duncan says, "Because 6 is greater than 3, 65 is greater than 344." Do you agree? Explain.

18. On Friday, 537 people attended a play. On Saturday, 812 people attended the same play. About how many more people attended the play on Saturday than on Friday? How did you estimate?

19. Andrew has the coins shown at the right. He wants to buy a comic book for $1.00. How much more money does he need to make 1 dollar?

20. Model with Math Lori lives 272 miles from her grandparents, 411 miles from her aunt, and 39 miles from her cousins. About how much closer does Lori live to her grandparents than to her aunt? Explain what math you used.

21. Higher Order Thinking Carl is estimating 653 – 644. His work is shown below.

700 – 600 = 100

What is the actual difference? Is Carl's estimate reasonable? If not, how could he have made a closer estimate?

22. Tyrel recorded the elevations of three cities. Estimate how many more feet Dallas's elevation is than Waco's.

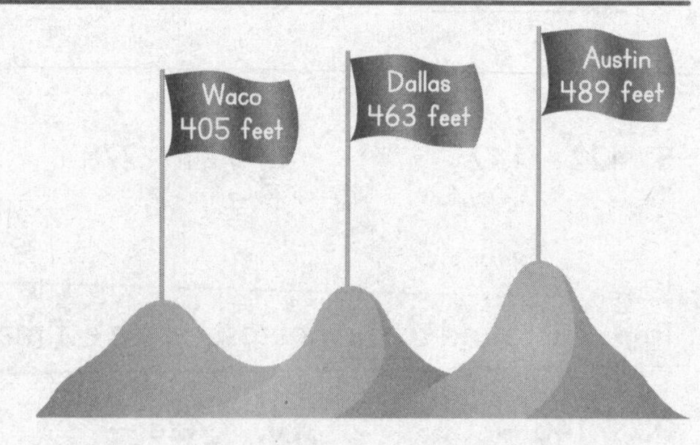

Assessment Practice

23. Estimate 851 – 242 by rounding each number to the nearest ten.

Ⓐ 620 Ⓑ 610
Ⓒ 600 Ⓓ 590

24. Estimate 904 – 312 by rounding each number to the nearest hundred.

Ⓐ 600 Ⓑ 500
Ⓒ 400 Ⓓ 300

Name ______________________________

Additional Practice 8-8
Model with Math

Another Look!

Don sold 180 books in the morning, 293 books in the afternoon, and 104 books in the evening. How many books did he sell in all?

Tell how you can model with math.

- I can use the math that I know.
- I can use a bar diagram and equations to represent and choose the operations I need.

One way you can model with math is by using bar diagrams to show the relationships between quantities in a problem.

Represent and solve this problem.

Find the hidden question:
How many books did Don sell in the morning and the evening?

? books sold in morning and evening

180	104

$180 + 104 = ?$
I can break apart by place value.
$(100 + 80) + (100 + 4)$
$= (100 + 100) + 80 + 4$
$= 284$ books

Use the answer to solve the problem.
How many books did Don sell in all?

? books sold in all

284	293

$284 + 293 = ?$
I can make a ten.
$293 + 7 = 300$
$284 - 7 = 277$
$300 + 277 = 577$ books in all

Model with Math

Vanessa spends $273. She donates $119. Vanessa started with $685. How much money does she have left?

1. Explain how you can represent this problem.

2. What is the hidden question you need to answer before you can solve the problem?

3. Solve the problem. Draw bar diagrams to represent the problem. Show any equations you used.

Stamp Collection

Scott has collected stamps for 4 years. The table at the right shows the number of stamps from foreign countries in Scott's stamp collection. Scott has 315 more stamps from the United States than from Canada. Each stamp from the United States is worth 49 cents. Scott wants to know the total number of stamps he has in his collection.

DATA

Stamps from Foreign Countries

Country	Number of Stamps
Canada	55
Mexico	221

4. **Reasoning** How are the numbers in this problem related?

5. **Model with Math** What is the hidden question you need to answer before you can solve the problem? How can you represent the hidden question?

6. **Model with Math** Solve the problem. Show the equations you used.

7. **Make Sense and Persevere** What are two ways that Scott can check that his answer is correct? Use one of those ways to check your answer.

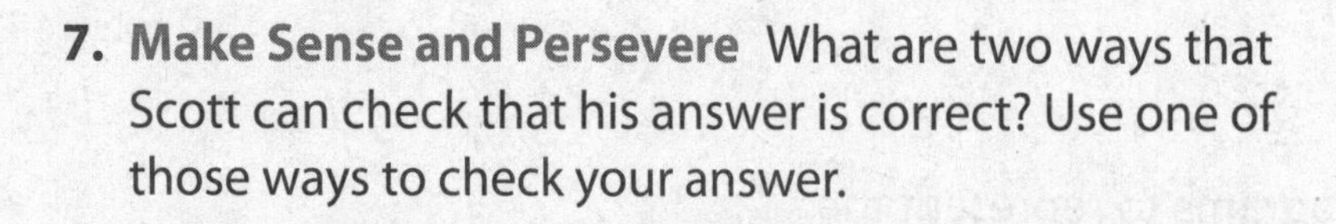

Name ______________________

Additional Practice 9-1
Use Partial Sums to Add

Another Look!

You can use place-value blocks to represent each number.

Find 234 + 451.

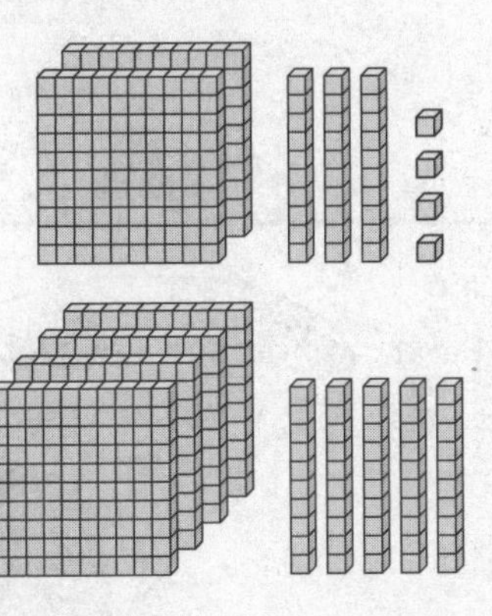

Break the problem into smaller problems.

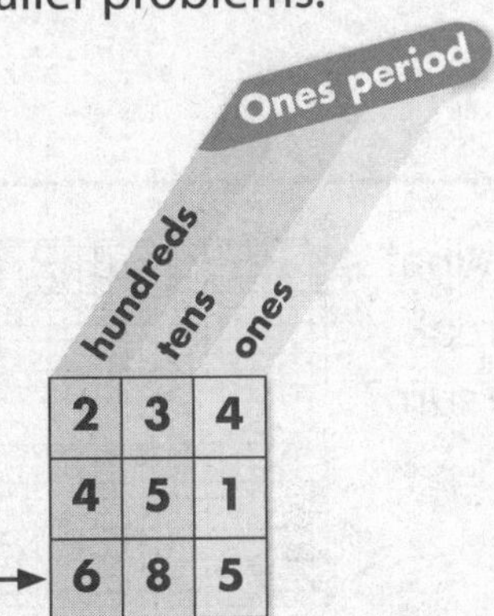

Add the sums.

$$\begin{array}{lr} & 234 \\ & +\,451 \\ \hline \text{Hundreds} \rightarrow & 600 \\ \text{Tens} \rightarrow & 80 \\ \text{Ones} \rightarrow & +\,5 \\ \hline & 685 \end{array}$$

In **1–11**, estimate each sum. Use place-value blocks or drawings and partial sums to add.

1.

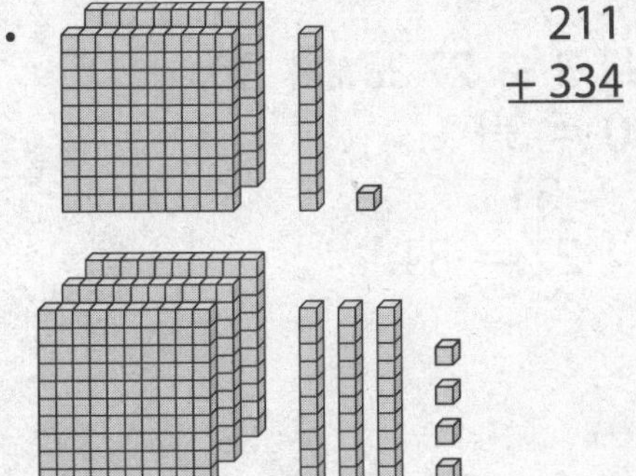

$$\begin{array}{r} 211 \\ +\,334 \\ \hline \end{array}$$

2.

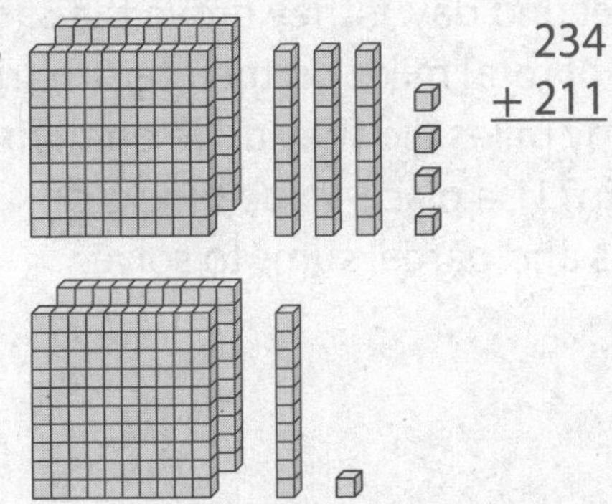

$$\begin{array}{r} 234 \\ +\,211 \\ \hline \end{array}$$

3. 516 + 142

4. 439 + 520

5. 721 + 176

6. 631 + 245

7. 580 + 315

8. 714 + 144

9. 128 + 441

10. 214 + 253

11. 661 + 127

12. Estimate first, and then use counting on to solve mentally. How many more students are in eighth grade than in sixth grade at North Middle School? Is your answer reasonable? Explain.

Students at North Middle School

Grade	Students
6th	352
7th	379
8th	421

13. Bill needs to find 318 + 230. Into what three smaller problems can Bill break this addition problem? What is the sum?

14. Higher Order Thinking The Smith family took a vacation. They drove 256 miles on the first day and 287 miles on the second day. If they drove the same number of total miles on their return trip, how many miles did they drive on their entire trip? Use place-value blocks or drawings and partial sums to solve.

15. Critique Reasoning Is Dale's work correct? If not, tell why and write a correct answer.

Find 64 − 27.
I can add 3 to 27 to get 30.
64 − 30 = 34
34 − 3 = 31
So, 64 − 27 = 31.

Assessment Practice

16. Which shows breaking 415 + 583 apart by place value to find the sum?

Ⓐ 400 + 800; 10 + 50; 5 + 3

Ⓑ 400 + 500; 10 + 83; 5 + 3

Ⓒ 400 + 580; 10 + 80; 5 + 3

Ⓓ 400 + 500; 10 + 80; 5 + 3

17. Break 627 + 361 apart by place value. Find the sum.

Ⓐ 889

Ⓑ 898

Ⓒ 988

Ⓓ 998

Name ____________________

Additional Practice 9-2
Use Regrouping to Add

Another Look!

Find 237 + 186.

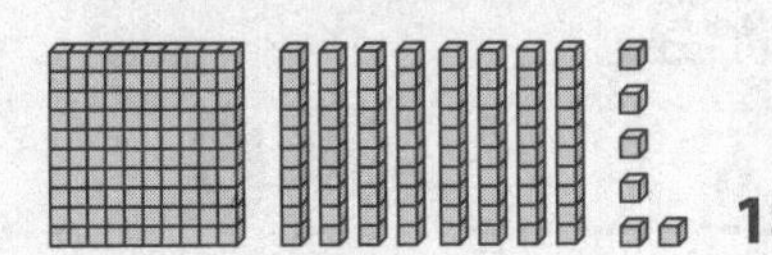

Add the ones, tens, and hundreds to find partial sums. Regroup to find the final sum.

	Hundreds	Tens	Ones
	2	3	7
+	1	8	6
	3	11	~~13~~
	3	~~12~~	3
	4	2	3

Regroup the ones.
Regroup the tens.

In **1** and **2**, use the place-value blocks to help add.

1.

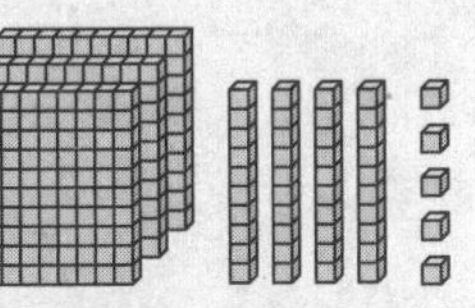

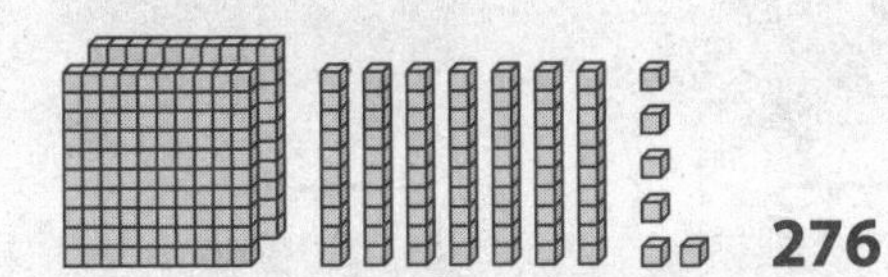

$$\begin{array}{r} 345 \\ +\,276 \\ \hline \end{array}$$

2.

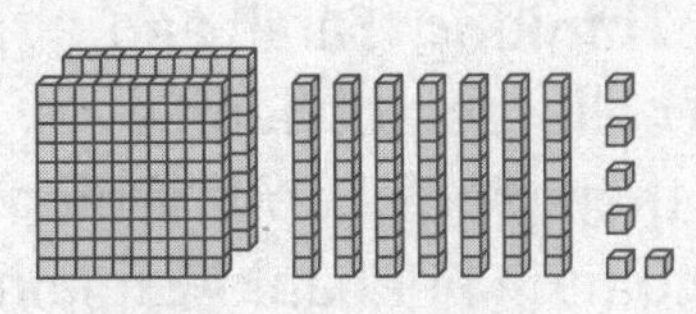

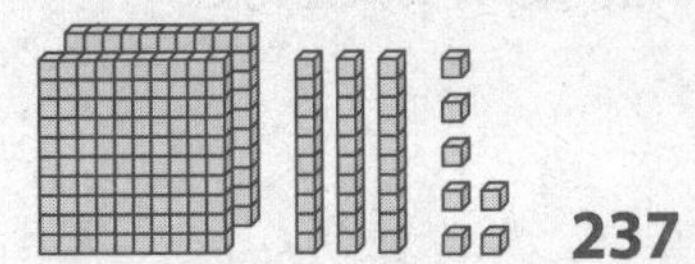

$$\begin{array}{r} 276 \\ +\,237 \\ \hline \end{array}$$

In **3–6**, estimate and then find each sum.

3. $\begin{array}{r} 118 \\ +\,146 \\ \hline \end{array}$

4. $\begin{array}{r} 283 \\ +\,147 \\ \hline \end{array}$

5. $\begin{array}{r} 542 \\ +\,109 \\ \hline \end{array}$

6. $\begin{array}{r} 220 \\ +\,479 \\ \hline \end{array}$

In **7** and **8**, use the table at the right.

7. How many points were scored by Howie and Theo? Estimate by rounding to the nearest hundred. Then solve. Write an equation that represents the problem.

Points Scored

DATA

Player	Points
Howie	272
Theo	325
Isabel	288

8. Make Sense and Persevere Is your answer to Exercise **7** reasonable? Explain.

9. A-Z **Vocabulary** Maria and her family drove 885 miles on their summer vacation. The first 8 on the left in this number has a

_______________ of 800.

10. Marc thinks a hexagon has 5 sides and 5 angles. Is Marc correct? Explain.

11. Higher Order Thinking Sarah and Angela have a collection of pennies and nickels in their piggy banks. Which girl has more coins in her bank? Explain how you know using numbers and symbols.

Assessment Practice

12. What is 252 + 163?

Ⓐ 415

Ⓑ 425

Ⓒ 515

Ⓓ 525

13. What is the value of the unknown in $256 + \square = 381$?

Ⓐ 115

Ⓑ 125

Ⓒ 135

Ⓓ 155

Name ______________________

 Practice  Video  Tools 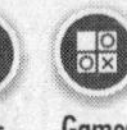 Games

Additional Practice 9-3

Add 3 or More Numbers

Another Look!

Find 137 + 201 + 109.

?		
137	201	109

To add three numbers, use partial sums or column addition.

You can use place value or properties of operations to add.

Use partial sums.

```
  137
  201
+ 109
  400
   30
+  17
  447
```

Use column addition.

	Hundreds	Tens	Ones
	1	3	7
	2	0	1
+	1	0	9
	4	3	17
	4	4	7

So, 137 + 201 + 109 = 447.

In **1–3**, estimate and then find each sum.

1. 35 + 63 + 76

2. 149 + 22 + 314

3. 255 + 128 + 312

In **4–9**, find each sum.

4.
```
  127
   39
+  87
```

5.
```
  293
  312
+  78
```

6.
```
   25
  238
   75
+ 180
```

7. 150 + 125 + 350

8. 382 + 164 + 267

9. 46 + 461 + 309

10. Generalize To subtract 178 − 135 mentally, Carmine adds 5 to each number. Karen adds 2 to each number. Will both methods work to find the correct answer? Why or why not?

11. Higher Order Thinking On Friday, 215 people went to the street fair. On Saturday, 163 more people went to the street fair than on Friday. On Sunday, 192 people went. In total how many people went to the fair? What are two ways you can use to find the answer?

12. The table shows what Carlos had for breakfast. How many calories did Carlos consume? Write an equation to solve the problem.

DATA

Food	Amount	Calories
Bran flakes	1 ounce	90
Banana	1	105
Orange juice	1 cup	110
Milk	1 cup	150

Assessment Practice

13. Use place value, partial sums, or properties of operations to find each sum.

Equation	Sum
22 + 257 + 178 = ?	
122 + 241 + 378 = ?	
252 + 167 + 314 = ?	

14. Use place value, column addition, or properties of operations to find each sum.

Equation	Sum
250 + 250 + 178 = ?	
131 + 32 + 68 = ?	
152 + 237 + 576 = ?	

Name

Practice Video Tools Games

Additional Practice 9-4
Use Partial Differences to Subtract

Another Look!

Greenwood School has 248 musical instruments. The students use 156 instruments for a concert. How many instruments are not used for the concert?

What You Think

I need to find 248 − 156.
156 is the same as 100 + 50 + 6.
I can subtract each addend, starting with hundreds and ending with ones.

There are not enough tens, so I will break apart 5 tens into 4 tens and 1 ten.

What You Write

248 − 100 = 148   108 − 10 = 98
148 − 40 = 108   98 − 6 = 92

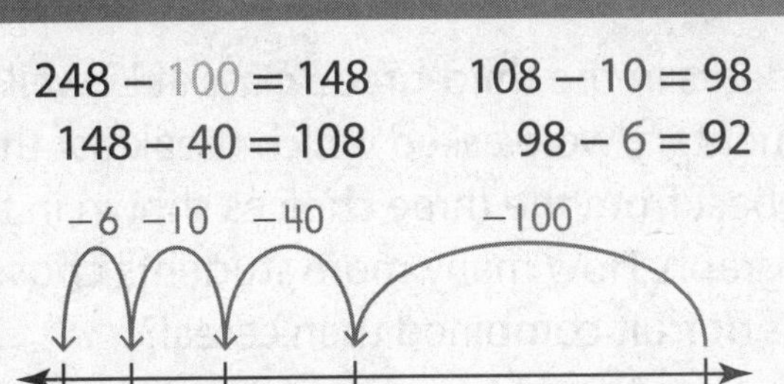

92 instruments are not used for the concert.

In **1–9**, estimate and then use partial differences to subtract. Use open number lines to help.

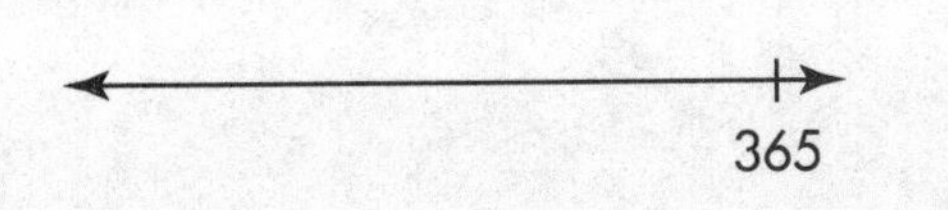

1. 365 − 138

2. 217 − 118

3. 267 − 138

365   217   267

4. 568 − 293

5. 928 − 374

6. 584 − 365

568   928   584

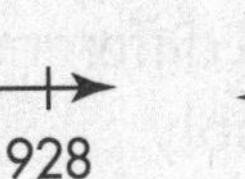 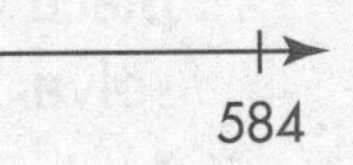

7. 756 − 642

8. 848 − 276

9. 641 − 139

756   848   641

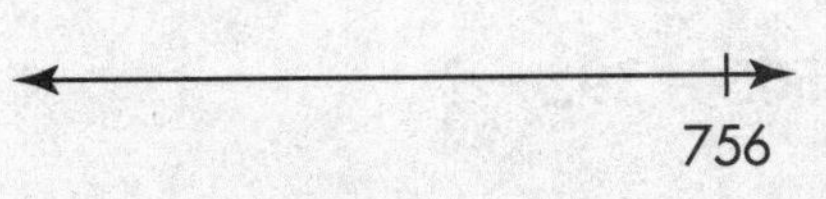

10. How many vertices does the cube below have?

11. Critique Reasoning Tamara needs to find 455 – 364. Her work is below. Explain what is incorrect and find the correct answer.

455 – 300 = 155
155 – 50 = 105
105 – 4 = 101

12. Students in the third-grade class at Lowell Elementary were asked which breakfast they like best from the three choices shown in the bar graph. How many more students chose eggs or fruit combined than cereal?

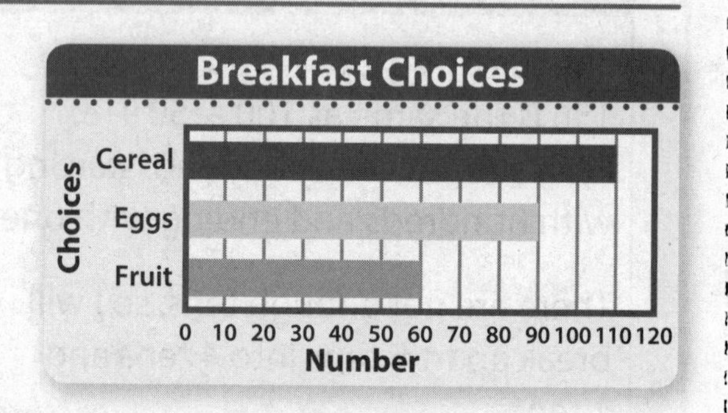

13. enVision® STEM Water boils at 212 degrees Fahrenheit. It freezes at 32 degrees Fahrenheit. How many degrees difference is there between these two temperatures? Explain how you found your answer.

14. Higher Order Thinking Tom had 347 marbles. He traded 28 of them for some marbles that he really wanted. Now he has 336 marbles. How many marbles did Tom get from the trade? Explain how you found the answer.

Assessment Practice

15. Which have a difference of 231? Use place value and partial differences to solve. Select all that apply.

☐ 428 – 197 = ?
☐ 561 – 330 = ?
☐ 489 – 268 = ?
☐ 875 – 644 = ?
☐ 496 – 275 = ?

16. Which have a difference of 173? Select all that apply.

☐ 877 – 704 = ?
☐ 422 – 259 = ?
☐ 652 – 489 = ?
☐ 700 – 527 = ?
☐ 565 – 392 = ?

Name ____________

Practice Video Tools Games

Additional Practice 9-5
Use Regrouping to Subtract

Another Look!

Find 726 − 238.
Estimate by rounding to the nearest ten: 730 − 240 = 490.

Subtract 8 ones.

First subtract 6 ones.
Regroup 1 ten as 10 ones.
Subtract 2 ones.

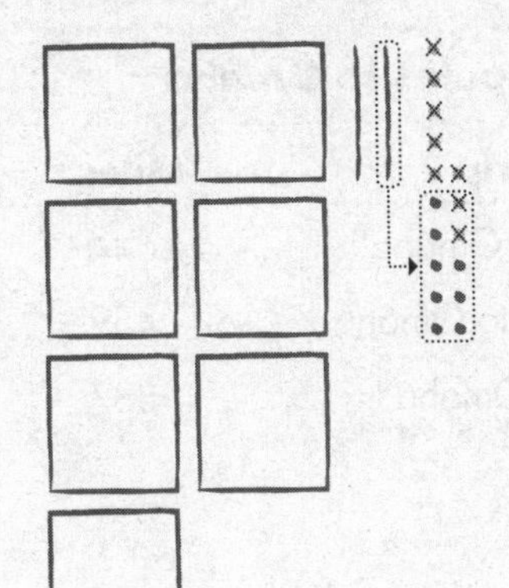

Subtract 3 tens.

First subtract 1 ten.
Regroup 1 hundred as 10 tens. Subtract 2 tens.

Subtract 2 hundreds.

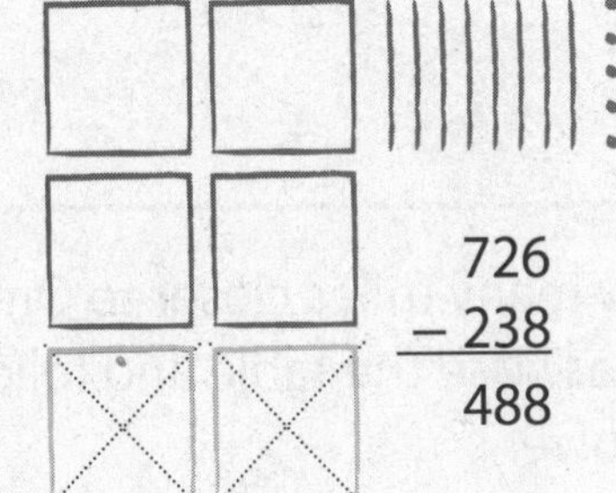

$$\begin{array}{r} 726 \\ -\ 238 \\ \hline 488 \end{array}$$

This answer is reasonable because 488 is close to the estimate, 490.

In **1–12**, estimate each difference and then use partial differences to subtract.

1. $\begin{array}{r} 914 \\ -\ 482 \\ \hline \end{array}$

2. $\begin{array}{r} 883 \\ -\ 388 \\ \hline \end{array}$

3. $\begin{array}{r} 375 \\ -\ 183 \\ \hline \end{array}$

4. $\begin{array}{r} 736 \\ -\ 295 \\ \hline \end{array}$

5. $\begin{array}{r} 478 \\ -\ 152 \\ \hline \end{array}$

6. $\begin{array}{r} 246 \\ -\ 127 \\ \hline \end{array}$

7. $\begin{array}{r} 816 \\ -\ 304 \\ \hline \end{array}$

8. $\begin{array}{r} 919 \\ -\ 284 \\ \hline \end{array}$

9. 318 − 123

10. 441 − 187

11. 334 − 275

12. 597 − 384

13. **Reasoning** A greenhouse grew tomato plants. It sold 276 tomato plants and 307 roses. There are 187 tomato plants left. How many tomato plants did the greenhouse originally grow? Explain which numbers and operation you used to solve.

14. Texas has 254 counties. California has 58 counties. Florida has 67 counties. How many more counties does Texas have than the number of counties in California and Florida combined?

15. How many miles closer to Omaha is Chicago than Dallas? Use the table and follow the steps below to solve.

a. Estimate the answer.
b. Write the solution to the problem in word form.
c. Explain why your answer is reasonable.

DATA

Routes to Omaha

Trip	Miles
Dallas to Omaha	644
Chicago to Omaha	459
Tulsa to Omaha	387

16. **Higher Order Thinking** Jill is going on a trip from Chicago to Omaha, and then from Omaha to Tulsa. Bill will travel from Dallas to Omaha. How much farther will Jill travel than Bill? Explain how you solved the problem.

You can use an inverse operation to check your solution to each part of a problem.

Assessment Practice

17. Which shows the estimate of 549 – 210 by rounding to the nearest ten, and then the correct difference?

Ⓐ 330; 338
Ⓑ 330; 328
Ⓒ 340; 339
Ⓓ 340; 329

18. Which shows the estimate of 967 – 502 by rounding to the nearest ten, and then the correct difference?

Ⓐ 460; 465
Ⓑ 460; 455
Ⓒ 470; 465
Ⓓ 470; 455

Name ____________________

Practice Video Tools Games

Additional Practice 9-6

Use Strategies to Add and Subtract

Another Look!

Find 207 − 98.

Remember, you can use addition to solve because addition and subtraction are inverse operations. You can also use estimation to see if your answer is reasonable.

One Way

Use the adding on strategy.

Find 98 + ? = 207.

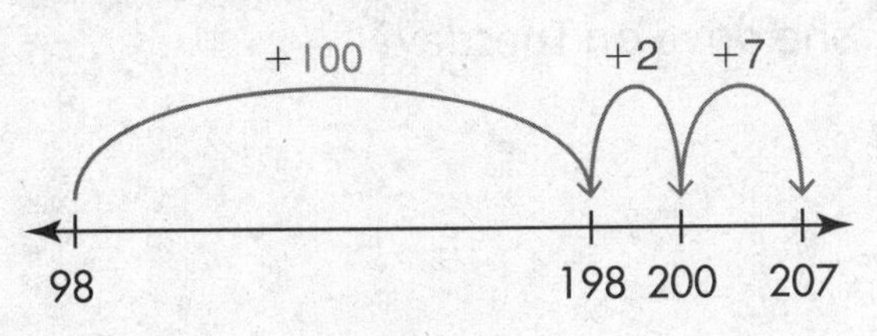

100 + 2 + 7 = 109

207 − 98 = 109

Another Way

Use partial differences to subtract.

Find 207 − 98 = ?.

$$\begin{array}{rl} 207 & \\ -\ \ \ 7 & \text{Subtract 7.} \\ \hline 200 & \\ -\ \ 90 & \text{Subtract 90.} \\ \hline 110 & \\ -\ \ \ 1 & \text{Subtract 1.} \\ \hline 109 & \end{array}$$

In **1–16**, find each sum or difference. Then use estimation to see if your answer is reasonable.

1. $\begin{array}{r} 518 \\ -\ 339 \\ \hline \end{array}$

2. $\begin{array}{r} 401 \\ -\ 137 \\ \hline \end{array}$

3. $\begin{array}{r} 856 \\ +\ 92 \\ \hline \end{array}$

4. $\begin{array}{r} 300 \\ +\ 523 \\ \hline \end{array}$

5. $\begin{array}{r} 946 \\ -\ 441 \\ \hline \end{array}$

6. $\begin{array}{r} 530 \\ -\ 157 \\ \hline \end{array}$

7. $\begin{array}{r} 600 \\ +\ 75 \\ \hline \end{array}$

8. $\begin{array}{r} 116 \\ +\ 850 \\ \hline \end{array}$

9. 155 + 109

10. 715 + 248

11. 922 − 39

12. 504 − 208

13. 300 + 145

14. 109 + 643

15. 200 − 188

16. 480 − 252

17. **Make Sense and Persevere** At a baseball game, the Gordon family bought 4 ham sandwiches and 4 drinks. How much did they pay for the food and drinks?

Ham sandwich	$4
Tuna sandwich	$5
Soft pretzel	$2
Drink	$1

18. Some seniors signed up for dance classes for the fall. Then 117 stopped taking classes. One hundred eighty-nine seniors continued taking classes. How many seniors started taking classes in the fall?

19. Mrs. Morris drove 116 more miles on Tuesday than on Monday. On Monday, she drove 235 miles. How many miles did she drive on Tuesday?

20. **Higher Order Thinking** Party Palace receives an order for 505 party favors. It packages 218 favors on Monday and 180 favors on Tuesday. How many more party favors does it still need to package? Show two different ways to solve the problem.

21. **enVision® STEM** A scientist was observing a group of wildebeests over two years. One year the herd consisted of 200 animals. In the next year there were 155 wildebeests. How many more animals were in the herd during the first year?

Assessment Practice

22. Use a place-value strategy to find the value of the unknown in $417 - ? = 312$.

Ⓐ 105
Ⓑ 115
Ⓒ 125
Ⓓ 225

23. Use the relationship between addition and subtraction to find the value of the unknown in $? + 635 = 902$.

Ⓐ 257
Ⓑ 267
Ⓒ 337
Ⓓ 367

Name ___________________

Practice Video Tools Games

Additional Practice 9-7
Construct Arguments

Another Look!

During the last two weeks, Max exercised for 446 minutes.
During the first week, he exercised for 220 minutes.
Did he exercise more during the first or second week?
Conjecture: Max exercised more during the second week.

Tell how you can justify the conjecture.

- I can use numbers, objects, drawings, or actions to explain.
- I can make sure my argument is simple, complete, and easy to understand.

When you construct an argument, you use reasoning to give a logical explanation.

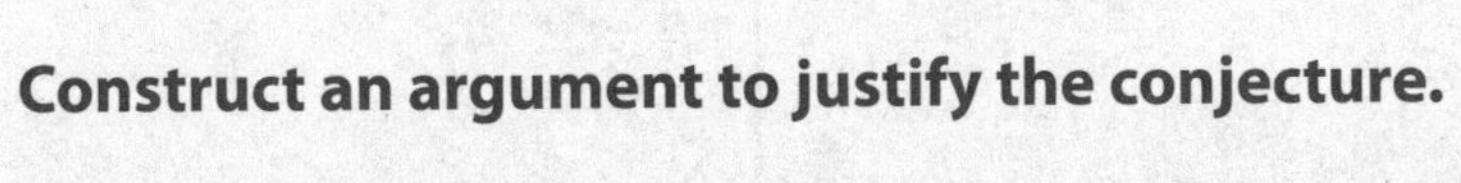

Construct an argument to justify the conjecture.

I can use place-value blocks to see that if Max exercised the same amount the second week, the time would only be 440 minutes. So Max must have exercised for more minutes the second week to get to a total of 446 minutes.

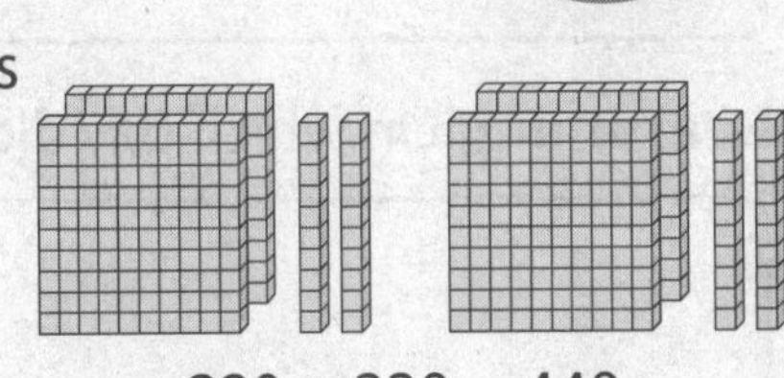

$220 + 220 = 440$

Construct Arguments

Central School has 758 students. There are 2 lunch periods at Central School. Three hundred seventy-one students eat during the first lunch period. Which lunch period has more students? *Conjecture: More students eat lunch during the second lunch period.*

1. Tell how you can justify the conjecture.

2. Construct an argument to justify the conjecture.

3. Explain another way you could justify the conjecture.

Performance Task

Family Vacation

The Willis family has 4 members. Some mornings and evenings the family traveled to different cities on their vacation. Below are the distances they drove. Mrs. Willis is trying to find which day they drove the most.

DATA	Saturday	Monday	Wednesday	Friday
Morning	174 miles	112 miles	121 miles	172 miles
Evening	106 miles	165 miles	168 miles	113 miles

4. Model with Math Write equations to represent the distances the family drove on the given days.

5. Reasoning On which day did the family drive the most?

6. Construct Arguments Construct a math argument to explain why your answer to Exercise **5** is correct.

7. Make Sense and Persevere How can you check that your answer is reasonable?

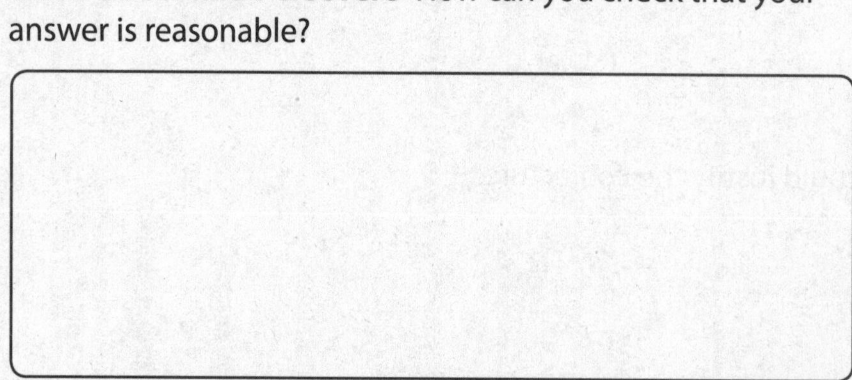

Name ___

Additional Practice 10-1
Use Patterns to Multiply

Another Look!

Herman's mother bought 4 tickets to the circus. Each ticket costs $40. How much did she spend on tickets?

Use place-value blocks.

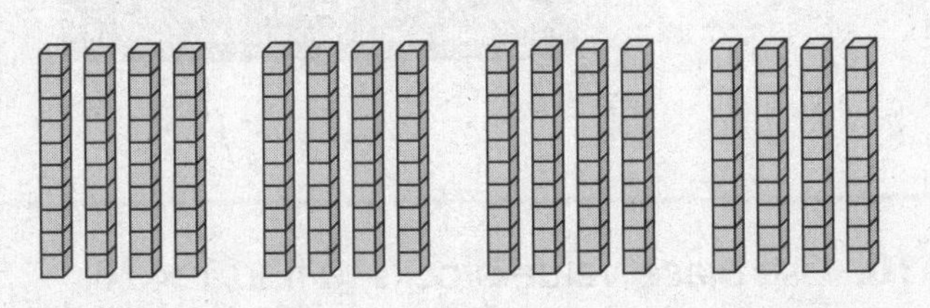

4×40 is 4 groups of 4 tens = 16 tens or 160.

4 tickets cost $160.

Use an open number line.

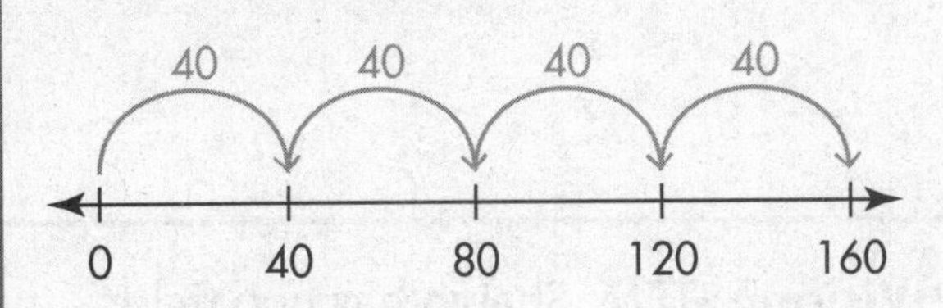

4 jumps of 40 are 160. $4 \times 40 = 160$

4 tickets cost $160.

In **1–6**, use an open number line or draw place-value blocks to find each product.

1. 4×90

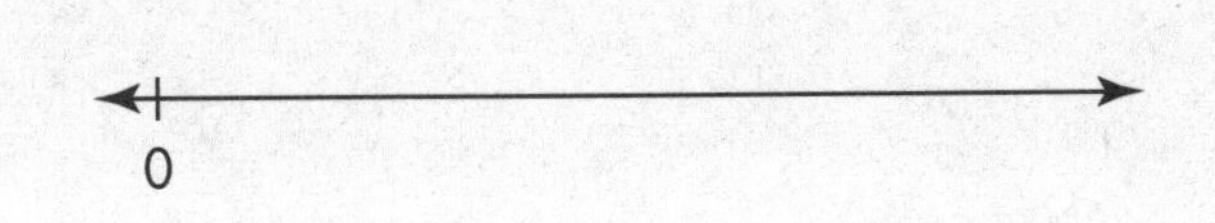

2. 8×40

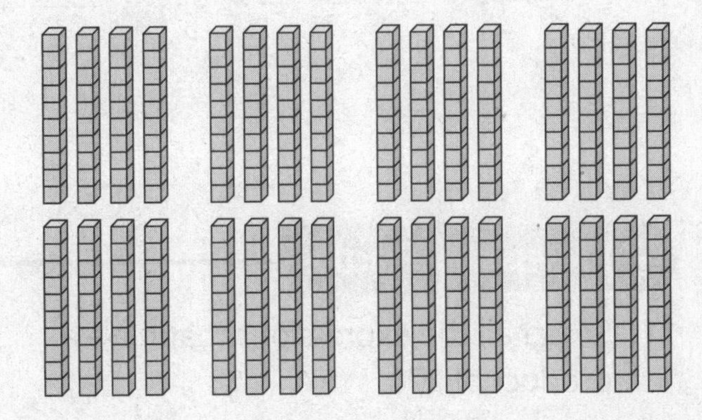

3. 7×50

4. 5×80

5. 7×80

6. 8×30

7. Model with Math Nursen collects trading cards. How many cards come in 3 packages? Show how to use an open number line to solve this problem.

8. Higher Order Thinking For his birthday, Gil got 4 packages of trading cards. He already had 75 cards. How many cards did he have after his birthday?

9. enVision® STEM Shawn has two fields on his farm. He plants two types of corn, one in each field. Each field has 60 rows of cornstalks. Type A grows better, so there are 8 cornstalks in each row. Type B does not grow as well, so there are only 3 cornstalks in each row. Use place-value blocks to find how many cornstalks are in each field.

10. Use place-value blocks to find 1×70, 2×70, 3×70, and 4×70. Describe any patterns you see in the products.

Assessment Practice

11. Select all the expressions that have a product of 270.

- ☐ 3×9
- ☐ 3×90
- ☐ 2×70
- ☐ 7×20
- ☐ 9×30

12. Select all the expressions that have a product of 160.

- ☐ 2×80
- ☐ 4×40
- ☐ 6×40
- ☐ 8×20
- ☐ 9×30

Name ______________

Practice Video Tools Games

Additional Practice 10-2
Use Mental Math to Multiply

Another Look!

You can use basic facts to help multiply by multiples of 10.

Find 6×40.

6×40 equals 6×4 tens.

6×4 tens equals 24 tens.

$6 \times 40 = 240$

You can use a basic fact or properties of multiplication to solve 2×70.

Below are different ways to solve 2×70.

2×70 equals 2×7 tens.	$2 \times 70 = 2 \times (7 \times 10)$
2×7 tens equals 14 tens.	$2 \times 70 = (2 \times 7) \times 10$
$2 \times 70 = 140$	$2 \times 70 = 14 \times 10$
	$2 \times 70 = 140$

In **1** and **2**, use basic facts to help multiply.

1. Find 3×80.

$3 \times 80 = (3 \times$ _____) tens

$3 \times 80 =$ _____ tens

$3 \times 80 =$ _____

2. Find 9×50.

$9 \times 50 = (9 \times$ _____) tens

$9 \times 50 =$ _____ tens

$9 \times 50 =$ _____

In **3–11**, complete each equation.

3. $5 \times 6 =$ _____

$50 \times 6 =$ _____

4. $8 \times 7 =$ _____

$80 \times 7 =$ _____

5. $3 \times 6 =$ _____

$3 \times 60 =$ _____

6. $30 \times 9 =$ _____

7. $9 \times 80 =$ _____

8. $60 \times 6 =$ _____

9. $5 \times 50 =$ _____

10. $7 \times 60 =$ _____

11. $4 \times 30 =$ _____

12. Explain why there are two zeros in the product of 5×40.

13. **enVision® STEM** There are 3 plots in Kevin's garden. Last year, Kevin planted 10 lilies in one plot. This year, there are 30 lilies on each plot. How many total lilies are on Kevin's land now?

14. **Use Appropriate Tools** Select and use one of the following tools to find the area of the rectangle: circular counters, square-inch tiles, or rulers.

1 in.

2 in.

15. Tonya lined up 4 rows of train tracks. In each row there are 20 trains. How many trains are there? Explain how you can represent this problem.

16. **Higher Order Thinking** Noah takes about 200 steps in an hour. About how many steps does Noah take in 4 hours? Fill in the table. Look for a pattern.

Time	1 hour	2 hours	3 hours	4 hours
Number of Steps				

Assessment Practice

17. Geena is taking inventory. She records the number of small, medium, large, and jumbo paper clips in the table at the right. Match each equation with its product to find the total number of each size of paper clip in stock.

	90	160
$2 \times 80 = ?$	☐	☐
$4 \times 40 = ?$	☐	☐
$3 \times 30 = ?$	☐	☐
$1 \times 90 = ?$	☐	☐

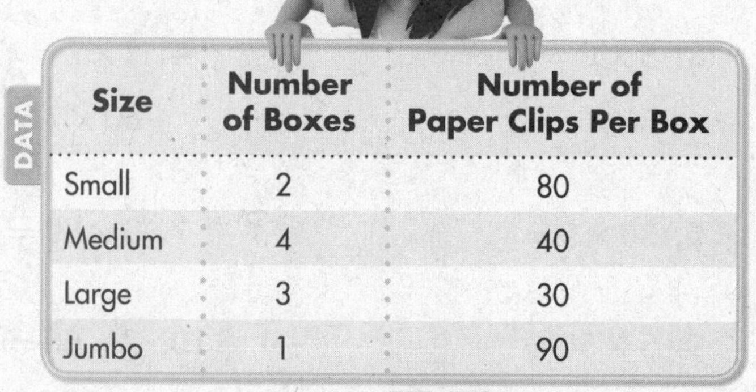

DATA

Size	Number of Boxes	Number of Paper Clips Per Box
Small	2	80
Medium	4	40
Large	3	30
Jumbo	1	90

Name ______________________

Practice Video Tools Games

Additional Practice 10-3
Use Properties to Multiply

Another Look!

Find 4×70.

Use equivalent expressions to solve a simpler problem.

It can be easy to multiply by 10! You can use properties to think of the problem as multiplying by 10.

You can group factors.

$4 \times 70 = 4 \times (7 \times 10)$

$4 \times 70 = (4 \times 7) \times 10$

$4 \times 70 = 28 \times 10 = 280$

So, $4 \times 70 = 280$.

You can decompose a factor.

$4 \times 70 = (2 + 2) \times 70$

$4 \times 70 = (2 \times 70) + (2 \times 70)$

$4 \times 70 = 140 + 140 = 280$

So, $4 \times 70 = 280$.

In **1–6**, show how to find each product using properties of multiplication.

1. $8 \times 40 = 8 \times (\_\_\_\_ \times 10)$

$8 \times 40 = (8 \times \_\_\_\_) \times 10$

$8 \times 40 = \_\_\_\_ \times 10 = \_\_\_\_$

2. $2 \times 90 = \_\_\_\_ \times (\_\_\_\_ \times 10)$

$2 \times 90 = (\_\_\_\_ \times \_\_\_\_) \times 10$

$2 \times 90 = (\_\_\_\_) \times 10 = \_\_\_\_$

3. 6×20

4. 4×80

5. 7×70

6. 8×60

7. 8×50

8. 3×40

9. Use Structure A warehouse has 9 crates. Each crate has 20 boxes of cereal. How many boxes of cereal does the warehouse have? Explain how to use properties to solve the problem.

10. Hank rents 9 cases of plates. He has 250 guests attending the banquet. There are 30 plates in each case. Did Hank rent enough plates? Explain.

11. $32 \div 4 =$ ____
List two other facts that belong to the same fact family.

12. Algebra Kelsey writes the equation $6 \times ? = 180$. What value makes Kelsey's equation true?

13. Josie bikes 40 miles each month for 5 months. She multiplies 40×5. What unit should she use for the product: miles or months? Explain.

14. Higher Order Thinking June says that $5 \times 28 = 140$. She uses the reasoning shown below. Explain whether you agree or disagree with June's reasoning.

$$
\begin{aligned}
5 \times 28 &= 5 \times (4 \times 7) \\
&= (5 \times 4) \times 7 \\
&= 20 \times 7 = 140
\end{aligned}
$$

Assessment Practice

15. Which products are equal to 490? Select all that apply.

- ☐ 4×9
- ☐ $7 \times (1 \times 10)$
- ☐ 7×70
- ☐ 4×90
- ☐ $7 \times (7 \times 10)$

16. Which products are equal to 300? Select all that apply.

- ☐ 3×10
- ☐ 6×50
- ☐ $6 \times (5 \times 10)$
- ☐ 5×60
- ☐ 30×10

Name ______________________

 Practice  Video  Tools  Games 

Additional Practice 10-4
Look For and Use Structure

Another Look!

Find the **missing products** in the table.

Tell how you can make use of structure to solve this problem.

- I can look for things in common to find a pattern.
- I can describe the patterns I find.
- I can extend a pattern.

Complete the table. Think about patterns or properties you know.

×	10	20	30	40	50	60	70	80	90
3	30	60	**90**	**120**	**150**	**180**	**210**	**240**	**270**
4	40	**80**	120	160	200	**240**	**280**	**320**	**360**
5	50	**100**	**150**	200	250	300	350	400	450

One factor is always a multiple of 10. I used patterns I know for multiplying by multiples of 10 to find each **missing factor**.

Use Structure
Clifton is making different types of necklaces. The necklaces will have either 10, 20, 30, or 40 beads. Clifton starts the table below to find the number of beads he will need if he makes 6, 7, or 8 of each type of necklace.

1. Tell how you can find the products in the table below.

2. Find the missing products in the table to show how many beads Clifton will need for each type of necklace. Think about patterns or properties you know.

×	10	20	30	40
6	60	120		
7	70			
8	80	160		

Performance Task

Exercise Routine

Bernard is training for a race. He performs the same exercise routine every day. In a 7-day week, how much more time does Bernard spend weight lifting than jogging? Answer Exercises **3–6** to solve the problem.

Activity	Time Each Day (minutes)	Time Each Week (minutes)
Walking	10	
Jogging	20	140
Weight lifting	30	
Stretching	5	

3. Model with Math Identify the hidden question in this problem. What operation can you use to answer the hidden question?

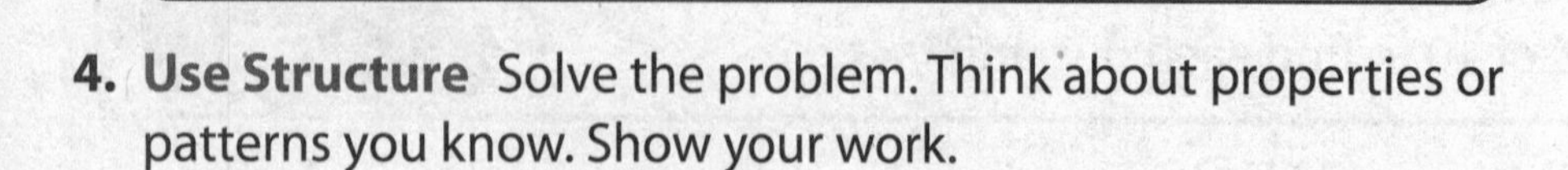

4. Use Structure Solve the problem. Think about properties or patterns you know. Show your work.

5. Generalize What step can you repeat to find the time Bernard spends on each activity in 1 week? Complete the table.

6. Critique Reasoning Jacob solves the problem by adding the time Bernard spends each day jogging and weight lifting. Then he multiplies this sum by 7. Does Jacob's reasoning make sense? Explain.

Name ______________________

 Practice  Video  Tools  Games

Additional Practice 11-1

Solve 2-Step Word Problems: Addition and Subtraction

Another Look!

Harry scores 394 points on Level 1 of a video game. On Level 2, he loses 248 points. He then scores an extra 138 points on Level 3. How many points does Harry have now?

Use bar diagrams and equations to solve.

Step 1

Find the hidden question.

Hidden question: How many points did Harry have left after he lost 248 points?

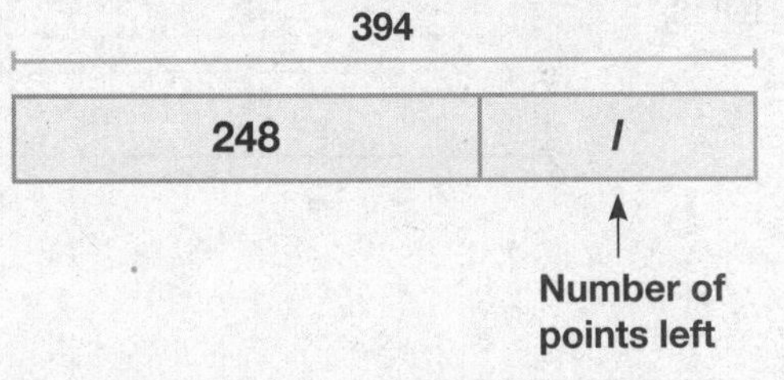

$l = 394 - 248$
$l = 146$

Harry had 146 points.

Step 2

Use the answer to the hidden question to answer the original question.

Original question: How many points does Harry have now?

p ← Number of points now

146	138

$p = 146 + 138$
$p = 284$

Harry has 284 points now.

In **1**, draw bar diagrams and write equations to solve.

1. Jamie has 875 building pieces in all. He gives his castle set to a friend. Jamie then buys the helicopter set. How many building pieces does Jamie have now?

2. How can you estimate to check if your answer is reasonable? Explain.

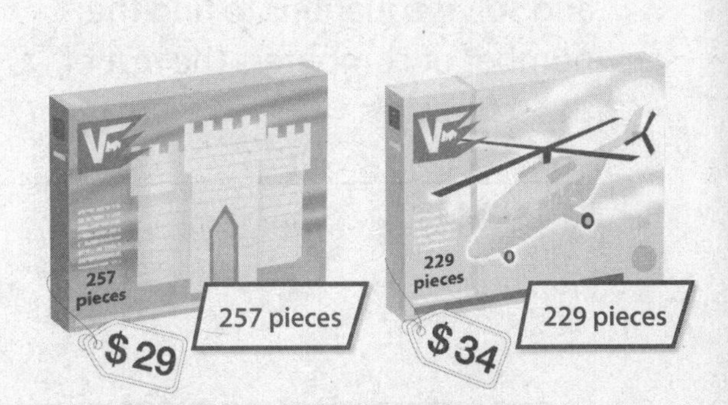

3. Reasoning What is another way to find how many points Harry had in the problem at the top of the previous page?

4. Number Sense Which has the greater sum, 468 + 153 or 253 + 209? Use estimates to tell how you know.

5. In a survey of 800 students, 548 said they liked pizza for lunch, 173 said they liked hamburgers, and 79 said they liked sloppy joes. Complete the bar diagrams and write equations to find how many more students liked pizza than liked hamburgers and sloppy joes combined. Use letters to represent unknown quantities in your equations. Check your work using estimation.

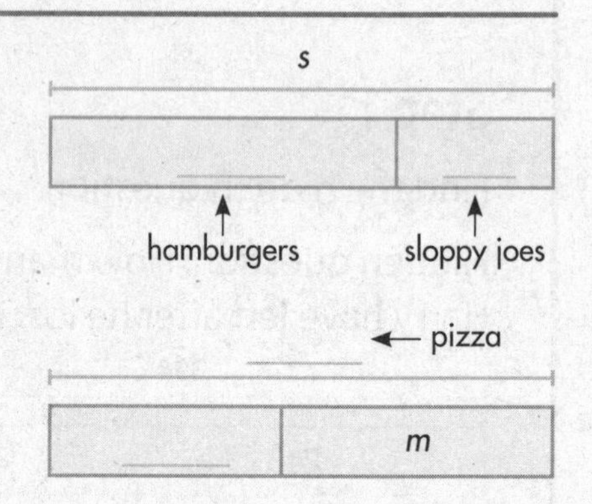

6. Higher Order Thinking Maria and John played a computer game. Who scored more points and won the game? Explain.

DATA

Computer Game Points

Player	Round 1 Points	Round 2 Points
Maria	256	345
John	325	273

Assessment Practice

7. Stewart School has 178 computers. Grade 3 has 58 computers and Grade 4 has 57 computers. Create and solve equations to find the number of computers the rest of the school has.

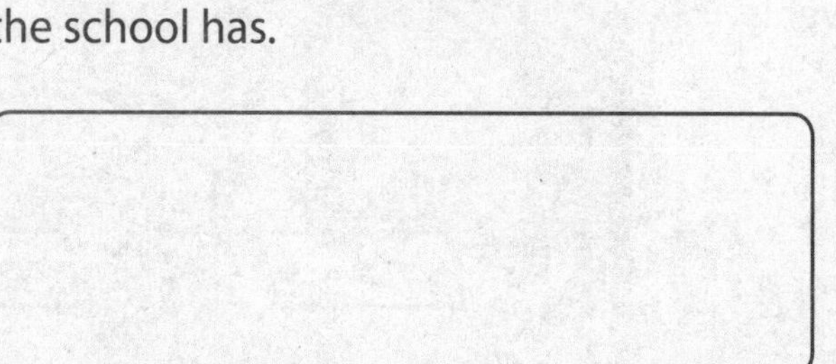

8. The school bookstore had 379 pencils. This week the bookstore sold 187 pencils. The manager then brought in 450 more pencils. Create and solve equations to find the number of pencils the bookstore has now.

Name ____________________

Practice

Video

Tools

Games

Additional Practice 11-2

Solve 2-Step Word Problems: Multiplication and Division

Another Look!

Each of the 6 members of the Recycling Club earned $3 recycling plastic bottles. They shared the money equally between 2 charities. How much money did they give to each charity?

First find and answer the hidden question.

Step 1

Find the hidden question and use a diagram and equation to answer it.

Hidden question: What is the total amount of money the club members earned?

d ← Total amount earned

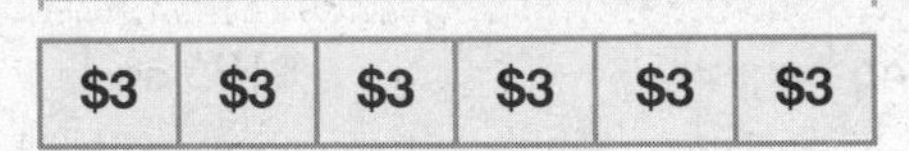

$d = 6 \times \$3$
$d = \$18$
The club members earned $18.

Step 2

Use the answer to the hidden question to answer the original question.

Original question: How much money did they give to each charity?

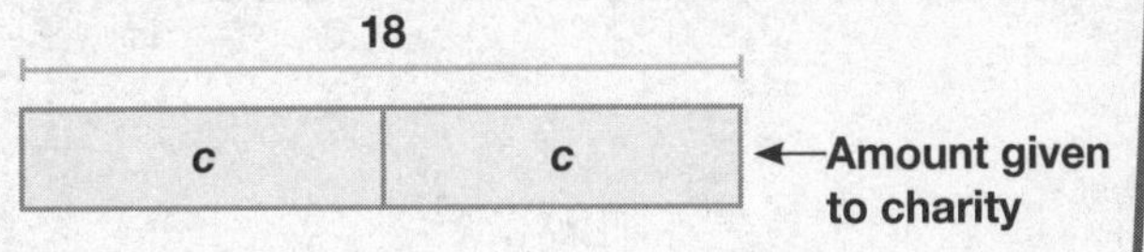

$c = 18 \div 2$
$c = \$9$
The club gave $9 to each charity.

In **1** and **2**, complete or draw diagrams and write equations to solve. Use letters to stand for unknown quantities.

1. A box of 6 trophies costs $5. How much would it cost to buy 48 trophies?

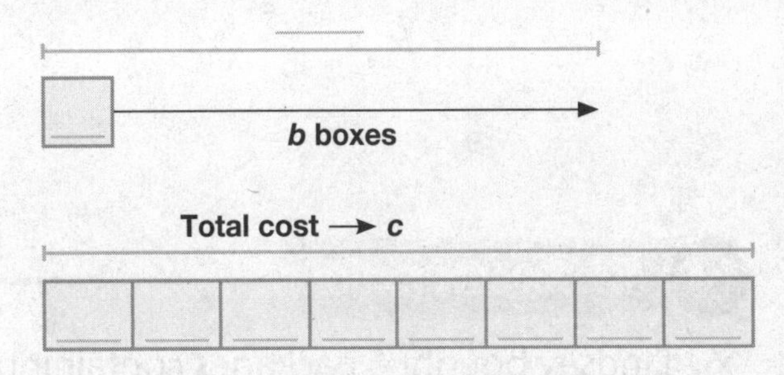

2. A third-grade gym class has 54 students. The gym teacher divides the class into 9 equal groups. She then divides each group into 2 teams. How many students are on each team?

3. **Make Sense and Persevere** Marco wants to buy 2 books that cost \$20 each. He can save \$5 a week. Complete the bar diagrams and write equations to find how many weeks it will take Marco to save enough money to buy the books. Use letters to represent unknown quantities in your equations.

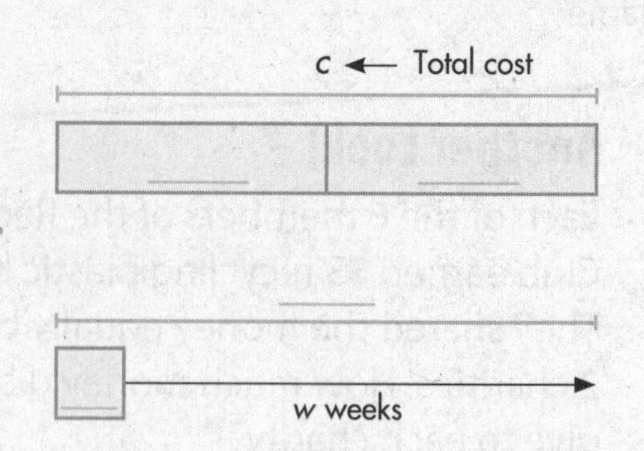

In **4** and **5**, use the table at the right.

4. **Number Sense** Use mental math to find the total cost of one tent and one sleeping bag. Explain how you found the answer.

Camping Equipment Sale	
Sleeping bags	\$195 each
Tents	\$238 each
Water bottles (box of 12)	\$10

5. **Higher Order Thinking** Angela buys 4 boxes of water bottles on Monday. She buys 1 more box of water bottles on Tuesday than she did on Monday. How much money did Angela spend on both days? Show how you found your answer.

Assessment Practice

6. Lindsey bought 5 packages containing 4 bracelets in each. She plans to decorate the bracelets and then sell them for \$3 each. How much money will she get if she sells all the bracelets?

   Ⓐ \$60
   Ⓑ \$50
   Ⓒ \$15
   Ⓓ \$12

7. Pierre runs the same distance around a track each day, 4 days a week. He runs a total of 12 miles each week. It takes 8 laps of the track to equal a mile. Which equation could you use to find how many laps Pierre runs each day?

   Ⓐ $y = 8 \div 4$
   Ⓑ $y = 12 \div 2$
   Ⓒ $y = 3 \times 8$
   Ⓓ $y = 4 \times 8$

Name ______________________

Additional Practice 11-3

Solve 2-Step Word Problems: All Operations

Another Look!

Some problems need more than one operation to solve.

Joseph had \$154. He then saved \$20 each week for 6 weeks. How much money does Joseph have now?

$n =$ amount Joseph saved

$m =$ total money Joseph has now

There is a hidden question in this problem.

What You Think	What You Do
First find and answer the hidden question: How much money did Joseph save? Find $6 \times \$20$. Then add the amount Joseph saved to the amount he had to solve the problem. Find $\$154 + \$120$.	First **multiply.** $6 \times \$20 = n$ $\$120 = n$ Then **add.** $\$154 + \$120 = m$ $m = \$274$

1. Rahmi bought 1 pair of jeans and 2 T-shirts. How much did Rahmi spend? Write equations to solve. Use letters to represent unknown quantities.

2. **Model with Math** Football party favors come in packages like the one shown. How much would it cost to buy 56 party favors? Think about how you can model with math to help solve the problem.

3. There are 12 seals, 4 whales, and 8 dolphins at the aquarium. Complete the picture graph to show the data.

4. One trainer fed the seals and whales, and another trainer fed the dolphins. How many more animals did the first trainer feed?

Mammals at the Aquarium	
Dolphins	
Seals	
Whales	
Each	= 2 animals.

5. **Higher Order Thinking** Serena has a toy train that is 32 inches long. She has an engine, a caboose, and a boxcar. The rest are passenger cars. How many passenger cars does Serena have?

Serena's Toy Train Cars

Type	Length in Inches
Engine	7
Boxcar	3
Passenger Car	9
Caboose	4

Assessment Practice

6. Use the table from Exercise **5**. If Serena's toy train had an engine and 3 passenger cars, then how long would her train be? Write equations to solve. Use letters to represent any unknown quantities.

Name ______________________________

 Practice  Video  Tools  Games

Additional Practice 11-4
Critique Reasoning

Another Look!

Frank needs \$169 to buy a bike. He already has \$46.
He earns \$20 for mowing a lawn.

Dan says Frank needs to mow 6 lawns at the same price to get enough money. His work is shown at the right.

Dan's work

$6 \times \$20 = \$120$
$\$120 + \$46$ is about $\$120 + \$50 = \$170$
$\$170 > \$169$
Frank has enough money.

Tell how you can critique Dan's reasoning.

- I can decide if his strategy makes sense.
- I can identify flaws in his thinking.

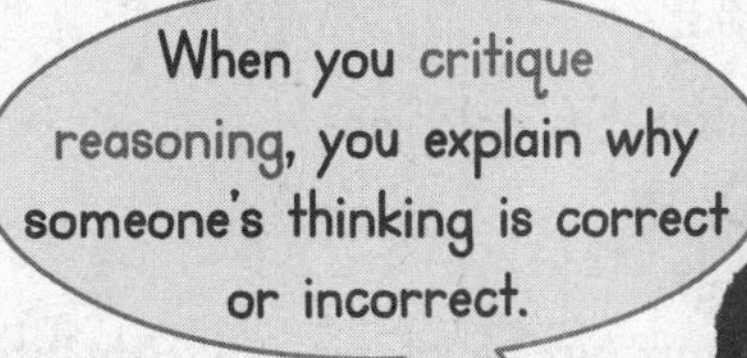

Critique Dan's reasoning.

The reasoning does not make sense.
Dan rounded \$46 to \$50, so his estimate of \$170 is more than Frank will actually have.
Compare the actual sum of \$120 + \$46 to \$169: $\$166 < \$169$.

Frank will not have enough money.

Critique Reasoning

A store made \$650 on Monday. It made \$233 on Tuesday morning and \$378 on Tuesday afternoon.

Leah says the store made more money on Tuesday. Her work is shown at the right.

Leah's work

$\$233 + \$378$ is about.
$\$300 + \$400 = \$700$

$\$700 > \$650$
The store made more money on Tuesday.

1. What is Leah's argument? How does she support it?

2. Tell how you can critique Leah's reasoning.

3. Critique Leah's reasoning.

Performance Task

Stocking a Fish Pond

About 200 people visit Mr. Ortiz's park each day. A fish pond in the park contains 636 fish. It cannot hold more than 700 fish. Mr. Ortiz has 7 bags of goldfish like the one at the right. Can Mr. Ortiz put all of his goldfish into the pond?

Jai solved the problem as shown.

$700 - 636$ is about $700 - 640$.
$700 - 640 = 60$

There are 8 goldfish in each bag.
$7 \times 8 = 56$
Mr. Ortiz has 56 goldfish.
$56 < 60$

Mr. Ortiz can put all of his goldfish into the pond.

4. Make Sense and Persevere Have you seen a problem like this before? If so, how can this help you solve it?

5. Critique Reasoning Does Jai's method make sense? Explain.

6. Be Precise Are Jai's calculations correct? Explain.

7. Reasoning Explain how Jai found the number of goldfish in each bag.

Name ______________________________

Practice

Video

Tools
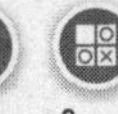
Games

Additional Practice 12-1
Partition Regions into Equal Parts

Another Look!

Divide these shapes into 6 equal parts in two different ways.

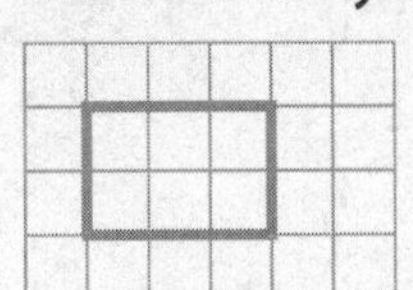
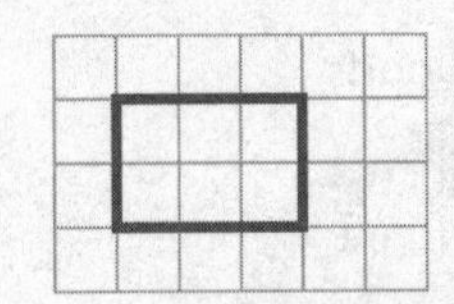

You can draw lines to divide the shapes into equal parts.

Equal parts do not need to be the same shape, but they must be equal in area.

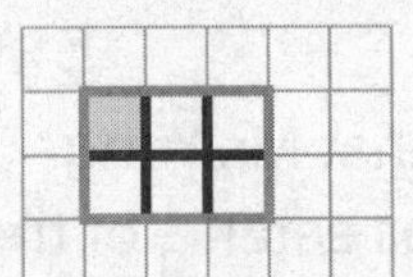
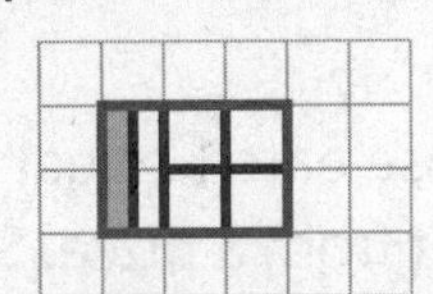

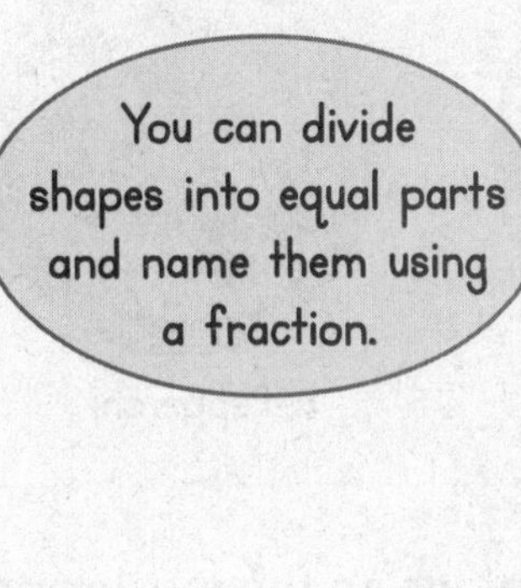

Both shapes are divided into six equal parts, or sixths. Each part is one sixth of the area of the shape. Each part can be written as $\frac{1}{6}$.

In **1–3**, tell if each shows equal or unequal parts. If the parts are equal, label one of the parts using a unit fraction.

1. 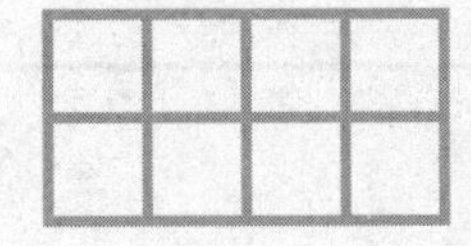

2. 

3. 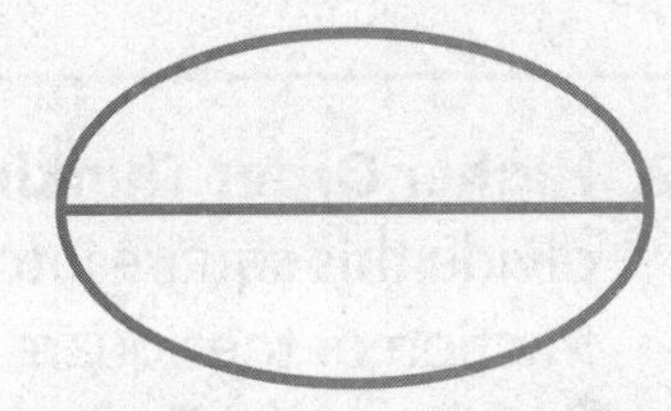

In **4–6**, draw lines to divide the shape into the given number of equal parts. Then write the fraction that represents one part.

4. 3 equal parts

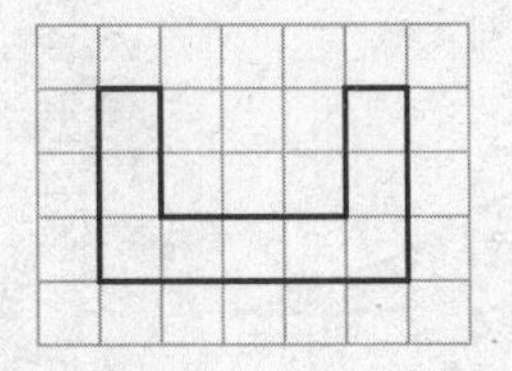

5. 4 equal parts

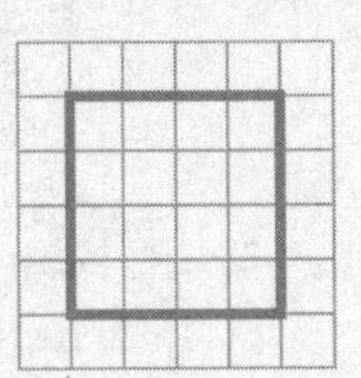

6. 6 equal parts

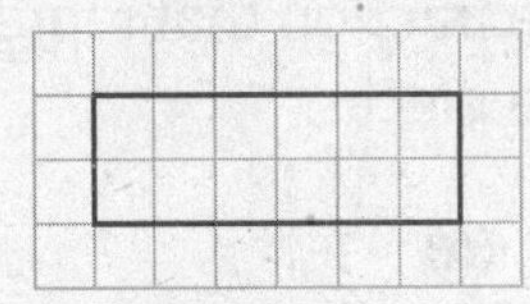

In **7–9**, use the pictures shown below.

7. Mr. Yung orders 3 pizzas. He cuts the pizzas into the number of equal parts shown. Draw lines to show how Mr. Yung could have cut the pizzas.

2 equal parts

Mushroom

8 equal parts

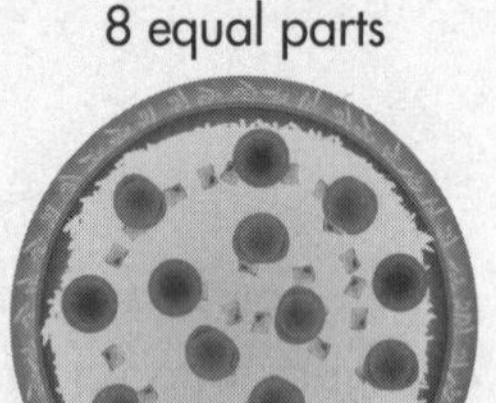

Pepperoni

4 equal parts

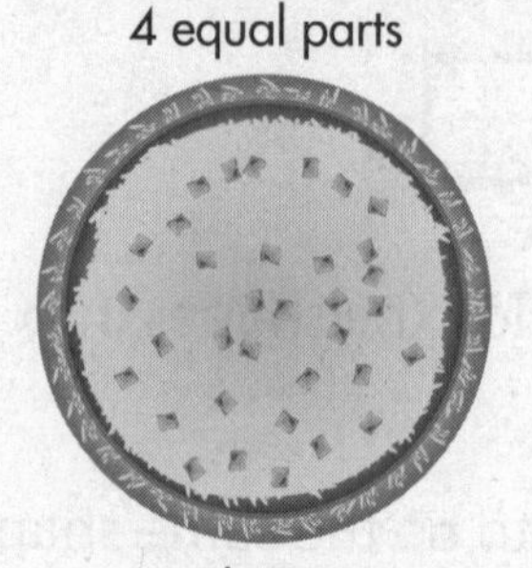

Cheese

8. Mr. Yung puts onions on the mushroom pizza. He puts onions on $\frac{1}{2}$ of that pizza. Shade the amount of pizza that has onions.

9. Rose eats 1 equal part that Mr. Yung cut from a pizza. She has eaten $\frac{1}{8}$ of the whole pizza. Which pizza did Rose eat?

10. Reasoning Ellen is drawing two polygons. One of the polygons has 3 more angles than the other. What shapes could she be drawing?

11. A-Z **Vocabulary** George cut a cake into 8 equal pieces. What is the unit fraction for the cake?

12. Higher Order Thinking Draw a line to divide this square into 8 equal parts. What fraction of the square was 1 part before you drew your line? After you drew your line?

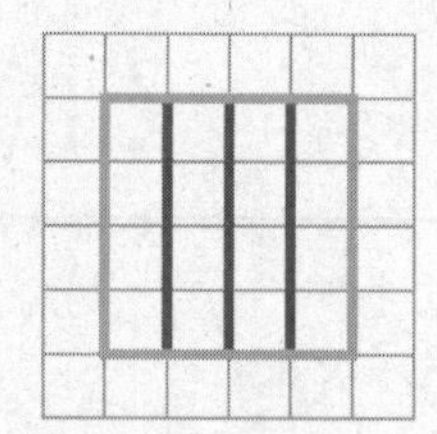

Assessment Practice

13. Draw lines to show how to divide this rectangle into 3 equal pieces. Then select the fraction that represents 1 of the pieces.

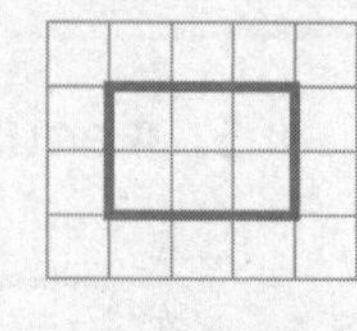

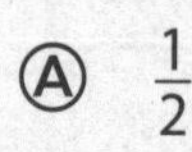

Ⓐ $\frac{1}{2}$

Ⓑ $\frac{1}{3}$

Ⓒ $\frac{1}{6}$

Ⓓ $\frac{1}{8}$

Name ________________

Practice Video Tools Games

Additional Practice 12-2
Fractions and Regions

Another Look!

A fraction can be used to name part of a whole.

The denominator shows the total number of equal parts in a whole. The numerator shows how many equal parts are described.

2 copies of $\frac{1}{4}$ is $\frac{2}{4}$. $\frac{2}{4}$ of the rectangle is shaded.

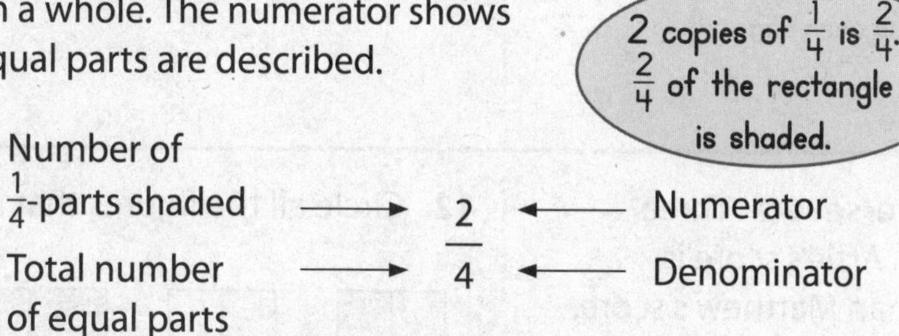

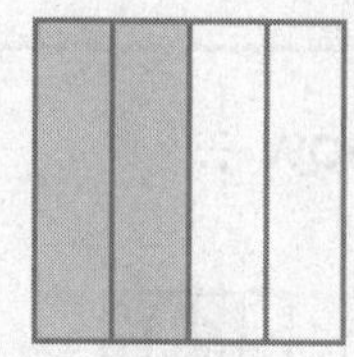

Number of $\frac{1}{4}$-parts shaded → $\frac{2}{4}$ ← Numerator

Total number of equal parts → 4 ← Denominator

In **1–6**, write the unit fraction that represents each part of the whole. Next write the number of shaded parts. Then write the fraction of the whole that is shaded.

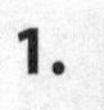

1. 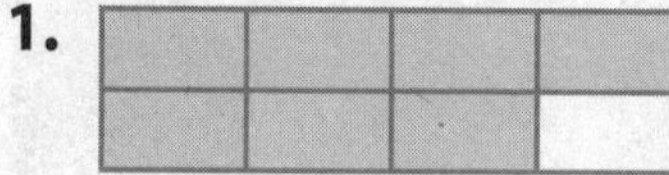

2. 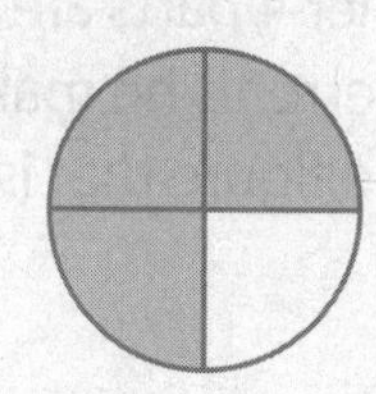

3. 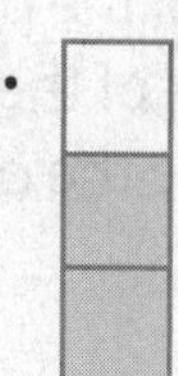

4. 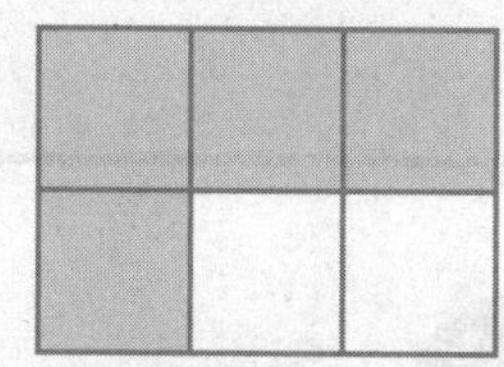

5. 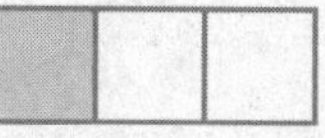

6. 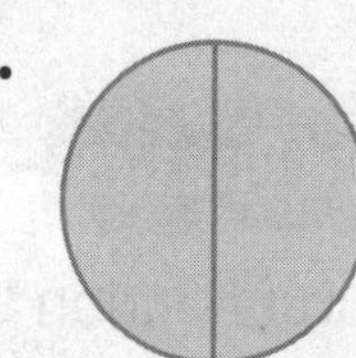

7. Draw a rectangle that shows 2 equal parts. Shade $\frac{1}{2}$ of the rectangle.

8. Draw a circle that shows 8 equal parts. Shade $\frac{2}{8}$ of the circle.

9. There are 6 cookies in 1 bag. How many cookies are in 5 bags? Use the bar diagram to write and solve an equation.

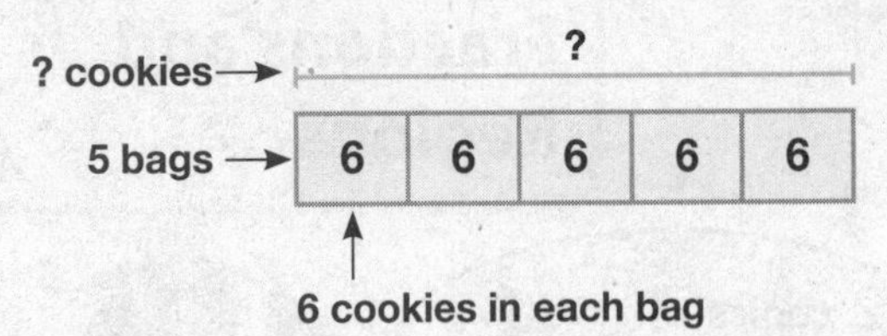

10. A banner is made of 8 equal parts. Five of the parts are green. Three of the parts are yellow. Draw and color the banner.

11. **Make Sense and Persevere** Three friends go bowling. Artie's score is 52 points greater than Matthew's score. Matthew's score is 60 points less than Greg's score. If Greg's score is 122, what is Artie's score?

12. Circle all the figures that show $\frac{3}{4}$.

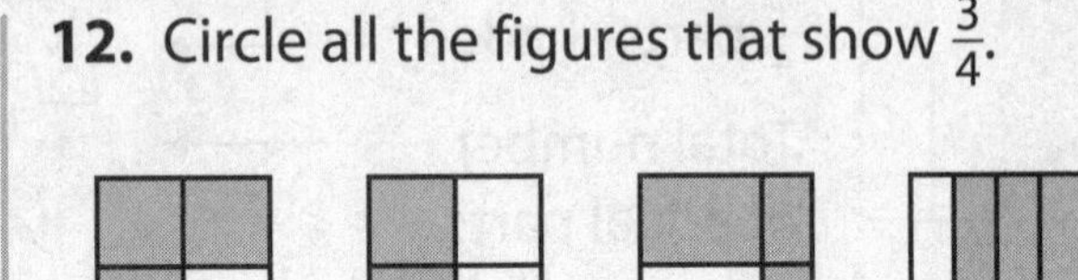

13. **Higher Order Thinking** Rashad draws a figure and divides it into equal parts. Two of the parts are red. The other 4 parts are blue. Rashad says that $\frac{2}{4}$ of the figure is red. What error is he making? Explain. Then write the correct fraction of the figure that is red.

You can draw a picture to help solve this problem.

Assessment Practice

14. Write the unit fraction that represents 1 square. Then write the fraction that represents the whole. Select numbers from the box to write the fractions.

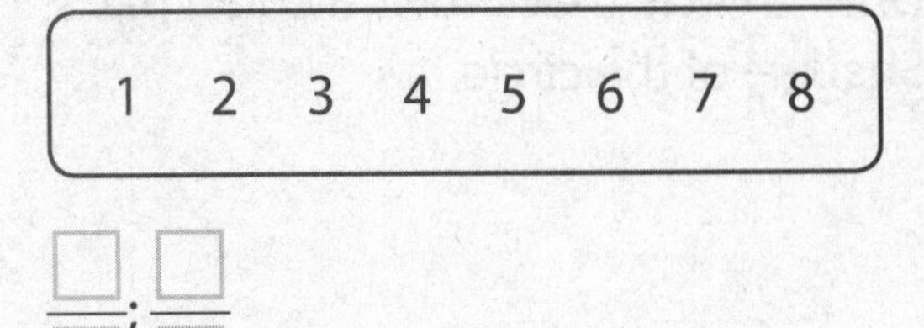

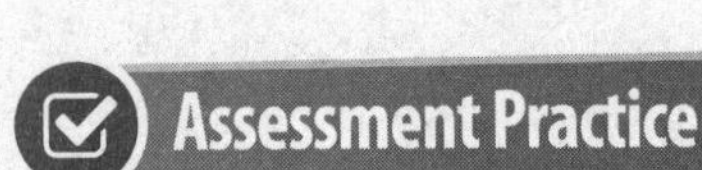

Name ______________________

Practice · Video · Tools · Games

Additional Practice 12-3
Understand the Whole

Another Look!

This is $\frac{3}{4}$ of a string cheese snack. How long is the whole string cheese snack?

$\frac{3}{4}$

$\frac{3}{4}$ is 3 lengths of $\frac{1}{4}$. Divide the snack into 3 equal lengths.

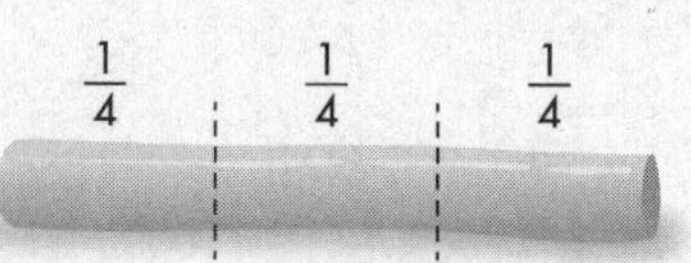

Four lengths of $\frac{1}{4}$ make $\frac{4}{4}$, or 1 whole. Draw one more fourth. The drawing shows the length of the whole string cheese.

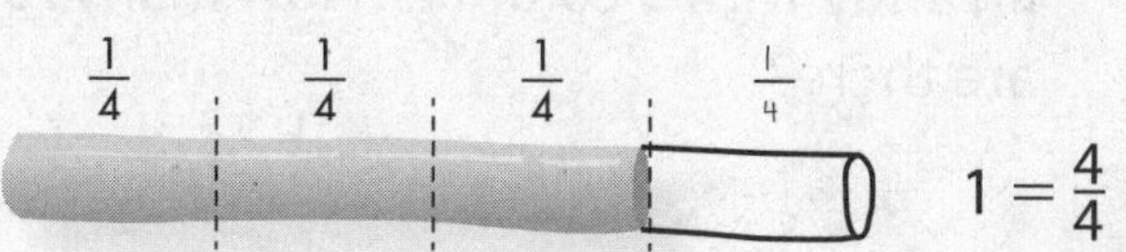

$1 = \frac{4}{4}$

The denominator of the fraction tells you how many lengths you need to make the whole.

In **1–4**, draw a picture of the whole and write a fraction to represent the whole.

1. $\frac{1}{3}$

$1 = \frac{\square}{\square}$

2. $\frac{1}{6}$

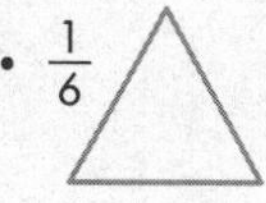

$1 = \frac{\square}{\square}$

3. $\frac{2}{4}$

$1 = \frac{\square}{\square}$

4. $\frac{3}{8}$

$1 = \frac{\square}{\square}$

5. Reasoning If the part shown is $\frac{3}{4}$ of a flag, what could the whole flag look like? Draw a picture and write a fraction to represent the whole.

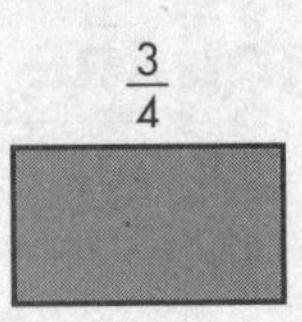

6. Jorge has $\frac{4}{8}$ of the fabric he needs to make a costume for the party. His fabric is shown. Draw a picture and write a fraction to represent the whole.

7. Jen's garden is 4 feet wide and 4 feet long. What is the area of Jen's garden?

8. Gary has 63 counters. He puts them in an array with 9 columns. How many rows are there?

9. Higher Order Thinking Megan and Mindy saw a plan for $\frac{2}{6}$ of a playground. They each drew a picture of the whole playground. Which drawing is **NOT** correct? Tell how you know.

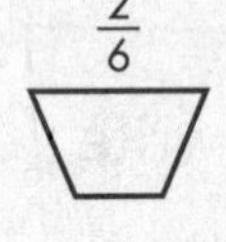

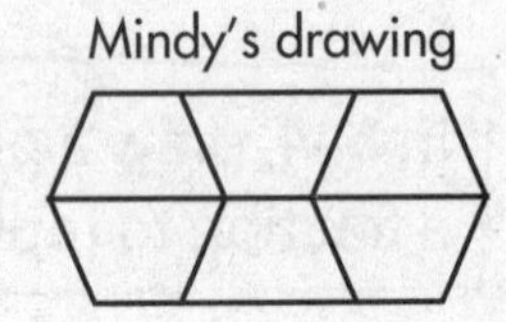

Assessment Practice

10. The picture shows $\frac{3}{4}$ of the distance Pedro lives from school.

Which shows the whole distance?

Ⓐ

Ⓑ

Ⓒ

Ⓓ

11. Each of these parts is $\frac{1}{8}$ of a different whole. Which is part of the largest whole?

Ⓐ

Ⓑ

Ⓒ

Ⓓ

Name ____________________

Practice Video Tools Games

Additional Practice 12-4

Number Line: Fractions Less Than 1

Another Look!

Show $\frac{3}{8}$ on a number line.

Start by drawing a number line from 0 to 1. Put tick marks at the ends. Label the tick marks 0 and 1.

Divide the number line into 8 equal lengths. Each length is $\frac{1}{8}$ of the whole.

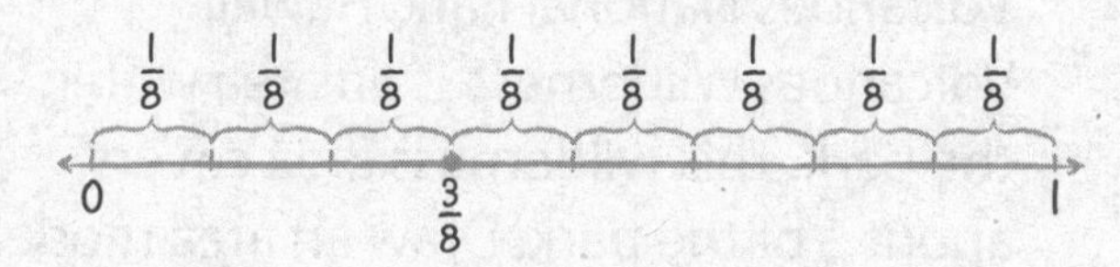

Start at 0. Go to the right until you come to the third tick mark. That mark represents $\frac{3}{8}$. Draw a point at $\frac{3}{8}$ on the line. Label the point $\frac{3}{8}$.

Be precise! You can use a number line to show fractions. The denominator tells you the number of equal parts on the number line.

In **1** and **2**, divide the number line into the given number of equal lengths. Then mark and label the given fraction on the number line.

1. 3 equal lengths; $\frac{2}{3}$

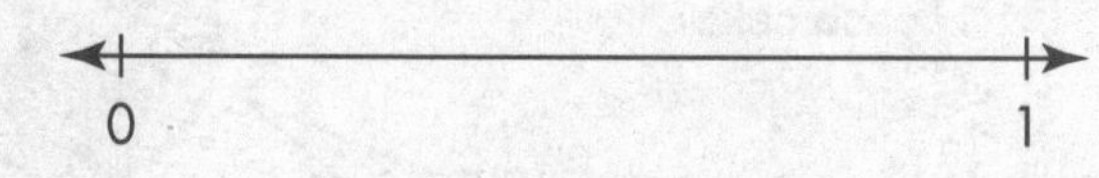

2. 6 equal lengths; $\frac{5}{6}$

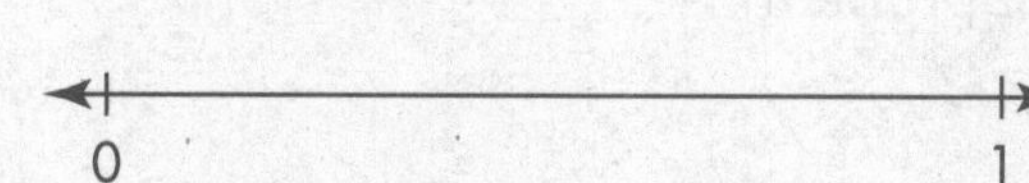

In **3–6**, draw a number line. Divide the number line into equal lengths for the given fraction. Then mark and label the fraction on the number line.

3. $\frac{3}{4}$

4. $\frac{4}{8}$

5. $\frac{1}{6}$

6. $\frac{7}{8}$

7. Algebra Ted writes the following equation. Write the number that makes the equation correct.

$824 = 20 + ? + 4$

$? =$ ______

8. Critique Reasoning Craig says that the dot on this number line shows $\frac{1}{3}$. Do you agree with Craig? Explain why or why not.

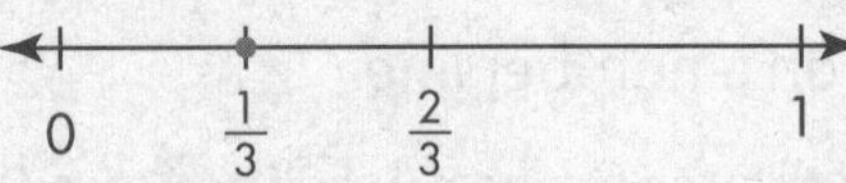

9. Higher Order Thinking Eddie is walking on a line that is painted on the sidewalk. It takes Eddie 8 equal-sized steps to get from one end of the line to the other. After Eddie has taken 5 steps, what fraction of the line is behind him? What fraction of the line is still in front of him?

10. enVision® STEM Fossilized footprints have been found within the Hawaii Volcanoes National Park. Hawaii Volcanoes Wilderness is an area within the park. This wilderness area covers about $\frac{1}{2}$ of the park. Draw an area model to show $\frac{1}{2}$.

11. Marty has 1 dozen eggs. He needs 4 eggs to bake a cake. How many cakes can he bake? Complete the bar diagram and write an equation to represent and solve the problem.

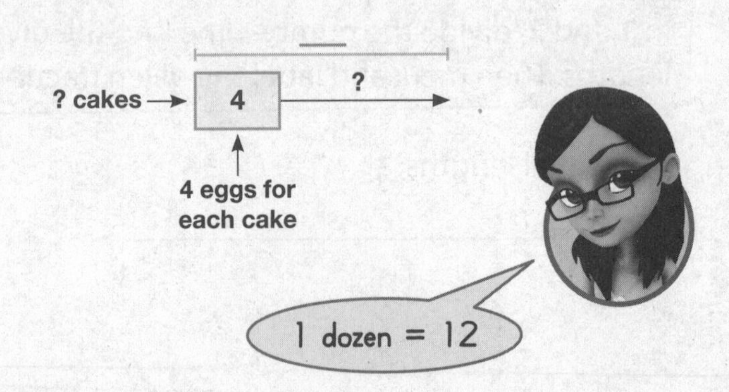

Assessment Practice

12. Which number line has a point at $\frac{3}{8}$?

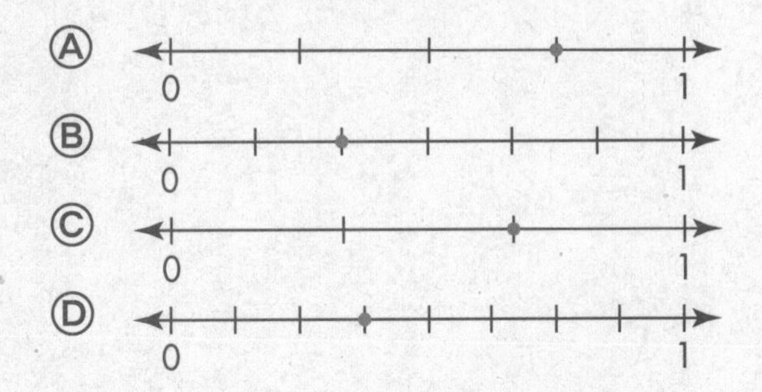

13. What fraction does the point on this number line represent?

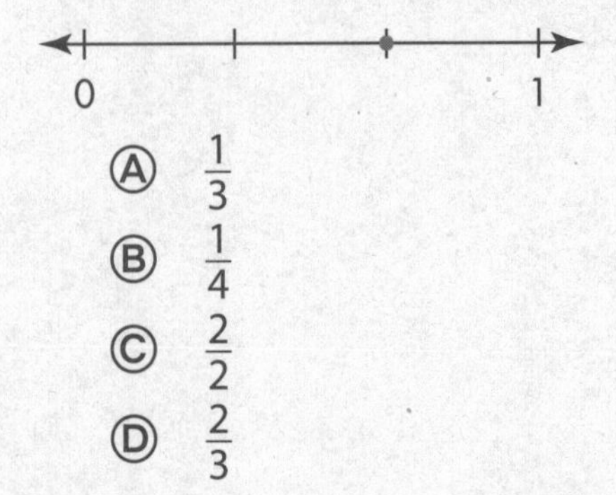

Name ____________________

Practice Video Tools Games

Additional Practice 12-5

Number Line: Fractions Greater Than 1

Another Look!

A point on a number line can be named using a fraction.

In the fractions below, the denominator shows the number of equal lengths that are between 0 and 1. The numerator shows the number of copies of the unit fraction.

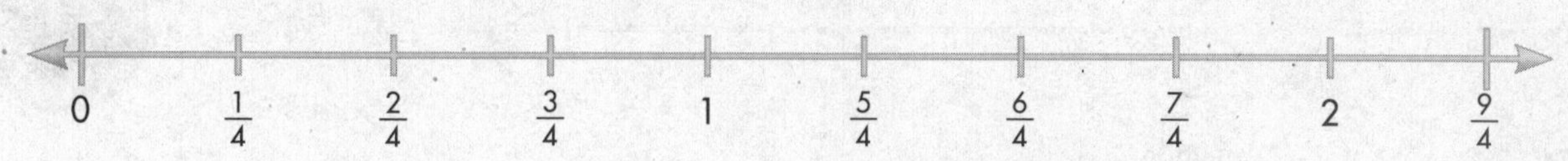

The numerator increases by 1 at each point. That is because each point means there is 1 more copy of the unit fraction!

In **1–6**, each number line has equal lengths marked. Write the missing fractions.

1. 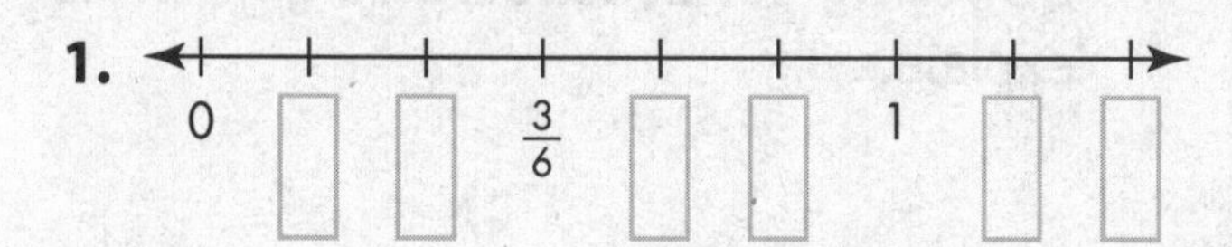

2. 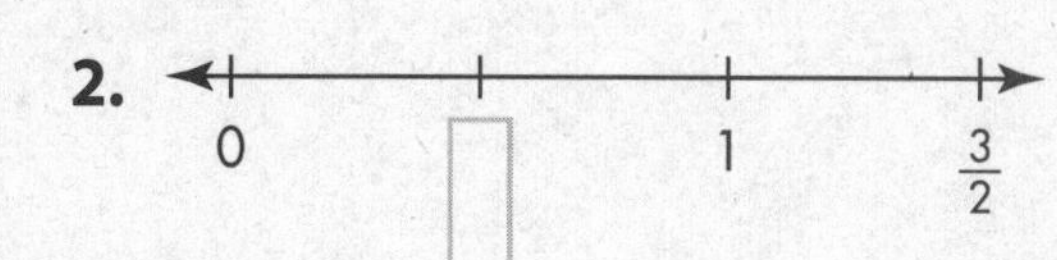

3. 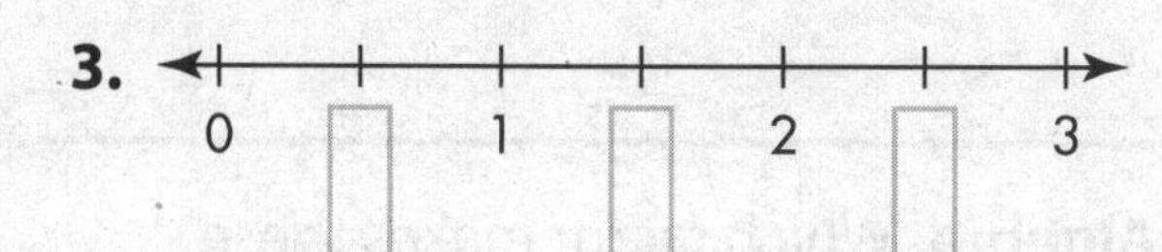

4. 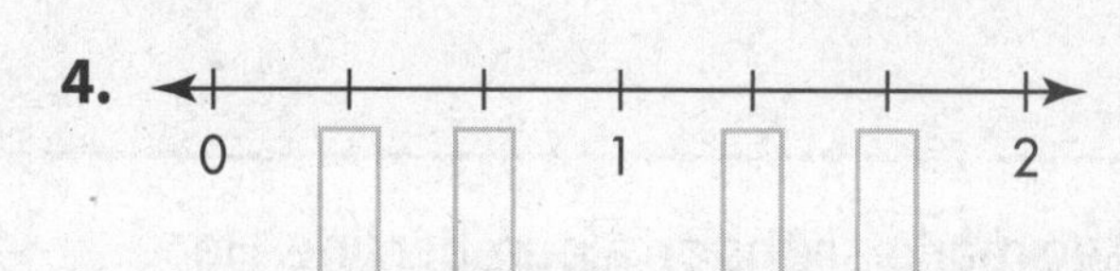

5. 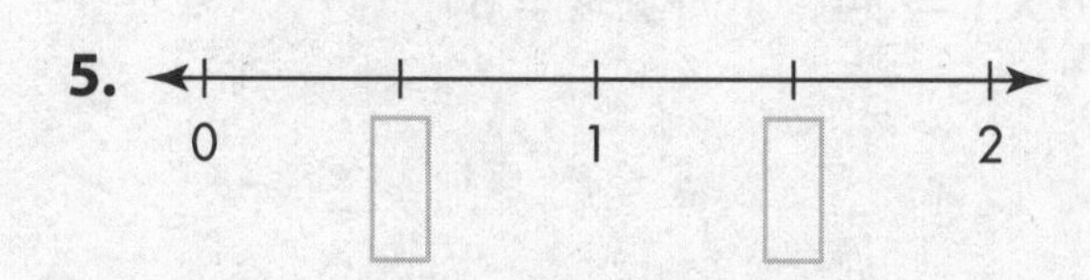

6. 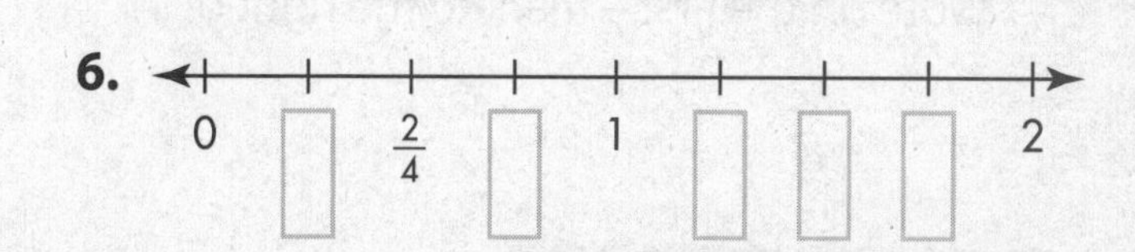

7. Divide the number line into thirds. Label each point.

0 1 2 3 4

In **8** and **9**, use the number line below.

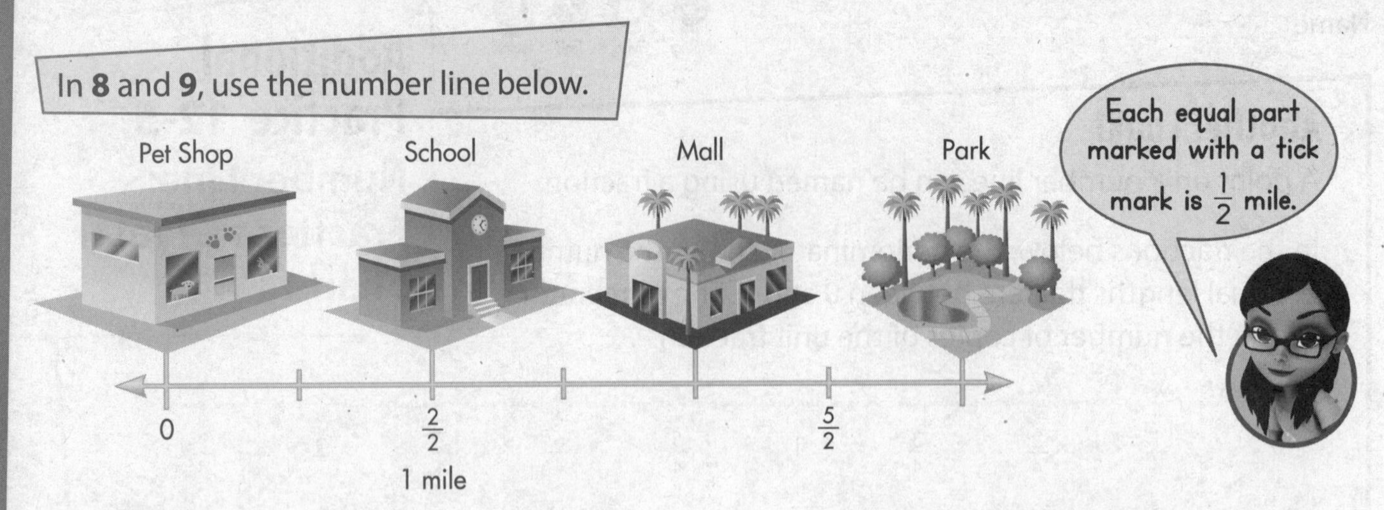

8. How far is the mall from the pet shop? Explain how you know.

9. Higher Order Thinking Ken lives at the point between the school and the pet shop. How far away is Ken's house from the park?

10. Draw a triangle in which all the sides are different lengths.

11. Construct Arguments Jan said that 2 is between 0 and $\frac{3}{4}$ on a number line. Do you agree? Construct an argument to explain.

12. Lee marks sixths on a number line. He writes $\frac{5}{6}$ just before 1. What fraction does he write on the first $\frac{1}{6}$ mark to the right of 1?

13. Algebra Which factor makes these equations correct?

$6 \times ? = 54$ $? \times 9 = 81$

Assessment Practice

14. What fraction is represented by the total length marked on the number line? Select the correct fraction from the box.

$\frac{1}{2}$ $\frac{2}{3}$ $\frac{3}{4}$ $\frac{4}{3}$ $\frac{5}{3}$

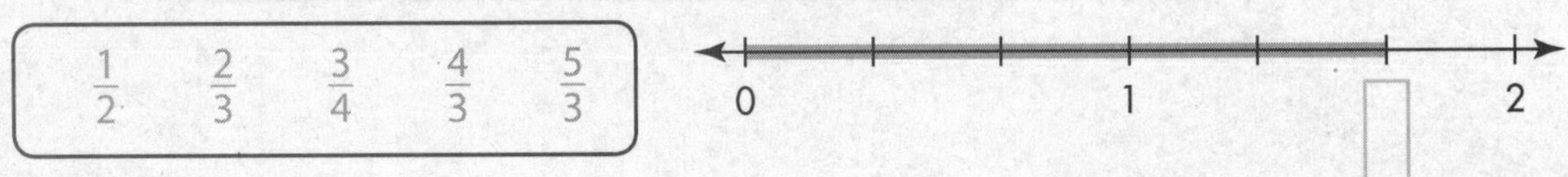

Name ______________________

Practice

Video

Tools

Games

Additional Practice 12-6
Line Plots and Length

Another Look!

This ruler shows half-inch marks. Franco used the ruler to measure a hexagon to the nearest half inch.

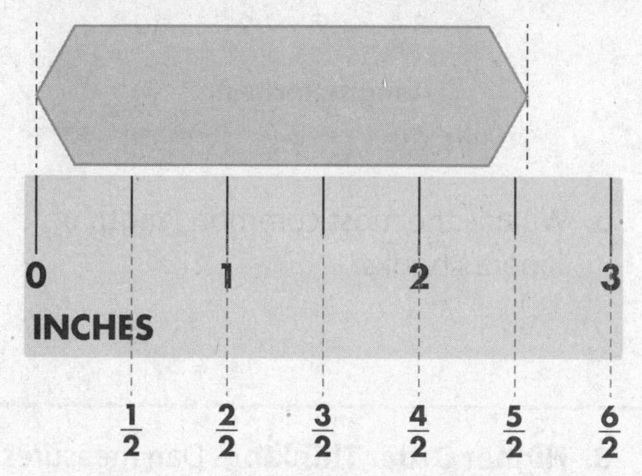

To the nearest half inch, the length of the hexagon is $2\frac{1}{2}$ inches. Franco recorded the lengths of other hexagons he measured. Then he made a line plot. The most common lengths were $1\frac{1}{2}$ inches and $2\frac{1}{2}$ inches.

1. Measure the length of each rectangle to the nearest half inch.

0 INCHES 1 2 3

Medium

Long

Short

2. Jamal drew 5 of the medium rectangles, 3 of the long rectangles, and 4 of the short rectangles. How many dots, or data points, should be on the line plot?

3. Complete the line plot to show the data.

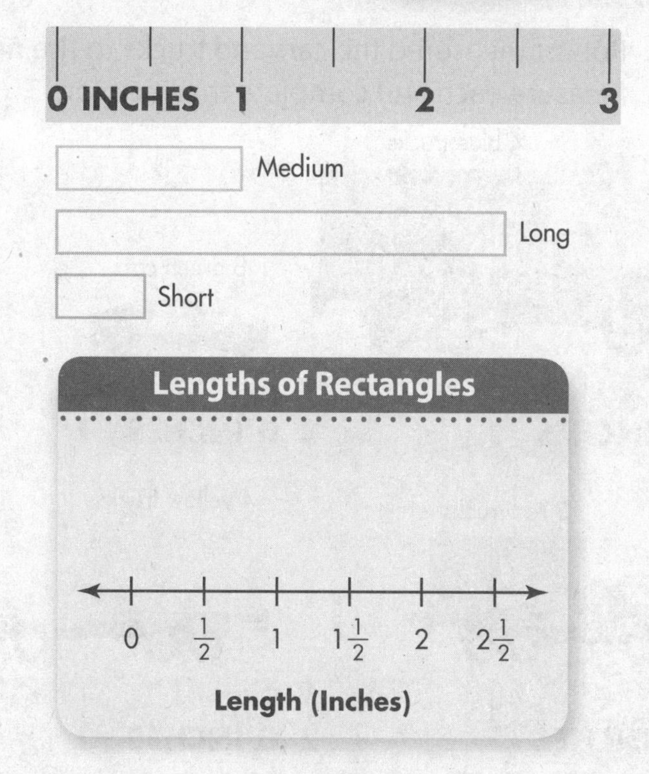

4. Japera measured the lengths of her books to the nearest half inch and listed their lengths. Complete the line plot to display the lengths of Japera's books.

$8\frac{1}{2}$ in., $9\frac{1}{2}$ in., $8\frac{1}{2}$ in., $9\frac{1}{2}$ in., 10 in., $9\frac{1}{2}$ in., $8\frac{1}{2}$ in., 9 in., $9\frac{1}{2}$ in.

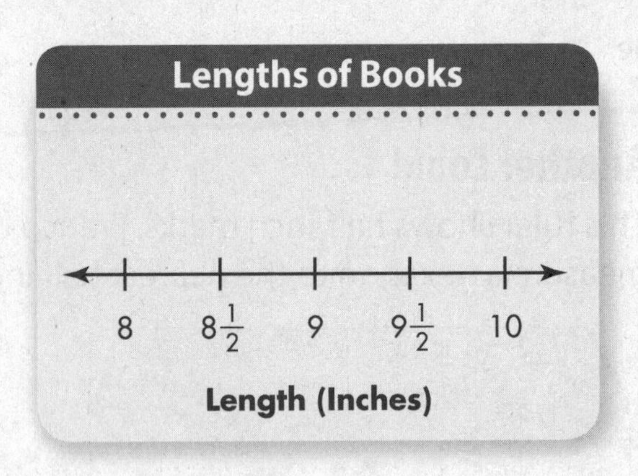

5. Eli has double the number of books that Japera has. How many books does Eli have?

6. What is the most common length of Japera's books?

---

7. **Model with Math** Peter bought 8 paint sets. He gives half of his sets to his sister. Each set has 5 bottles. How many bottles does Peter's sister have? Use math you know to represent the problem.

8. **Higher Order Thinking** Dan measures an object to the nearest half inch. He records the length as $4\frac{1}{2}$ inches. Geri measures the same object to the nearest inch. Could Dan and Geri get the same measurement? Explain.

Assessment Practice

9. Robert measured the cars and trucks to the nearest half inch. Measure each and complete the line plot.

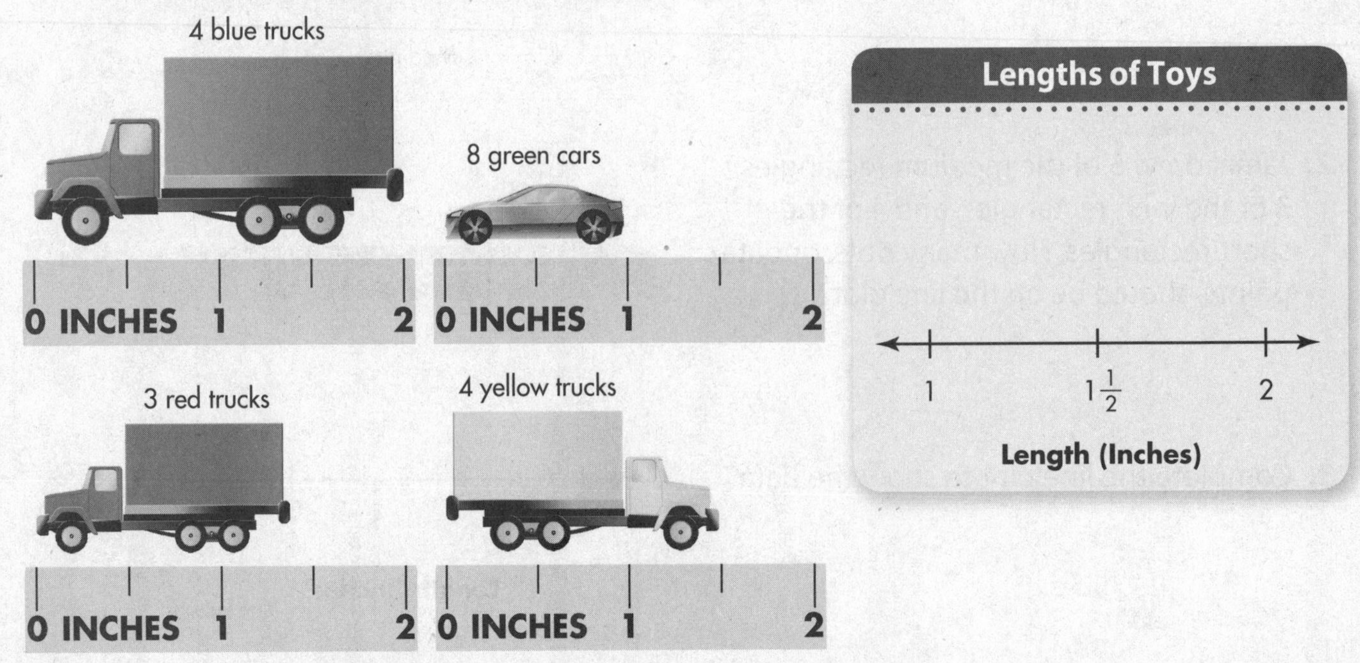

Name ______________________

Additional Practice 12-7
More Line Plots and Length

Another Look!

This ruler shows fourth-inch marks. Serena used the ruler to measure a ribbon to the nearest fourth inch.

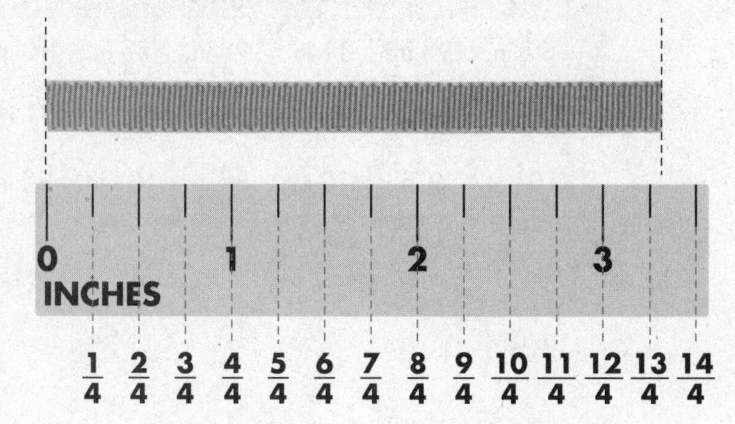

$\frac{1}{4}$ $\frac{2}{4}$ $\frac{3}{4}$ $\frac{4}{4}$ $\frac{5}{4}$ $\frac{6}{4}$ $\frac{7}{4}$ $\frac{8}{4}$ $\frac{9}{4}$ $\frac{10}{4}$ $\frac{11}{4}$ $\frac{12}{4}$ $\frac{13}{4}$ $\frac{14}{4}$

A ruler can help you be precise when measuring. A line plot can organize the data.

To the nearest fourth inch, the length of the ribbon is $3\frac{1}{4}$ inches.

Serena recorded the measurements of all the ribbons she has. Then she made a line plot.

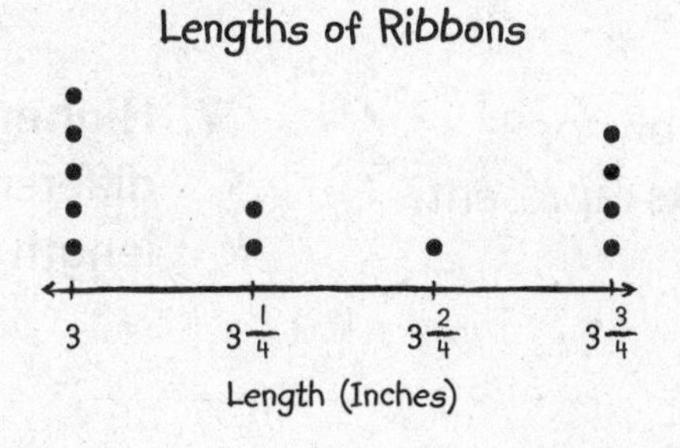

1. Toby's toy insects are shown at the right. Measure each insect to the nearest fourth inch. Record each measurement.

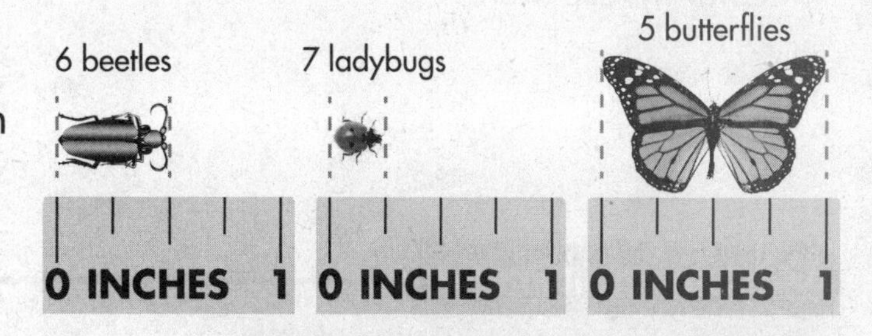

2. How many dots, or data points, should be on the line plot to show all of Toby's toy insects?

3. Complete the line plot to show the data.

4. How many more dots did you draw for beetles than for butterflies?

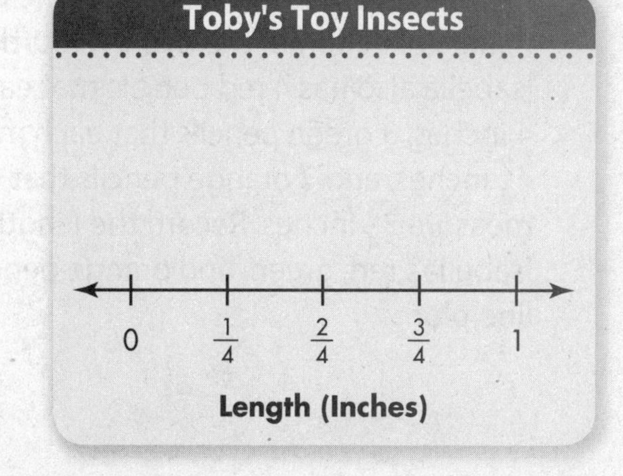

In **5–7**, use the table at the right. The table shows the lengths of fish that scientists studied, to the nearest fourth inch.

5. Make a line plot to show the data.

Fish Lengths

DATA

$9\frac{1}{4}$ in.	$9\frac{3}{4}$ in.	11 in.	$9\frac{3}{4}$ in.	$8\frac{3}{4}$ in.	10 in.
$8\frac{3}{4}$ in.	$9\frac{2}{4}$ in.	$10\frac{2}{4}$ in.	$8\frac{2}{4}$ in.	$9\frac{3}{4}$ in.	11 in.
$10\frac{1}{4}$ in.	9 in.	10 in.	$8\frac{3}{4}$ in.	$10\frac{3}{4}$ in.	$9\frac{3}{4}$ in.

6. How many dots do you show for $9\frac{3}{4}$ inches? What do these dots represent?

7. Higher Order Thinking What is the difference in length between the longest length and the shortest length?

8. Owen arranges 48 beads into an array. There are 6 rows of beads. How many columns are there?

9. Make Sense and Persevere On Wednesday, Connor spent $65. On Thursday, he spent $130. Connor has $311 left. How much money did Connor have to start?

Assessment Practice

10. Isabella recorded the lengths of the blue pencils in her collection to the nearest fourth inch. Isabella also has 4 red pencils that each measure 4 inches, 3 green pencils that each measure $4\frac{2}{4}$ inches, and 7 orange pencils that each measure $3\frac{3}{4}$ inches. Record the lengths of Isabella's red, green, and orange pencils in the line plot.

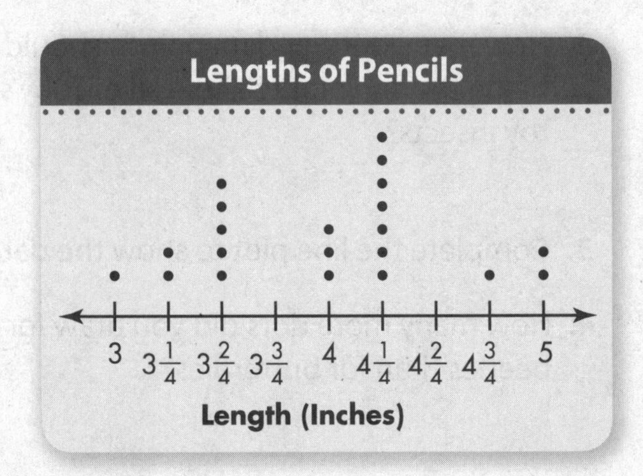

Name ______________________________

Additional Practice 12-8
Make Sense and Persevere

Another Look!

Becky divides a rectangle into 8 equal parts. She colors 4 parts yellow. The rectangle has 4 sides and 4 angles. Becky colors 1 part red and the rest blue. What fraction of the rectangle does Becky color blue?

Tell how to make sense of the problem.

- I can identify the quantities given.
- I can understand which quantities are needed to solve the problem.

You can make sense and persevere in solving the problem by identifying the quantities needed. Then use what you know to solve the problem.

Use what you know to solve the problem.

The rectangle has 4 sides and 4 angles is extra information. There are 8 equal parts. So, each part is $\frac{1}{8}$ of the whole. There are 3 parts left to color blue: 3 copies of $\frac{1}{8}$ is $\frac{3}{8}$. So, $\frac{3}{8}$ is blue.

Y	Y	R	B
Y	Y	B	B

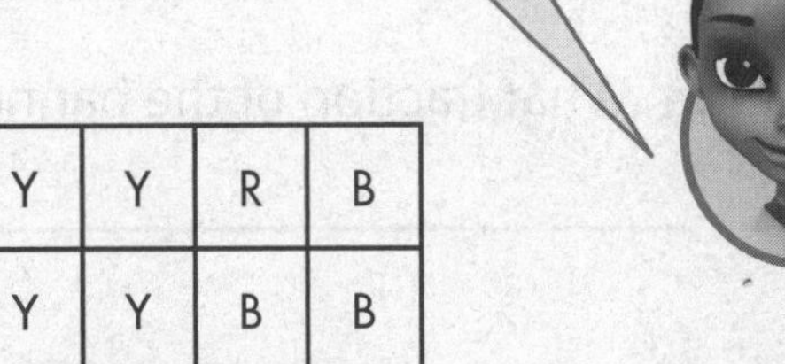

Make Sense and Persevere

Three friends get to a party at 2:00. They cut a pizza into 4 pieces. The friends each eat one slice of pizza. What fraction of the pizza is left?

1. Tell how to make sense of the problem.

2. Is there any missing or extra information? Explain.

3. Solve the problem. If information you need is missing, make up some reasonable information for the problem. You can draw a picture to help.

Performance Task

School Banner

Four students are making the banner shown at the right. They have 1 week to finish the banner. Anja makes the green parts. Michael makes the white part. Adeeba makes the same number of parts as Lee.

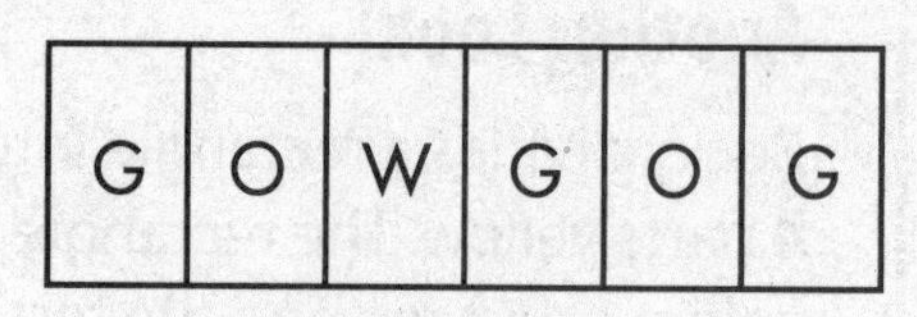

4. Make Sense and Persevere The teacher wants to know what fraction of the banner Lee makes. Is there any extra or missing information?

5. Reasoning What fraction of the banner does Anja make?

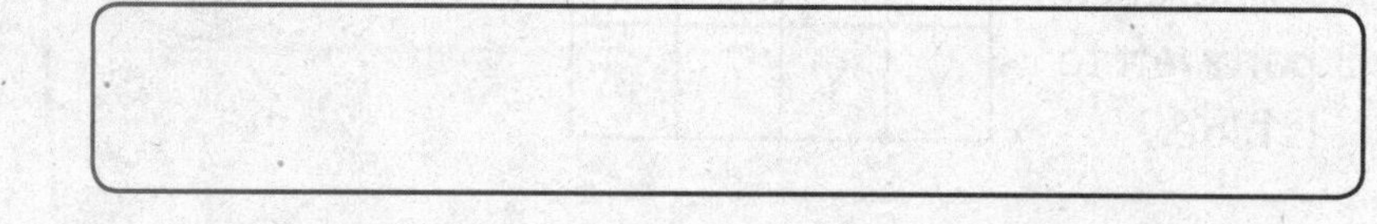

6. Reasoning What fraction of the banner does Michael make?

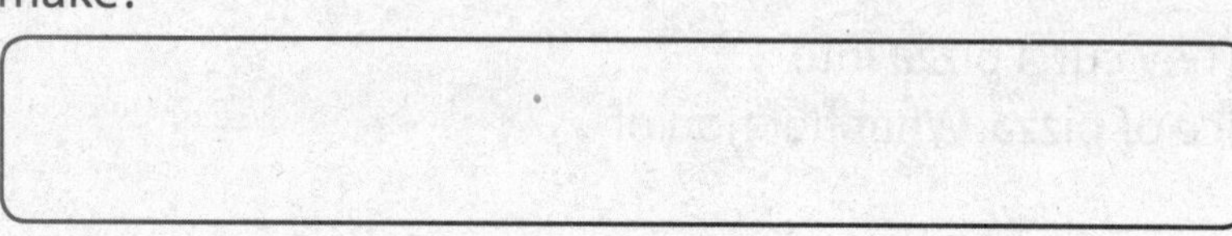

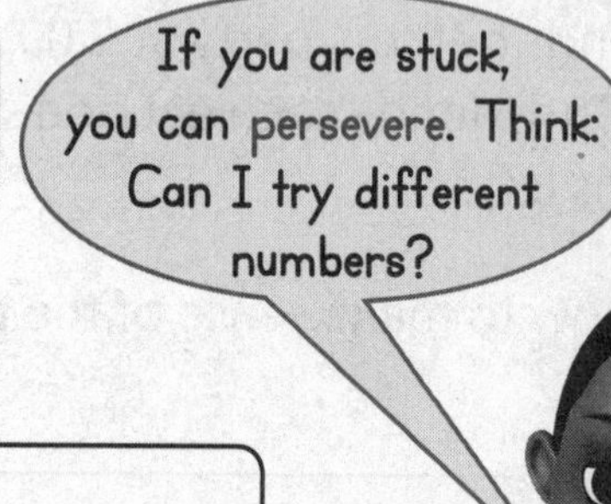

7. Be Precise Explain how you know the fraction of the banner that is **NOT** made by either Anja or Michael.

8. Construct Arguments What fraction of the banner does Lee make? Explain.

Name ____________________

Additional Practice 13-1

Equivalent Fractions: Use Models

Another Look!

You can use fraction strips to find equivalent fractions.

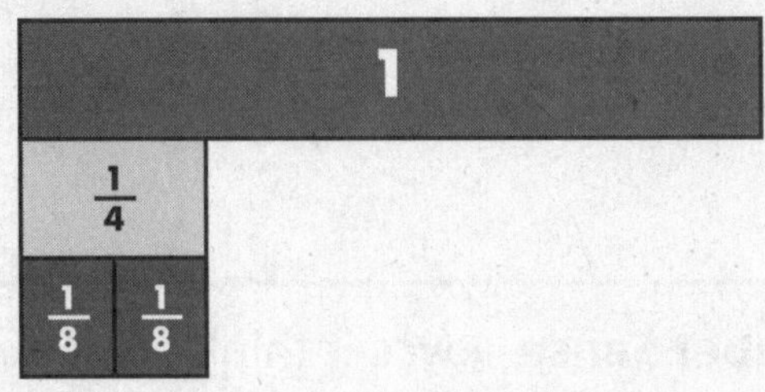

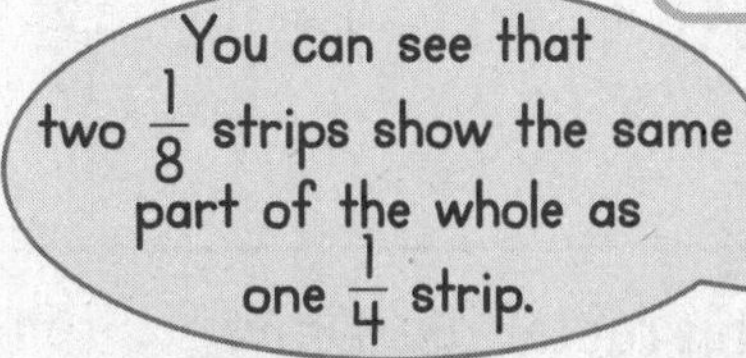

$\frac{1}{4}$ and $\frac{2}{8}$ are equivalent fractions because they name the same amount. You can write $\frac{1}{4} = \frac{2}{8}$.

You also can use area models to show that $\frac{1}{4}$ and $\frac{2}{8}$ are equivalent. The two fractions name the same part of the whole.

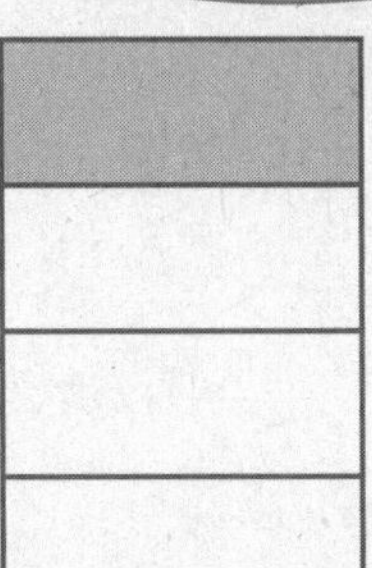

In **1–8**, find the equivalent fractions. Use fraction strips or draw area models to help.

1.

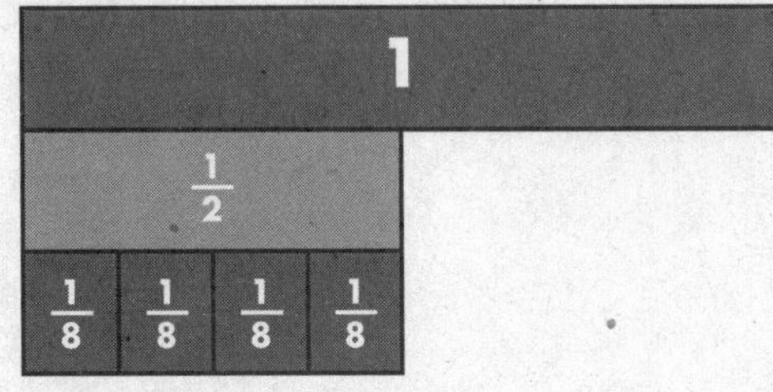

$\frac{1}{2} = \square$

2.

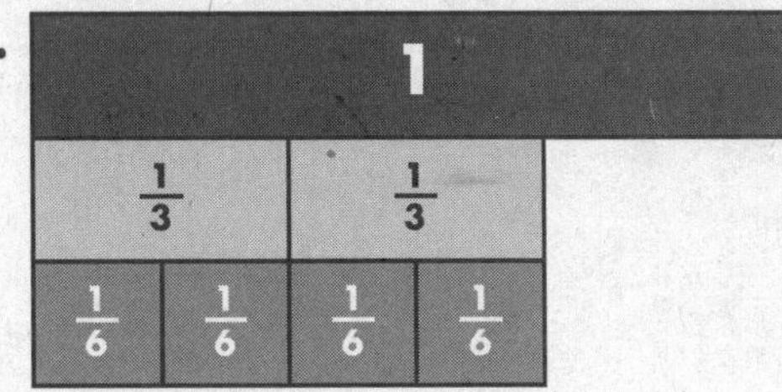

$\frac{2}{3} = \square$

3.

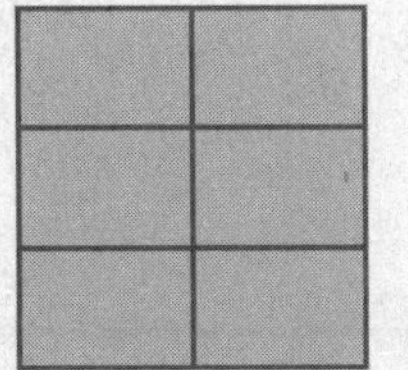

$\frac{6}{6} = \square$

4.

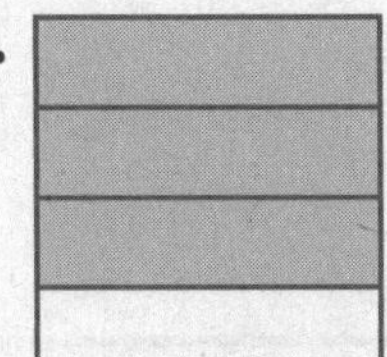

$\frac{3}{4} = \square$

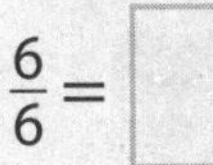

5. $\frac{1}{3} = \frac{\square}{6}$

6. $\frac{4}{4} = \frac{\square}{3}$

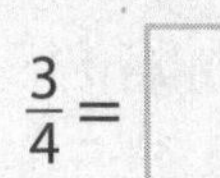

7. $\frac{1}{2} = \frac{\square}{4}$

8. $\frac{3}{6} = \frac{\square}{2}$

9. **Vocabulary** Explain what equivalent fractions are and give an example.

10. **Use Appropriate Tools** When you use fraction strips, how can you tell if two fractions are **NOT** equivalent?

11. Taylor colored $\frac{1}{4}$ of this rectangle. Draw an area model showing a fraction equivalent to $\frac{1}{4}$. Use the picture to help.

12. **Number Sense** Joyce is thinking of a 3-digit number. Her number has the digits 8, 4, and 6. To the nearest hundred, it rounds to 600. What is the number?

13. Dinner plates are arranged on 5 shelves, with 8 plates on each shelf. How many dinner plates are on all of the shelves? Draw a bar diagram and write an equation to solve.

14. **Higher Order Thinking** Fred says that $\frac{1}{2}$ and $\frac{7}{8}$ are equivalent fractions. Draw area models for $\frac{1}{2}$ and $\frac{7}{8}$ to show if Fred's statement is correct. Name two fractions that you know are equivalent to $\frac{1}{2}$.

Assessment Practice

15. Which fraction pairs are **NOT** equivalent? Select all that apply.

- ☐ $\frac{1}{3}$ and $\frac{1}{6}$
- ☐ $\frac{1}{3}$ and $\frac{3}{6}$
- ☐ $\frac{2}{6}$ and $\frac{1}{3}$
- ☐ $\frac{4}{6}$ and $\frac{2}{3}$
- ☐ $\frac{2}{3}$ and $\frac{3}{6}$

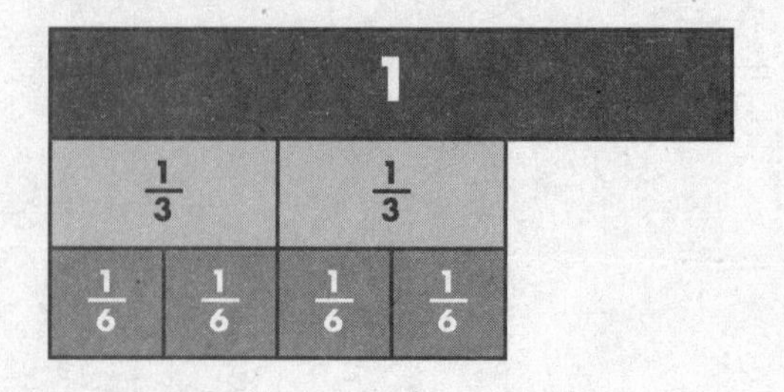

Name

Practice Video Tools Games

Additional Practice 13-2

Equivalent Fractions: Use the Number Line

Another Look!

Leah shares a fruit roll with her sister. Her sister says that Leah took $\frac{1}{3}$ of the fruit roll. Leah thought that she took $\frac{2}{6}$ of the fruit roll. She drew two number lines to see if the two fractions were equivalent.

The fractions are at the same location on the number line, so the fractions are equivalent.

$\frac{1}{3} = \frac{2}{6}$

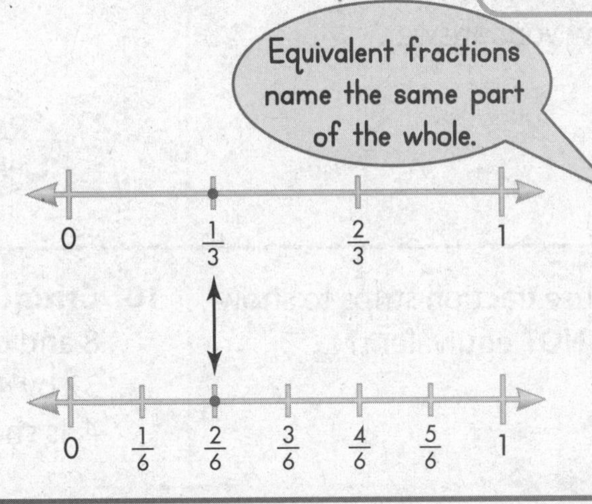

In **1–4**, find the missing equivalent fractions on the number line. Then write the equivalent fractions below. In **5** and **6**, write equivalent fractions.

1.

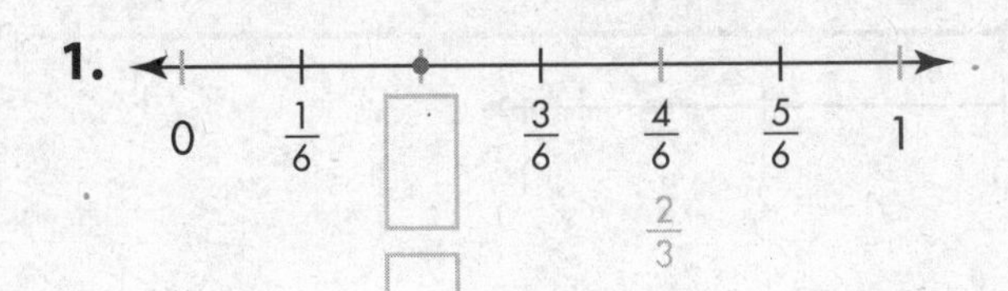

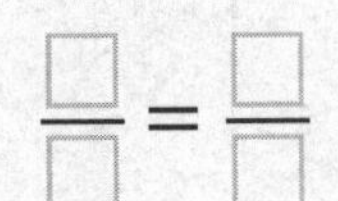

2.

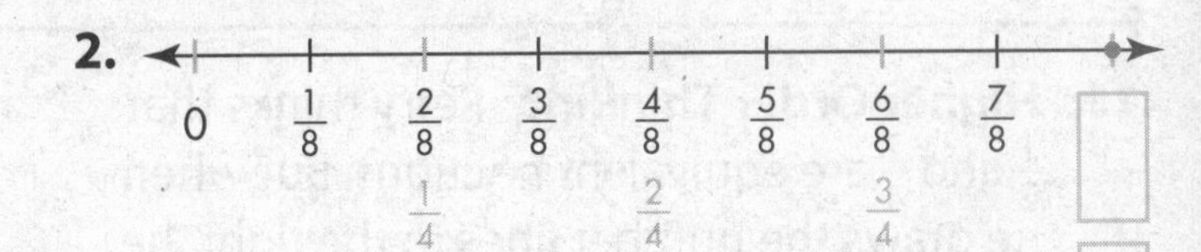

$\frac{\square}{\square} = \frac{\square}{\square}$

3.

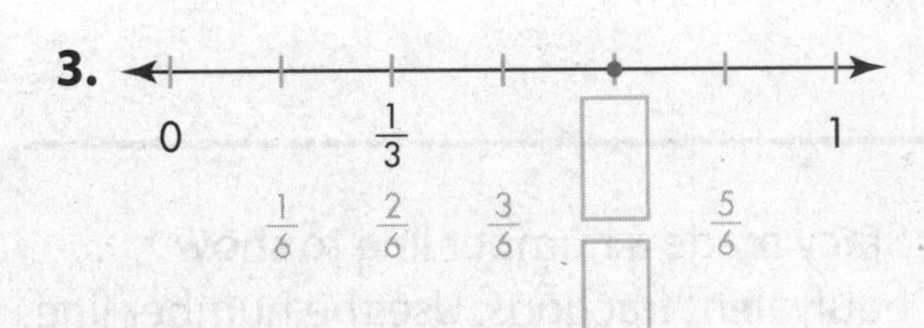

4.

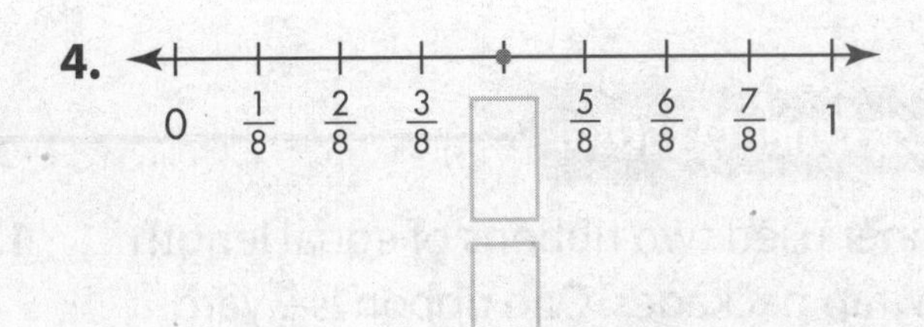

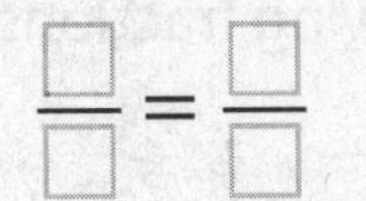

5.

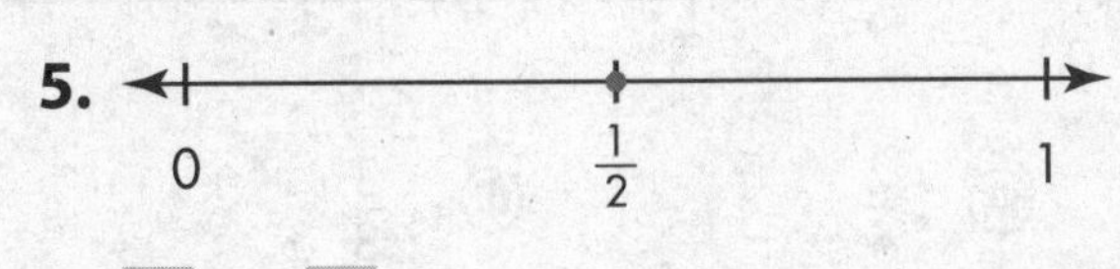

6.

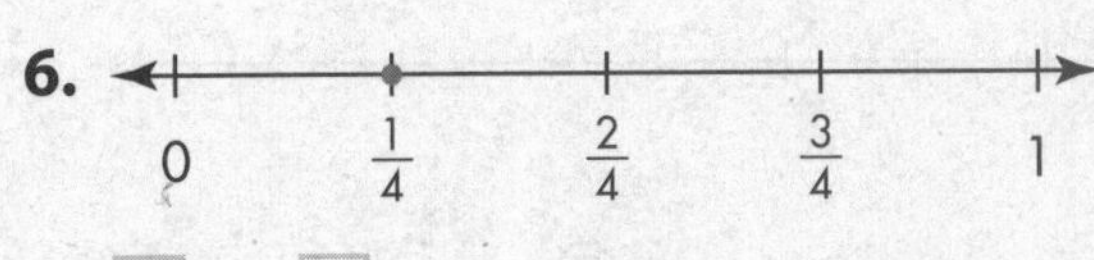

7. Oliver and Peter had the same length of string. Oliver used $\frac{3}{4}$ of his string to tie a bundle of newspapers. Peter used $\frac{6}{8}$ of his string to tie a bundle of magazines. Did they use the same amount of string? Draw a number line and write the fractions to show your answer.

8. Eric divides a strip of paper into 8 equal parts. He cuts off 2 of the parts. He shades 4 of the remaining parts blue. What fraction of the remaining whole does Eric shade blue?

9. How can Brady use fraction strips to show that $\frac{3}{4}$ and $\frac{7}{8}$ are **NOT** equivalent?

10. Critique Reasoning Isabel divided 32 by 8 and got 4. She says that if she divides 32 by 4, the quotient will be greater than 4. Is she correct? Explain.

11. Higher Order Thinking Perry thinks that $\frac{1}{2}$ and $\frac{2}{4}$ are equivalent fractions. But when he draws the number lines to the right, he sees that $\frac{1}{2}$ and $\frac{2}{4}$ do not name the same location. Explain what Perry did wrong.

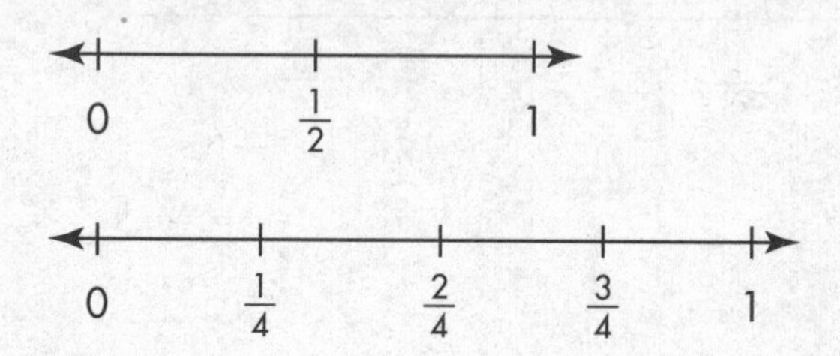

Assessment Practice

12. Tanner used two ribbons of equal length to wrap packages. One ribbon is $\frac{4}{8}$ yard. Use the number line to find which of the following is **NOT** a possible length for the second ribbon.

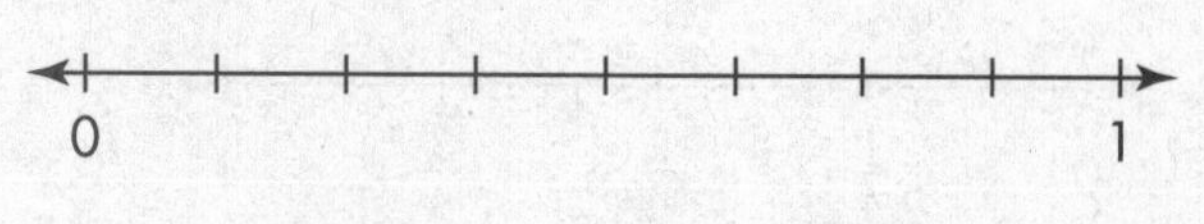

Ⓐ $\frac{3}{8}$ yard
Ⓑ $\frac{4}{8}$ yard
Ⓒ $\frac{1}{2}$ yard
Ⓓ $\frac{2}{4}$ yard

13. Stacy made a number line to show equivalent fractions. Use the number line to find which of the following fractions is equivalent to $\frac{6}{8}$.

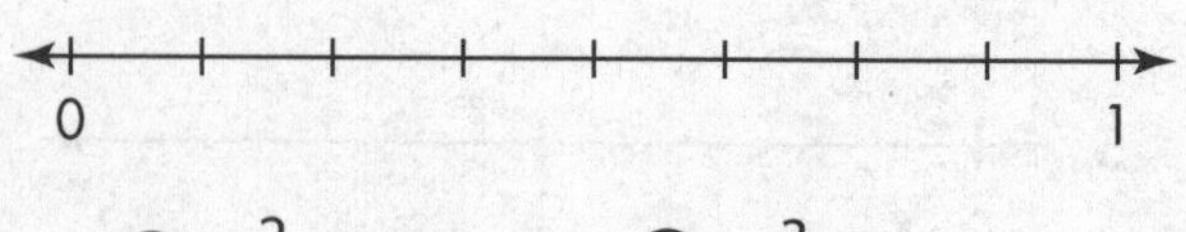

Ⓐ $\frac{2}{4}$
Ⓑ $\frac{1}{2}$
Ⓒ $\frac{3}{8}$
Ⓓ $\frac{3}{4}$

Name ______________________

Additional Practice 13-3

Use Models to Compare Fractions: Same Denominator

Another Look!

You can use fraction strips to compare fractions that have the same denominator.

Compare $\frac{1}{4}$ and $\frac{3}{4}$.

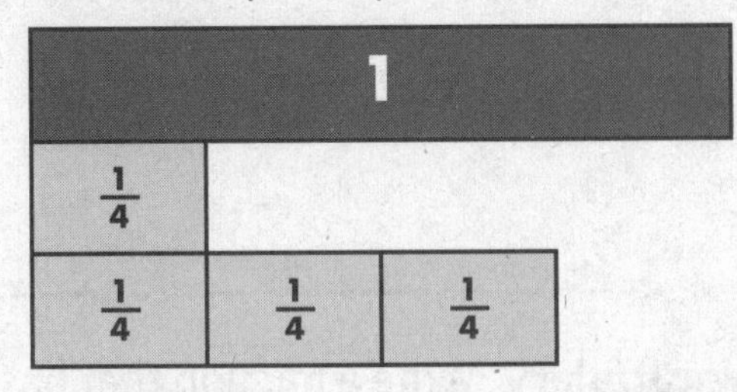

Fractions that you compare must be part of the same whole or of equal-sized wholes.

The denominator for each fraction is 4.
Use fraction strips to help compare the fractions.

Use one $\frac{1}{4}$ strip to show $\frac{1}{4}$ and three $\frac{1}{4}$ strips to show $\frac{3}{4}$.
More $\frac{1}{4}$ strips are used to show $\frac{3}{4}$. So, $\frac{3}{4} > \frac{1}{4}$ and $\frac{1}{4} < \frac{3}{4}$.

In **1–12**, compare. Write <, >, or =. Use or draw fraction strips to help. The fractions refer to the same whole.

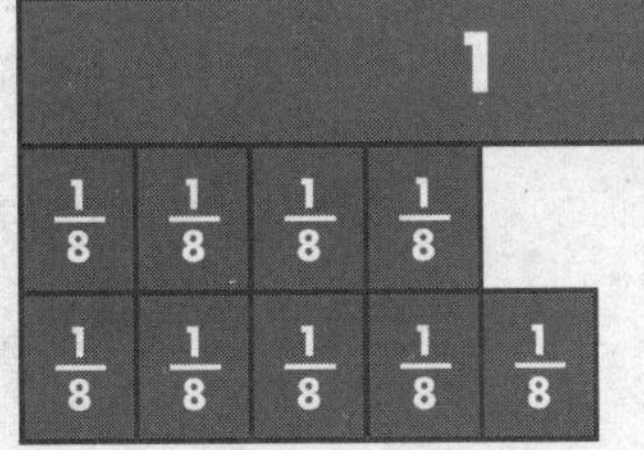

$\frac{4}{8} \bigcirc \frac{5}{8}$

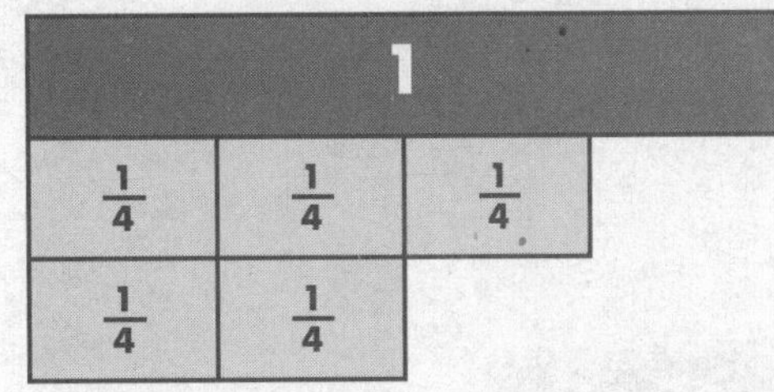

$\frac{3}{4} \bigcirc \frac{2}{4}$

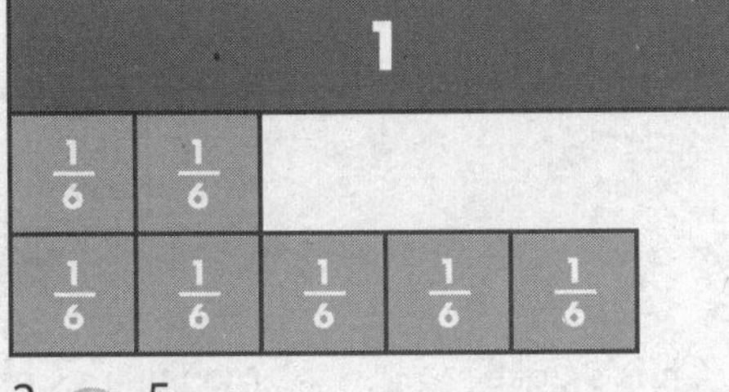

$\frac{2}{6} \bigcirc \frac{5}{6}$

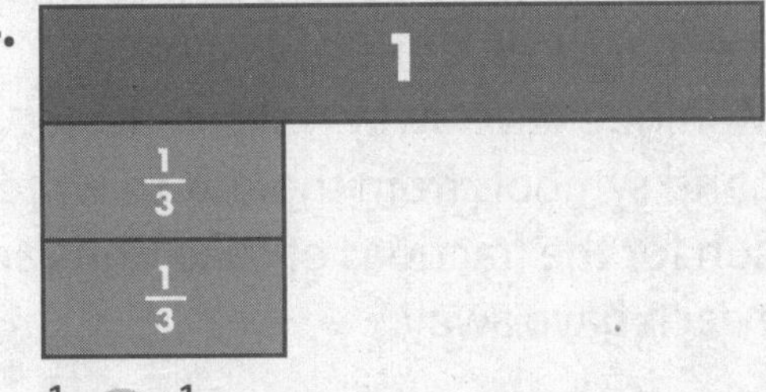

$\frac{1}{3} \bigcirc \frac{1}{3}$

5. $\frac{4}{8} \bigcirc \frac{4}{8}$

6. $\frac{2}{4} \bigcirc \frac{1}{4}$

7. $\frac{7}{8} \bigcirc \frac{1}{8}$

8. $\frac{2}{6} \bigcirc \frac{3}{6}$

9. $\frac{5}{6} \bigcirc \frac{5}{6}$

10. $\frac{1}{8} \bigcirc \frac{2}{8}$

11. $\frac{4}{6} \bigcirc \frac{2}{6}$

12. $\frac{1}{6} \bigcirc \frac{5}{6}$

13. Be Precise Ali is comparing fractions using fraction strips. Using the symbols > and <, write two different comparisons for the fractions.

1		
$\frac{1}{6}$	$\frac{1}{6}$	$\frac{1}{6}$
$\frac{1}{6}$	$\frac{1}{6}$	

14. How could you decide which fraction is greater, $\frac{5}{8}$ or $\frac{6}{8}$?

15. Number Sense Keisha has 10 coins. Two of the coins are nickels, 6 are pennies, and the rest are dimes. What is the value of Keisha's coins?

16. A-Z **Vocabulary** Write a fraction that has 6 as the *denominator*. Write an equivalent fraction that does not have 6 as the denominator.

17. Higher Order Thinking Draw fraction strips to show the following fractions: $\frac{4}{6}$, $\frac{1}{6}$, and $\frac{5}{6}$. Then write the three fractions in order from least to greatest.

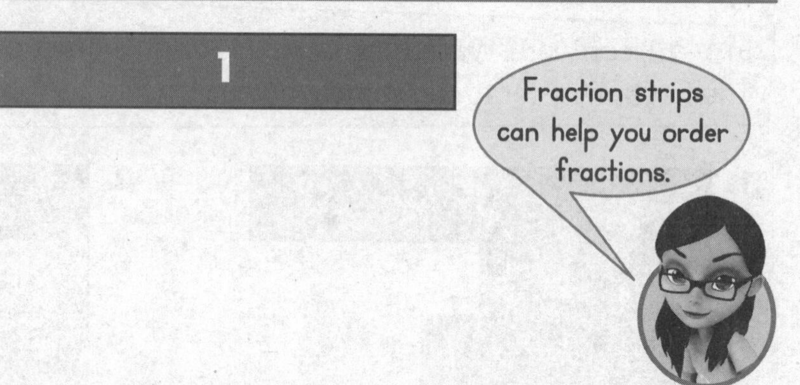

18. Chris and Monique have equal-sized cookie cakes cut into 8 equal slices. Chris gave away 3 slices. Monique gave away 4 slices. Select numbers and symbols from the box to write a comparison for the fractions of cake Chris and Monique each gave away.

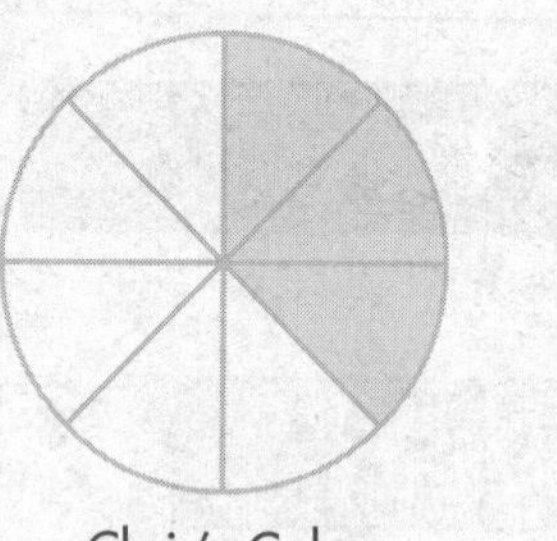
Chris's Cake

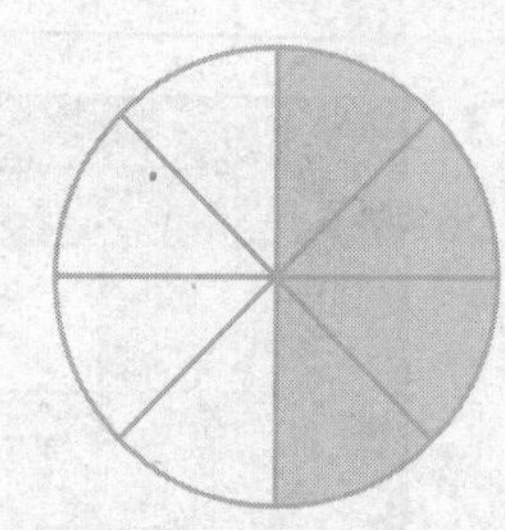
Monique's Cake

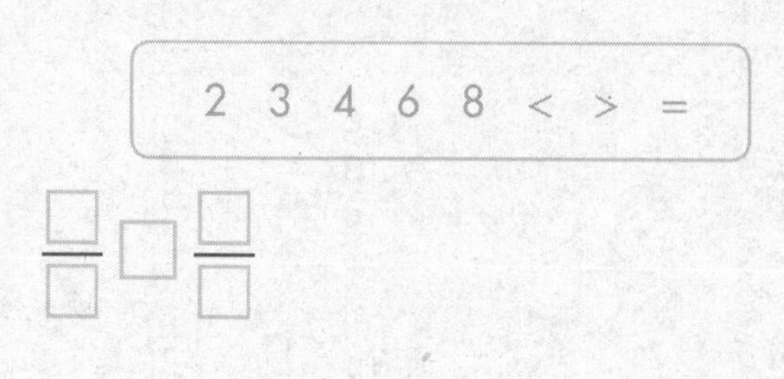

Name ______________________

Additional Practice 13-4

Use Models to Compare Fractions: Same Numerator

Another Look!

Compare $\frac{1}{4}$ and $\frac{1}{3}$. $\frac{1}{4}$ ← Same numerators → $\frac{1}{3}$; ← Different denominators →

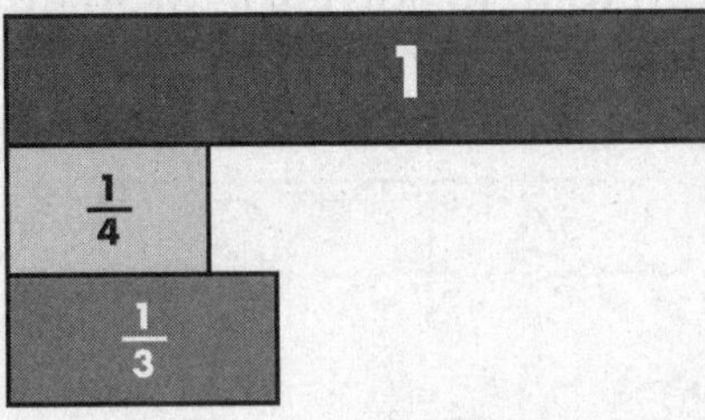

You can use fraction strips to represent and compare fractions with the same numerator. The $\frac{1}{3}$ strip represents a greater part of the whole.

The $\frac{1}{4}$ strip is not as long as the $\frac{1}{3}$ strip. These fractions have the same numerator, which means the fraction with the lesser denominator is greater.

So, $\frac{1}{4} < \frac{1}{3}$.

In **1–12**, compare. Write <, >, or =. Use or draw fraction strips to help. The fractions refer to the same whole.

1.

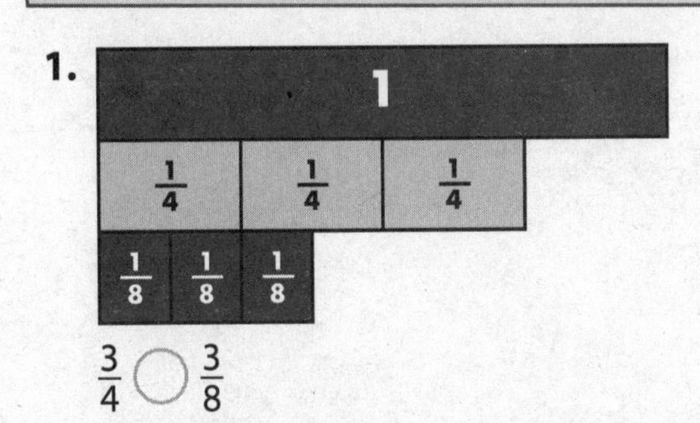

$\frac{3}{4}$ ◯ $\frac{3}{8}$

2.

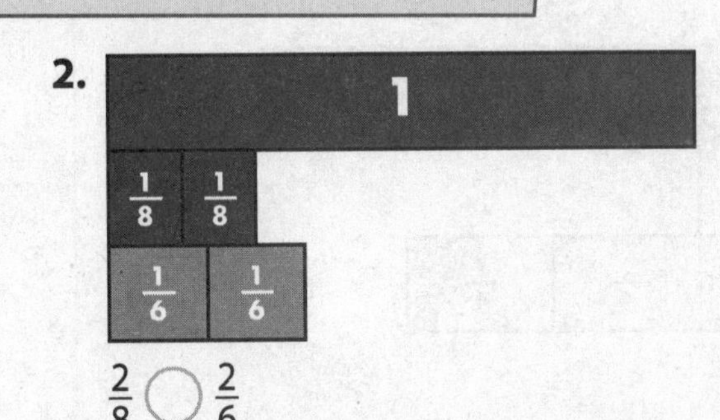

$\frac{2}{8}$ ◯ $\frac{2}{6}$

3. 1

$\frac{4}{6}$ ◯ $\frac{4}{6}$

4.

$\frac{2}{3}$ ◯ $\frac{2}{8}$

5. $\frac{2}{3}$ ◯ $\frac{2}{4}$

6. $\frac{1}{8}$ ◯ $\frac{1}{4}$

7. $\frac{3}{6}$ ◯ $\frac{3}{6}$

8. $\frac{1}{2}$ ◯ $\frac{1}{3}$

9. $\frac{4}{4}$ ◯ $\frac{4}{6}$

10. $\frac{2}{3}$ ◯ $\frac{2}{6}$

11. $\frac{3}{4}$ ◯ $\frac{3}{4}$

12. $\frac{6}{8}$ ◯ $\frac{6}{6}$

13. Ivan played basketball for two thirds of an hour on Tuesday and two fourths of an hour on Wednesday. On which day did he spend more time playing basketball? Use the symbols >, <, or = to compare.

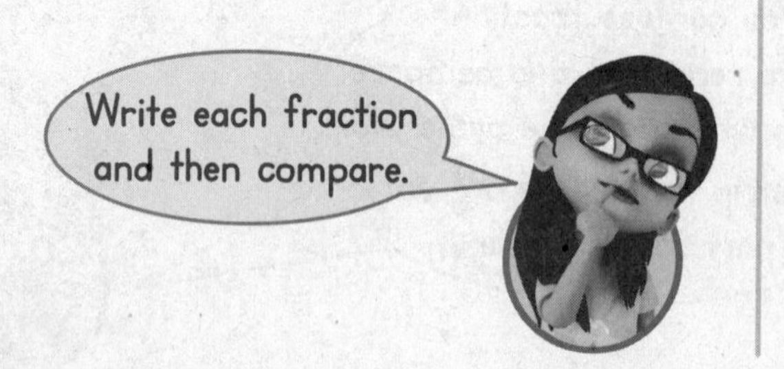

14. Model with Math On a trip to the beach, Josie collected 64 shells. Her father collected 57 shells, and her mother collected 73 shells. How many shells did Josie's parents collect? Complete the bar diagram to help solve the problem.

? shells parents collected →

57	____

15. enVision® STEM A plant's life has different stages. Leah measured the length of a seed. It was $\frac{1}{4}$-inch long. She then planted the seed. It grew into a seedling that was $\frac{3}{4}$-inch long. Use the fraction strips to compare the two fractions. Write <, >, or =.

1		
$\frac{1}{4}$		
$\frac{1}{4}$	$\frac{1}{4}$	$\frac{1}{4}$

$\frac{1}{4} \bigcirc \frac{3}{4}$

16. Higher Order Thinking There are 4 people in Mitchell's family and 3 people in Paul's family. Each family buys a same-sized bag of trail mix to share equally. Who gets more trail mix, Mitchell or Paul? Use reasoning about fraction size to explain how you know.

17. Circle the solid figure that has 2 flat surfaces and 0 vertices. What is this solid figure called?

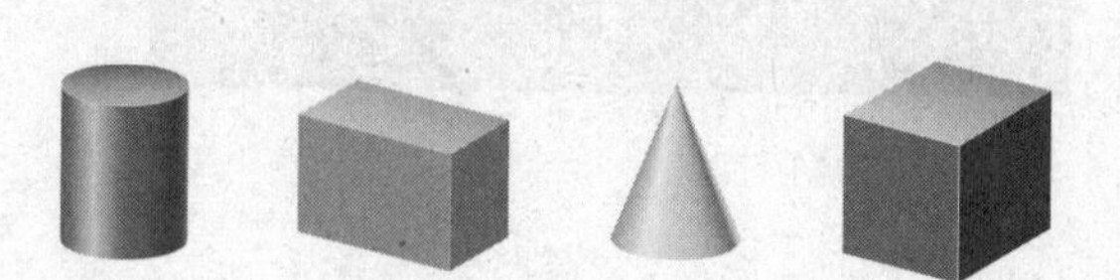

Assessment Practice

18. These fractions refer to the same whole. Which of these comparisons are correct? Select all that apply.

- ☐ $\frac{3}{4} = \frac{3}{4}$
- ☐ $\frac{2}{8} = \frac{2}{3}$
- ☐ $\frac{1}{6} < \frac{1}{4}$
- ☐ $\frac{4}{6} < \frac{4}{8}$
- ☐ $\frac{5}{8} > \frac{5}{6}$

Name ______________________

Additional Practice 13-5

Compare Fractions: Use Benchmarks

Another Look!

Compare $\frac{3}{8}$ and $\frac{7}{8}$.

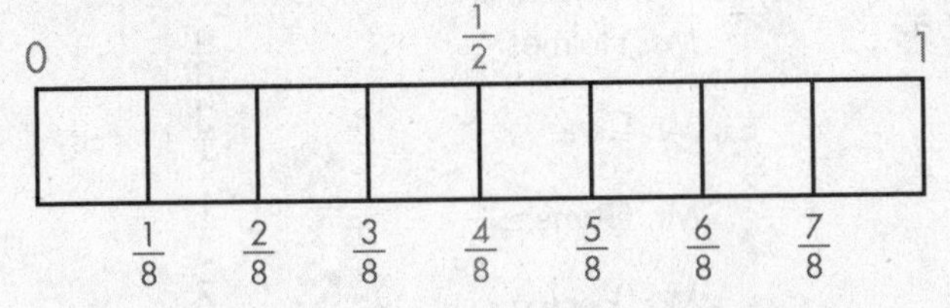

The denominator for each fraction is 8. Use the benchmark numbers 0, $\frac{1}{2}$, and 1 to reason about the relative sizes of the numerators in $\frac{3}{8}$ and $\frac{7}{8}$.

$\frac{1}{2}$ and $\frac{4}{8}$ are equivalent fractions. $\frac{3}{8}$ is less than $\frac{4}{8}$ and closer to 0. $\frac{7}{8}$ is greater than $\frac{4}{8}$ and closer to 1. So, $\frac{3}{8}$ is less than $\frac{7}{8}$.

In **1** and **2**, choose from the fractions $\frac{1}{3}$, $\frac{5}{6}$, $\frac{3}{4}$, and $\frac{3}{8}$.

1. Which of the fractions are closer to 1 than to 0?

2. Which of the fractions are closer to 0 than to 1?

3. Write two fractions with a denominator of 8 that are closer to 0 than to 1.

4. Use the benchmark $\frac{1}{2}$ and the fractions $\frac{1}{8}$ and $\frac{5}{8}$ to write three comparison statements.

In **5–10**, use a strategy to compare. Write <, >, or =.

5. $\frac{2}{6}$ ◯ $\frac{2}{4}$

6. $\frac{1}{4}$ ◯ $\frac{1}{8}$

7. $\frac{3}{6}$ ◯ $\frac{5}{6}$

8. $\frac{2}{3}$ ◯ $\frac{2}{3}$

9. $\frac{1}{6}$ ◯ $\frac{1}{4}$

10. $\frac{3}{3}$ ◯ $\frac{3}{8}$

In **11–14**, use the table at the right.

11. The third-grade classes at Haines Elementary are each making a class banner. The banners are all the same size. The table shows how much of a banner each class has completed so far. Has Ms. Holmes's class or Mrs. Johnson's class completed the greater fraction of a banner?

DATA

Class	Fraction of Class Banner Completed
Ms. Holmes	$\frac{6}{8}$
Mr. Cline	$\frac{3}{6}$
Mr. Gomez	$\frac{1}{3}$
Mrs. Johnson	$\frac{7}{8}$
Ms. Park	$\frac{3}{4}$

12. In whose classes are the fractions of the banners completed equivalent?

13. In whose classes is the fraction of a completed banner closer to 1 than to 0?

14. Construct Arguments In whose class is the fraction of a completed banner closer to neither 0 nor 1? Use benchmark numbers to explain.

15. Using the denominators 2, 3, 6, or 8, write two fractions less than 1. Then tell if the fractions are closer to 0 than to 1.

16. Natalie has 28 erasers. She divided some of her erasers equally among 3 friends. Natalie has 10 erasers left. How many erasers did each friend get?

17. Higher Order Thinking Write two fractions using the numbers from the cards at the right. One fraction should be closer to 0 than to 1. The other fraction should be closer to 1 than to 0. Explain which fraction meets each rule.

1	2	3	4

Assessment Practice

18. Each of the fractions in the comparisons at the right refers to the same whole. Use benchmark fractions to reason about the size of each fraction. Select all the correct comparisons.

- ☐ $\frac{2}{8} = \frac{2}{4}$
- ☐ $\frac{2}{4} < \frac{2}{2}$
- ☐ $\frac{5}{8} > \frac{3}{8}$
- ☐ $\frac{3}{4} < \frac{2}{4}$
- ☐ $\frac{3}{6} > \frac{3}{4}$

Name ____________________ Practice Video Tools Games

Additional Practice 13-6

Compare Fractions: Use the Number Line

Another Look!

Ben has $\frac{1}{2}$ yard of string. John has $\frac{1}{3}$ yard of string. Who has more string?

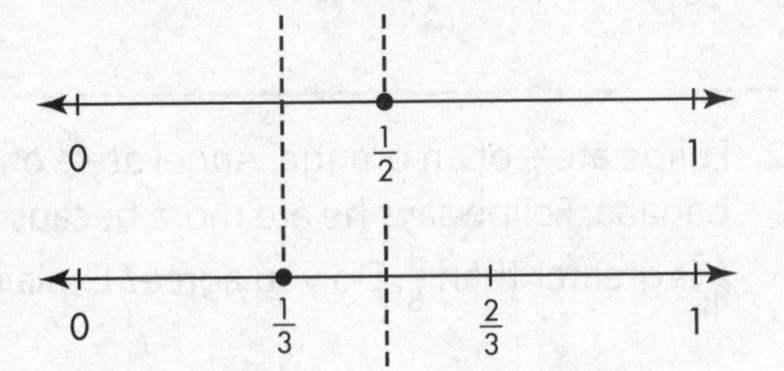

Mark 0 and 1 on both number lines.
Divide the first number line into 2 equal parts. Mark $\frac{1}{2}$.
Divide the second number line into 3 equal parts. Mark $\frac{1}{3}$.
$\frac{1}{2}$ is farther from zero than $\frac{1}{3}$.
So, $\frac{1}{2} > \frac{1}{3}$. Ben has more string than John.

In **1–4**, use the number lines to compare the fractions. Write >, <, or =.

1. 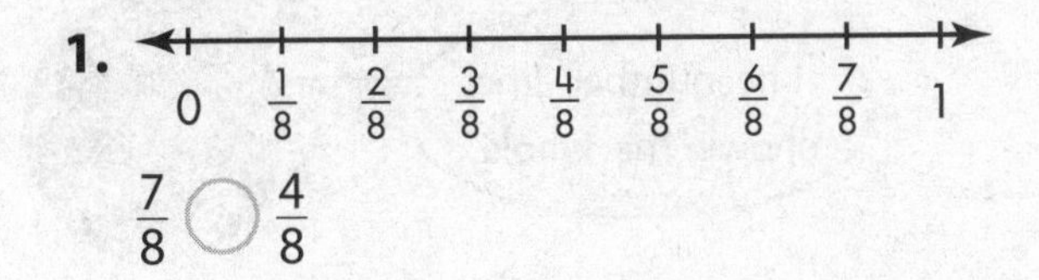

$\frac{7}{8}$ ◯ $\frac{4}{8}$

2. 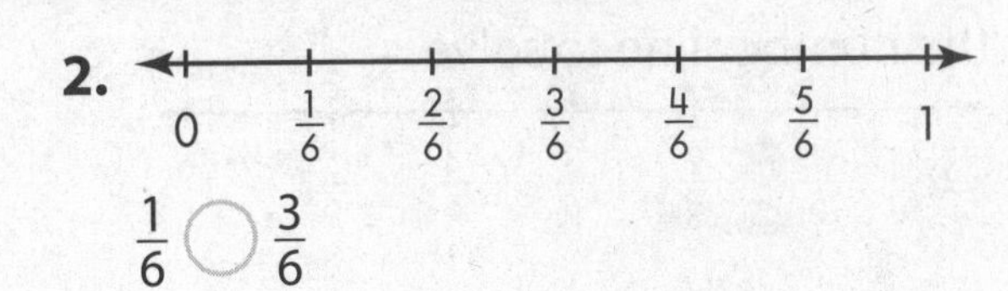

$\frac{1}{6}$ ◯ $\frac{3}{6}$

3. 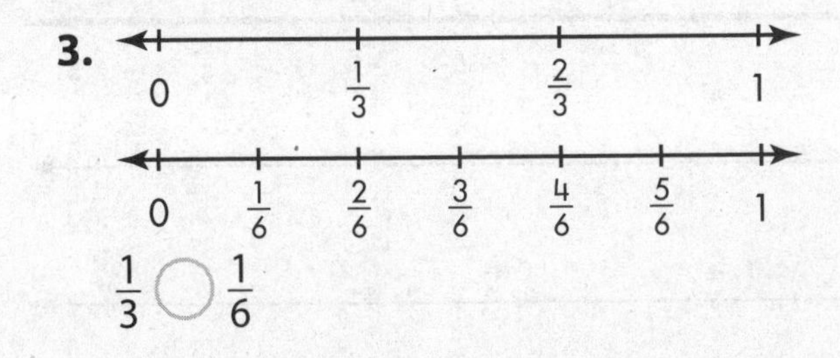

$\frac{1}{3}$ ◯ $\frac{1}{6}$

4. 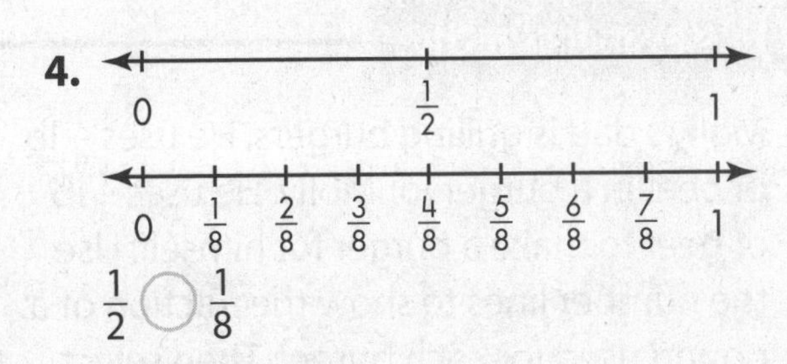

$\frac{1}{2}$ ◯ $\frac{1}{8}$

In **5–8**, compare the fractions. Use number lines to help. Write >, <, or =.

5. $\frac{1}{4}$ ◯ $\frac{1}{8}$

6. $\frac{3}{6}$ ◯ $\frac{3}{4}$

7. $\frac{4}{8}$ ◯ $\frac{4}{6}$

8. $\frac{2}{3}$ ◯ $\frac{2}{4}$

9. Number Sense Angela drove 82 miles on Monday. She drove 94 miles on Tuesday. To the nearest hundred, how many miles did Angela drive over the two days?

10. I have 4 sides. The lengths of all my sides are equal. Which shape am I?

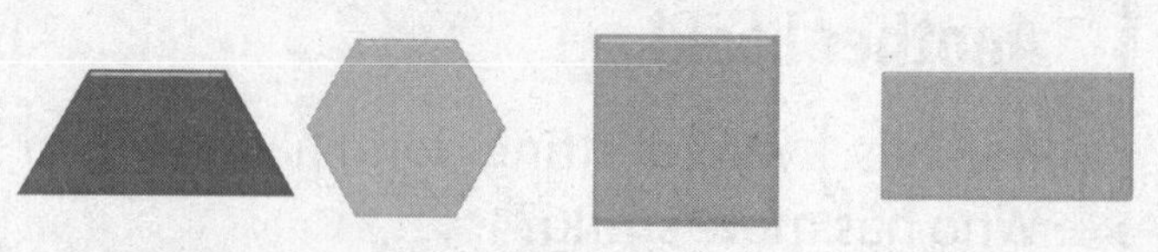

11. Be Precise Dylan and Javier each had a same-sized serving of vegetables for dinner. Dylan finished $\frac{2}{3}$ of his vegetables. Javier ate $\frac{2}{6}$ of his serving. Who ate more vegetables? Draw two number lines to justify your answer.

12. Felipe ate $\frac{7}{8}$ of an orange. Angel ate $\frac{5}{8}$ of a banana. Felipe says he ate more because $\frac{7}{8}$ is greater than $\frac{5}{8}$. Do you agree? Explain.

13. Higher Order Thinking Some friends are sharing a watermelon. Simone eats $\frac{2}{6}$ of the watermelon. Ken eats $\frac{3}{6}$ of the watermelon and Claire eats the rest. Alex has his own watermelon equal in size to the one shared by his friends. He eats $\frac{5}{6}$ of his watermelon. Which of the friends eats the smallest amount of watermelon? Use the number line to solve.

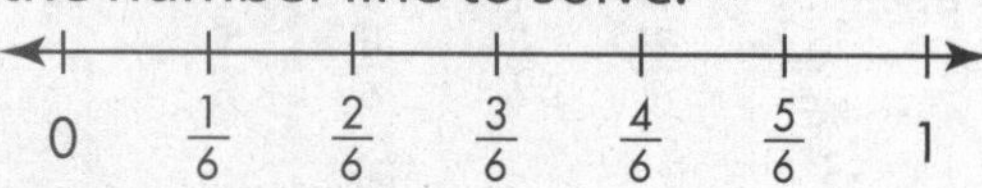

The number line shows the whole.

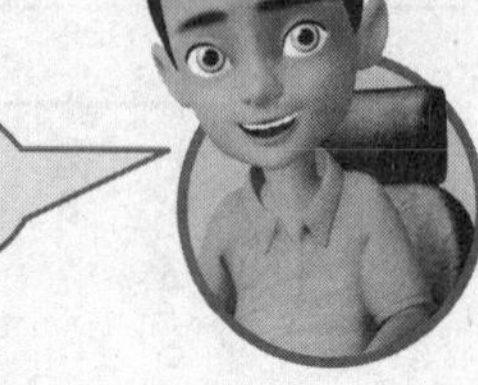

Assessment Practice

14. Molly's dad is grilling burgers. He uses $\frac{1}{4}$ lb of beef in a burger for Molly. He uses $\frac{1}{3}$ lb of beef to make a burger for himself. Use the number lines to show the fraction of a pound used for each burger. Then select all the correct statements that describe the fractions.

- ☐ $\frac{1}{4}$ is equivalent to $\frac{1}{3}$ because the fractions mark the same point.
- ☐ $\frac{1}{3}$ is greater than $\frac{1}{4}$ because it is farther from zero.
- ☐ $\frac{1}{3}$ is less than $\frac{1}{4}$ because it is farther from zero.
- ☐ $\frac{1}{4}$ is less than $\frac{1}{3}$ because it is closer to zero.
- ☐ $\frac{1}{4}$ is greater than $\frac{1}{3}$ because it is closer to zero.

Name ________________

Additional Practice 13-7
Whole Numbers and Fractions

Another Look!

Whole numbers have equivalent fraction names.

1 whole divided into 1 equal part can be written as $\frac{1}{1}$.

2 wholes each divided into 1 equal part can be written as $\frac{2}{1}$.

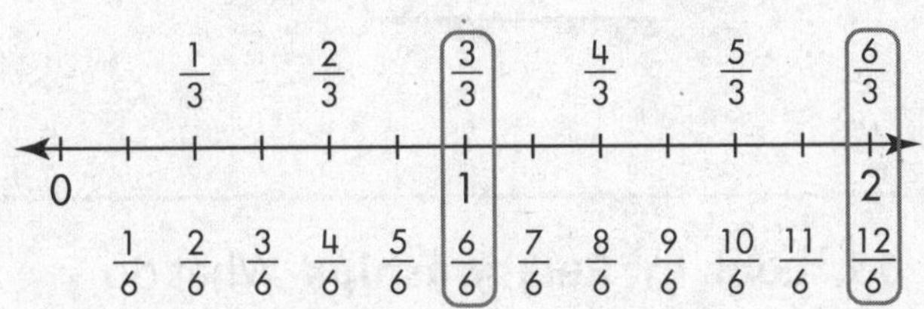

You can name fractions as whole numbers and whole numbers as fractions.

This number line shows other equivalent fractions for 1 and 2. You can see how many equal parts make up 1 or 2 wholes.

$1 = \frac{1}{1} = \frac{3}{3} = \frac{6}{6}$

$2 = \frac{2}{1} = \frac{6}{3} = \frac{12}{6}$

In **1–4**, complete each number line by naming all of the tick marks or making tick marks and naming the fractions for the given denominator.

1. Sixths

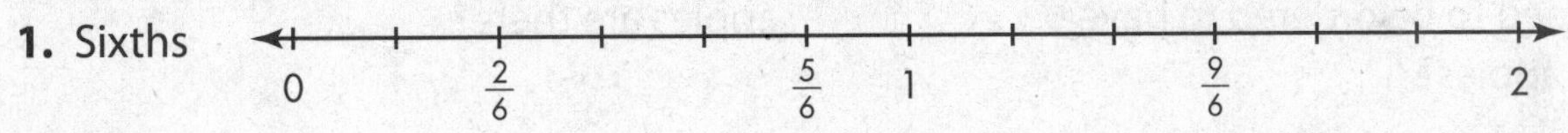

2. Thirds

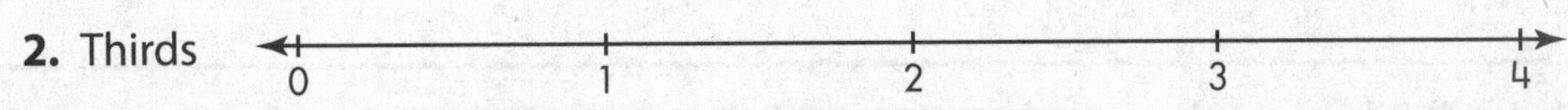

3. Fourths

0 1 2

4. Halves

0 1 2 3

In **5–8**, write two equivalent fractions for each whole number. You can draw number lines to help.

5. $3 = \frac{\square}{1} = \frac{\square}{3}$ **6.** $2 = \frac{\square}{1} = \frac{\square}{4}$ **7.** $8 = \frac{\square}{1} = \frac{\square}{2}$ **8.** $1 = \frac{\square}{2} = \frac{\square}{3}$

In **9–12**, for each pair of fractions, write the equivalent whole number.

9. $\frac{12}{3} = \frac{4}{1} =$ **10.** $\frac{18}{3} = \frac{6}{1} =$ **11.** $\frac{5}{5} = \frac{3}{3} =$ **12.** $\frac{15}{3} = \frac{5}{1} =$

13. Andy earned $38 on Monday and $34 on Tuesday. How many lucky bamboo plants can he buy with the total money he earned?

14. Julio says, "To turn the whole number 3 into an equivalent fraction, I just put 3 under a numerator of 3." Is he correct? Explain.

15. Look for Relationships What do you notice about all fractions that are equivalent to 2? Explain and give an example.

16. The kid's meal at Happy Time Diner comes with an apple slice that is $\frac{1}{4}$ of a whole apple. How many kid's meals would need to be ordered to have 3 whole apples?

17. Kevin is selling apples at the farmer's market. He arranges 32 apples into an array with 4 rows. How many columns of apples are there?

18. Higher Order Thinking Look at the fraction strip diagram. Write the whole number represented and its equivalent fraction name. Then write a story problem in which the same whole number equals the fraction.

1			1			1		
$\frac{1}{3}$	$\frac{1}{3}$	$\frac{1}{3}$	$\frac{1}{3}$	$\frac{1}{3}$	$\frac{1}{3}$	$\frac{1}{3}$	$\frac{1}{3}$	$\frac{1}{3}$

Assessment Practice

19. Complete the equations. Match the fractions with their equivalent whole numbers.

	1	2	3	5
$\frac{2}{1} = \frac{4}{2} = ?$	☐	☐	☐	☐
$\frac{15}{3} = \frac{5}{1} = ?$	☐	☐	☐	☐
$\frac{9}{3} = \frac{12}{4} = ?$	☐	☐	☐	☐
$\frac{8}{8} = \frac{1}{1} = ?$	☐	☐	☐	☐

Name

Practice Video Tools Games

Additional Practice 13-8
Construct Arguments

Another Look!

Tonya and Josh have aquariums that are the same size. Tonya poured enough water to fill $\frac{4}{6}$ of her aquarium. Josh poured enough water to fill $\frac{3}{6}$ of his aquarium.

Conjecture: Tonya and Josh each poured the same amount of water.

Tell how you can justify the conjecture.

- I can use numbers, objects, drawings, or actions to explain.
- I can make sure my argument is simple, complete, and easy to understand.

When you construct an argument, you can explain why your work is mathematically correct.

Construct an argument to justify the conjecture.

Both fractions are for the same whole. The number line shows sixths. Because $\frac{4}{6} > \frac{3}{6}$, Tonya and Josh did not pour the same amount.

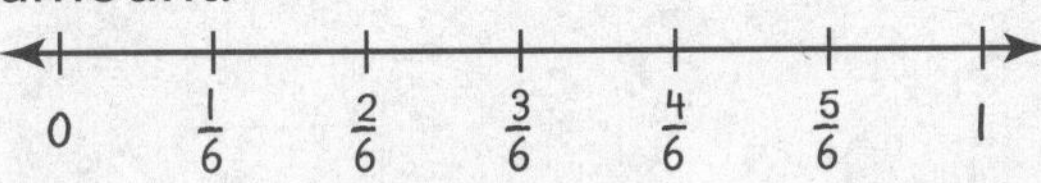

Construct Arguments Mr. Demming jogs for $\frac{13}{8}$ of a mile. Mrs. Demming jogs for $\frac{13}{6}$ of a mile.

Conjecture: Mrs. Demming jogs farther than Mr. Demming.

1. What are important things to think about when justifying a conjecture?

2. Construct an argument to justify the conjecture.

3. Explain another way you could justify the conjecture.

Performance Task

Fruit Smoothie
Liza found a recipe for a fruit smoothie. She wants to know if any ingredients make up an equal amount of the smoothie.

DATA

Ingredient	Cups
Vanilla Yogurt	$\frac{2}{8}$
Pineapples	$\frac{2}{4}$
Bananas	$\frac{2}{6}$
Strawberries	$\frac{2}{2}$
Oranges	$\frac{2}{3}$

4. **Make Sense and Persevere** What comparisons do you need to make to find which ingredients have equal amounts in the smoothie?

5. **Be Precise** What is the whole for the fractions in this problem? Do all the fractions have the same whole?

6. **Model with Math** Use the number lines to represent the fraction of each ingredient. What do equivalent fractions represent?

7. **Construct Arguments** Do any ingredients make up an equal amount of the smoothie? Construct a math argument to explain why or why not.

Name ____________________

Practice

Video

Tools

Games

Additional Practice 14-1
Time to the Minute

Another Look!

You can tell time to the minute in different ways. The hour and minute hands of the clock face show the time.

In digital form, this time is written as 10:15. You can also write the same time as 15 minutes after 10 o'clock.

In **1–3**, write the time shown on each clock in two ways.

1. 

2. 

3. 

In **4–9**, write the time in digital form. Use clocks to help.

4. 12 minutes before noon

5. 21 minutes after 2

6. 30 minutes after 9

7. 2 minutes after 7

8. 45 minutes before 6

9. 4 o'clock

10. Be Precise Tonya's family went to see a movie. The movie started at 4:30 and ended at 6:36. Show the time the movie ended on the clock.

11. enVision® STEM The Hubble Space Telescope has been moving in its orbit for 1 hour. In 37 more minutes, it will complete an orbit. How many minutes does it take the Hubble Space Telescope to complete 1 orbit?

12. Ross started walking his dog at 3:15. He finished before 4:00. Use digital form to write a time he could have finished walking his dog.

13. Higher Order Thinking Jake rode his bike from 2:30 to 3:30. Then he took a shower. He finished his shower 30 minutes after the bike ride ended. What time was it when he finished his shower? How would you show this time on a clock face?

Assessment Practice

14. Jody and her family went to the swimming pool at the time shown on the clock. Which of the following are other ways to write this time? Select all that apply.

- ☐ 3:13
- ☐ 2:16
- ☐ 16 minutes after 2 o'clock
- ☐ 44 minutes before 4 o'clock
- ☐ 13 minutes after 3 o'clock

15. Phil is reading a magazine. He stops reading at the time shown on the clock. Which of the following are **NOT** other ways to write this time? Select all that apply.

- ☐ 20 minutes after 3 o'clock
- ☐ 3:20
- ☐ 7 minutes after 4 o'clock
- ☐ 4:07
- ☐ 20 minutes after 1 o'clock

Name

Additional Practice 14-2

Units of Time: Measure Elapsed Time

Another Look!

A children's museum is open from 1:00 P.M. to 6:35 P.M. every day. How long is the museum open?

Step 1

Begin at the starting time.

Step 2

Count the hours.

There are 5 hours.

Step 3

Count the minutes.

There are 35 minutes.

The museum is open 5 hours, 35 minutes.

In **1–6**, find the elapsed or end time. You may use the clock faces or a number line to help.

1. Start Time: 3:30 P.M.
End Time: 7:00 P.M.
Elapsed Time: ______

2. Start Time: 8:10 A.M.
End Time: 10:55 A.M.
Elapsed Time: ______

3. Start Time: 3:20 P.M.
End Time: 6:00 P.M.
Elapsed Time: ______

4. Start Time: 1:20 P.M.
End Time: 2:00 P.M.
Elapsed Time: ______

5. Start Time: 8:00 A.M.
Elapsed Time: 5 hours, 15 minutes
End Time: ______

6. Start Time: 7:30 A.M.
Elapsed Time: 2 hours, 20 minutes
End Time: ______

7. Algebra Mindy divides a rectangular piece of fabric into 8 equal-sized pieces for two sewing projects. For Project A, she will use $\frac{1}{2}$ of the fabric. For Project B, she will use $\frac{1}{4}$ of the original fabric. Draw a model to show how the fabric was divided and which pieces will be used. What unit fraction represents one of the pieces? Write an equation to find how much of the fabric will not be used. Let *f* represent the fraction of leftover fabric.

A unit fraction represents 1 equal part of the whole.

8. On Monday, Tanner folds 569 shirts and 274 pairs of shorts for his job. How many items does Tanner fold on Monday?

9. Make Sense and Persevere A movie starts at 2:30 P.M. and ends at 4:15 P.M. After the movie, Anne and her friends go out for ice cream. They eat ice cream from 4:30 P.M. to 5:00 P.M. How much time elapses from the start of the movie to the time the friends finish their ice cream?

10. Gary's father dropped him off at soccer practice at 2:45 P.M. Gary's mother picked him up at 5:00 P.M. How long did soccer practice last?

11. Higher Order Thinking Raquel attended a volleyball game that began at 9:30 A.M. and ended at 11:45 A.M. She began her lunch at 12:00 P.M., and ended lunch at 1:00 P.M. How much time did Raquel spend at the game and at lunch?

Assessment Practice

12. A picnic starts at 12:10 P.M. Kevin arrives at 1:40 P.M. The picnic continues until 3 P.M. How much time elapsed between the time the picnic starts and Kevin's arrival? Use a number line to help.

12:10 P.M. Picnic Starts

1:40 P.M. Kevin Arrives

Ⓐ 30 minutes Ⓑ 1 hour Ⓒ 1 hour 30 minutes Ⓓ 2 hours

Name ______________________

Additional Practice 14-3

Units of Time: Solve Word Problems

Another Look!

Jed has 2 homework assignments. He spends 15 minutes doing his math homework. Then, he spends 38 minutes doing his reading homework. How much time does Jed spend doing his homework?

Draw a number line.

First show the number of minutes Jed spends doing his math homework. Then add the number of minutes Jed spends doing his reading homework.

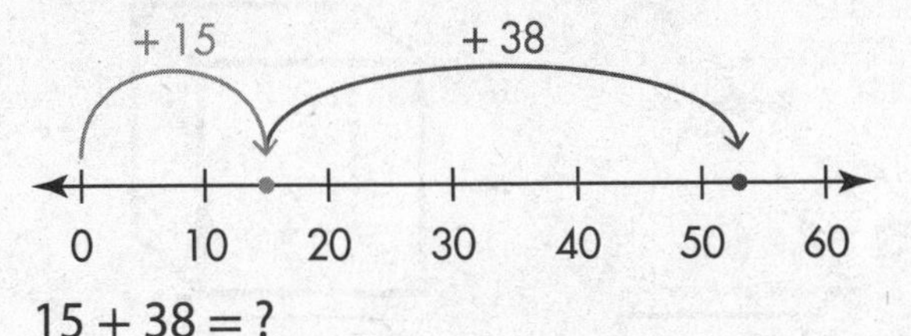

$15 + 38 = ?$

$15 + 38 = 53$. So, Jed spends 53 minutes doing homework.

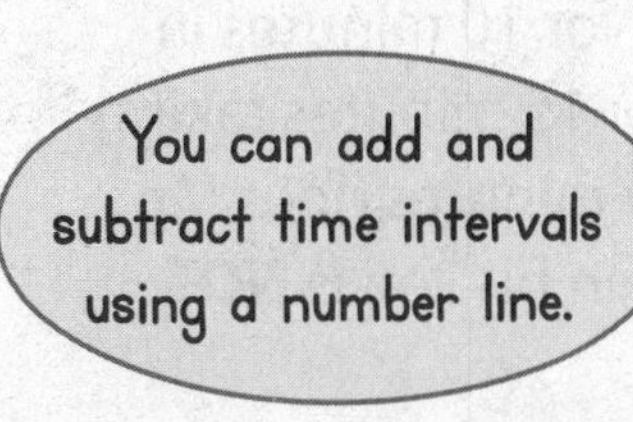

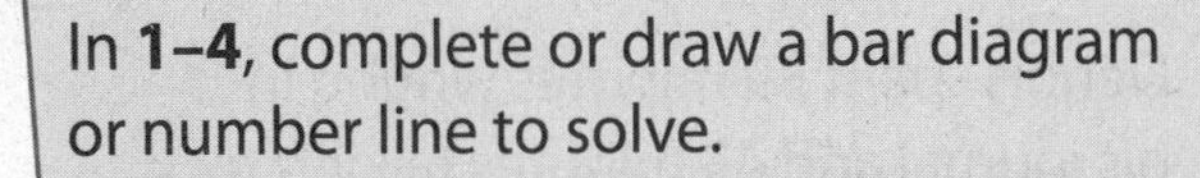

1. A bus travels for 22 minutes from Greensburg to Pleasant Valley. Then it travels 16 minutes from Pleasant Valley to Red Mill. How many minutes does it travel?

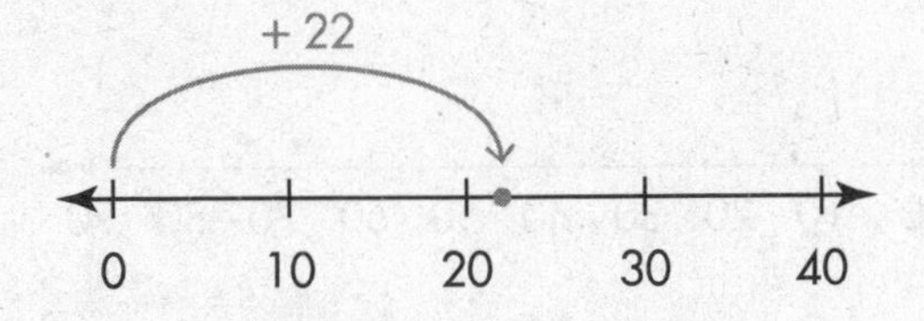

2. Ethan needs to spend 35 minutes cleaning his room. So far, he has been cleaning for 11 minutes. How many more minutes does he need to spend cleaning?

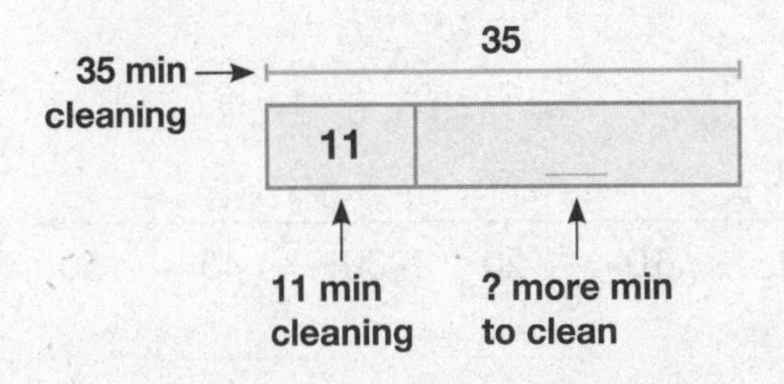

3. James plans on spending 60 minutes each day practicing pitching for baseball. He only has 14 minutes left to practice today. How many minutes has James already practiced today?

4. Margot helps out at a horse farm. She spends 26 minutes one morning brushing a horse. She spends 39 minutes that same day brushing another horse. How many minutes does she brush horses in all?

5. **Make Sense and Persevere** A barber cuts 3 people's hair in 35 minutes. Each haircut takes at least 10 minutes, and the first haircut takes the most time. List one way the barber could cut 3 people's hair given this information.

6. **Vocabulary** Write a word problem that uses the phrase *time interval*.

7. **Higher Order Thinking** Mr. Maxwell spends 34 minutes working in his garden and 25 minutes raking leaves. His son helps him for 10 minutes in the garden and for 15 minutes raking leaves. How many minutes does Mr. Maxwell work when his son is **NOT** helping him?

8. Lisa drew the two geometric figures below. Write a statement describing one way the figures are different.

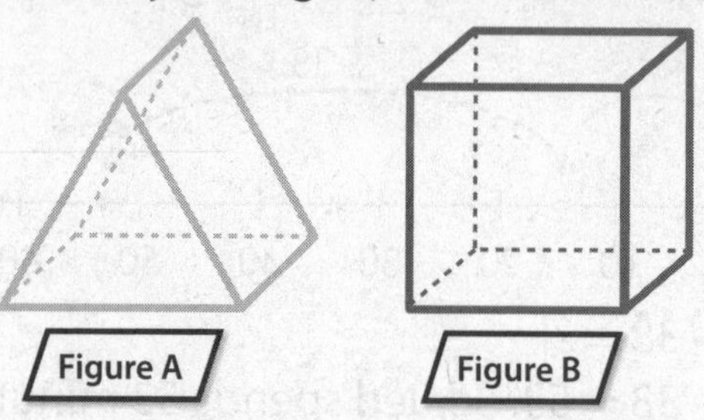

Assessment Practice

9. Colby's art class is 50 minutes. She spends 21 minutes cutting paper and the rest of the time making a collage. Use the number line and complete the table to show the number of minutes Colby spends making her collage.

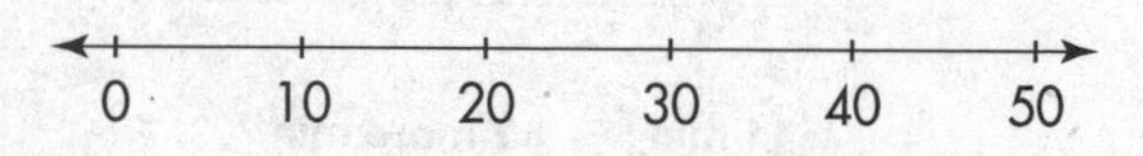

Activity	Time (min)
Cutting Paper	21
Making a Collage	
Total	

10. Dennis spent 39 minutes writing in his journal and 43 minutes talking to a friend. Use the number line and complete the table to show how much time Dennis spent writing and talking.

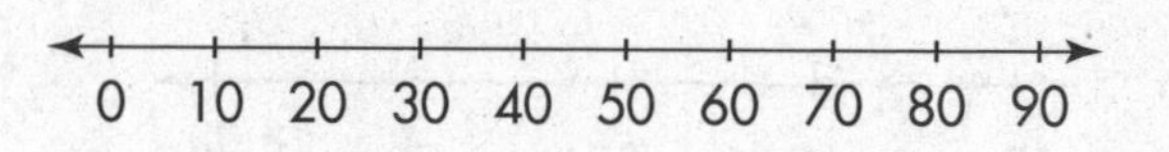

Activity	Time (min)
Writing	39
Talking	
Total	

Name ____________________

Practice Video Tools Games

Additional Practice 14-4
Estimate Liquid Volume

Another Look!

One unit of capacity in the metric system is the liter (L).

A liter is slightly larger than a quart.

Many beverages are sold in 1-liter and 2-liter bottles.

The capacity of this bottle is 2 liters.

In **1–12**, circle the better estimate for each if full.

1.

$\frac{1}{4}$ L or 35 L

2.

$\frac{1}{4}$ L or 10 L

3.

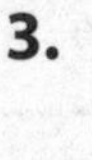

$\frac{1}{10}$ L or 1 L

4.

2 L or 20 L

5. Wading pool

1 L or 85 L

6. Fish bowl

$\frac{1}{4}$ L or 6 L

7. Small water bottle

$\frac{1}{2}$ L or 5 L

8. Soup ladle

$\frac{1}{4}$ L or 7 L

9. Small milk carton

$\frac{1}{4}$ L or 25 L

10. Soup can

$\frac{1}{2}$ L or 5 L

11. Sports cooler

2 L or 20 L

12. Salt shaker

$\frac{1}{4}$ L or 1 L

13. Write an estimate for the capacity of a glass of juice. ____________

14. Write an estimate for the capacity of a pitcher of water. ____________

15.  **Vocabulary** Describe a liter.

16. Reasoning A gym membership costs \$19 each month. If Miss Lacey joins the gym for one year, will she pay more or less than \$190? Explain your answer.

In **17** and **18**, use the grid at the right.

17. The area of a rectangle is 16 square units. Use the grid to draw what the rectangle could look like. Then shade the area. What are its dimensions?

18. Is there another rectangle you could draw on the grid that has an area of 16 square units? If so, what are its dimensions? Draw and shade it on the grid.

19. Find a container you think might hold about 2 liters of liquid. Use a liter container to measure and find how much it actually holds. Write about what you found.

20. Higher Order Thinking Essie has two identical containers. She fills one with milk and the other with water. If the first container holds about 10 liters of milk, how much water does the second container hold? How do you know?

Assessment Practice

21. Which container does **NOT** have a capacity that is close to 1 liter?

Ⓐ 

Ⓑ 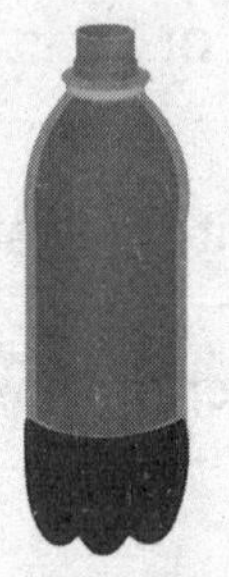

Ⓒ 

Ⓓ 

Name ______________________

Practice

Video

Tools

Games

Additional Practice 14-5
Measure Liquid Volume

Another Look!

The capacity of the can is $\frac{1}{2}$ liter.

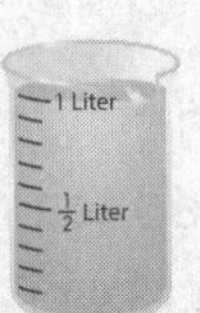

The capacity of the bottle is 2 liters.

In **1–6**, find the total capacity represented in each picture.

1. 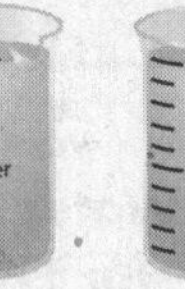 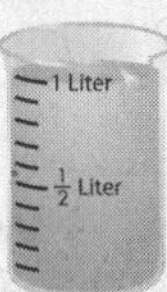 

____

2. 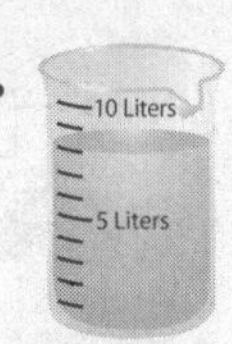

____

3. 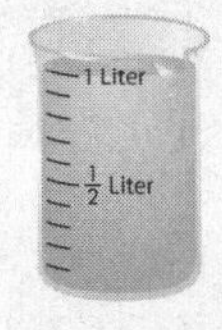 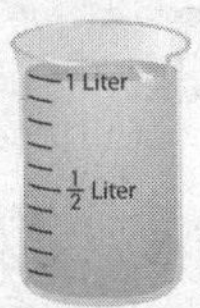 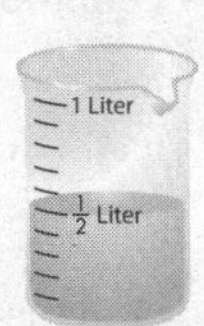

____

4.  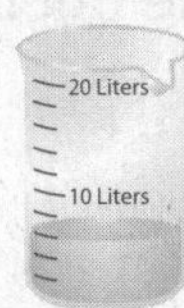

____

5. 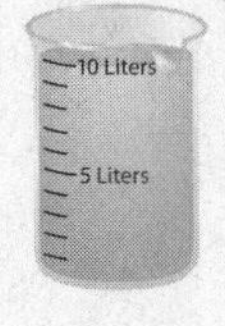 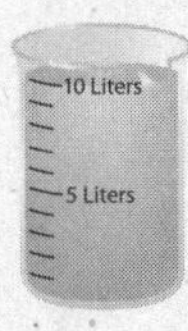 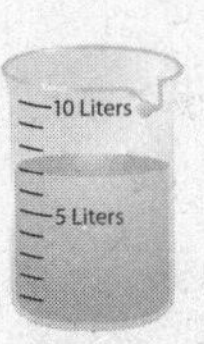

____

6. 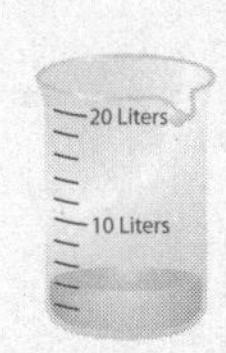

____

7. **Model with Math** The capacity of a large container of glue is 8 liters. How much glue is there in 3 large containers? Use math you know to represent and solve the problem.

8. Meg counts 62 bottles of orange juice at the store. If each bottle contains 2 liters, how many liters of bottled orange juice are at the store?

9. Tomas orders 210 liters of iced tea for his restaurant. He serves 115 liters of iced tea. How many liters of iced tea remain?

10. June measured a 500-liter vat of milk and then emptied 350 liters from the vat. She says that she has more than 200 liters of milk left in the vat. Is June correct? Explain.

11. **Higher Order Thinking** Some people use a chart like the one shown to help them decide how many fish they can put in their fish tank. Harrison has a 40-liter fish tank. How many 4-centimeter fish can he put in his fish tank?

DATA

Length of Fish	Water Needed for Each Fish
1 centimeter	2 liters
2 centimeters	4 liters
3 centimeters	6 liters
4 centimeters	8 liters

Assessment Practice

12. Benito made a small pitcher of fruit punch. He mixed together lemonade and cherry juice. Use the picture to find the amount of fruit punch Benito made.

Ⓐ 1 liter

Ⓑ 3 liters

Ⓒ 9 liters

Ⓓ 20 liters

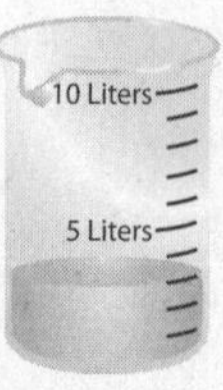

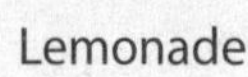
Lemonade

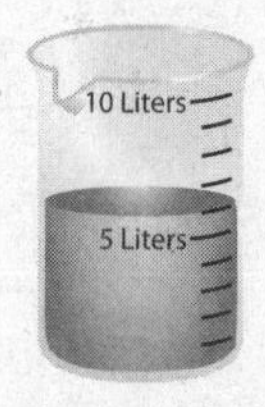

Cherry Juice

Name ______________________________

 Practice  Video  Tools  Games

Additional Practice 14-6
Estimate Mass

Another Look!

Units of mass include grams (g) and kilograms (kg).

1 kilogram = 1,000 grams

Mass is a measure of the amount of matter in an object.

A paper clip has a mass of about 1 gram.

A large wooden baseball bat has a mass of about 1 kilogram.

You can estimate the mass of different objects based on the mass of the paper clip and mass of the baseball bat.

In **1–16**, circle the better estimate for each.

1. 

150 g or 150 kg

2. 

1 g or 100 g

3. 

200 g or 2 kg

4. 

15 g or 150 g

5. Soccer ball

500 g or 5 kg

6. Tiger

30 kg or 300 kg

7. Dime

2 g or 2 kg

8. Baseball glove

100 g or 1 kg

9. Large dog

400 g or 40 kg

10. Flat screen TV

15 kg or 100 kg

11. Lemon

100 g or 1 kg

12. Cell phone

150 g or 15 kg

13. Boat anchor

40 g or 40 kg

14. Calculator

95 g or 1 kg

15. Sweatshirt

50 g or 300 g

16. Dinner plate

300 g or 3 kg

17. **Use Appropriate Tools** Choose the best tool to measure each item. Write the letter in the blank.

The mass of a peach ______

The capacity of a bowl ______

The time you finish breakfast ______

The length of a crayon ______

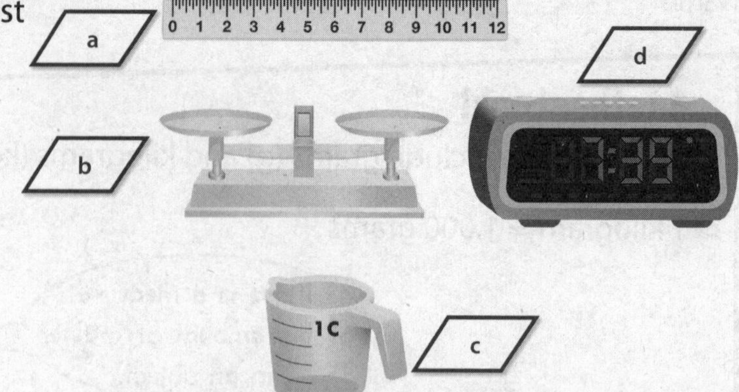

18. **enVision® STEM** A science class estimated the mass of objects that a magnet lifted. The magnet lifted 2 keys and 1 wrench. What was the total estimated mass that the magnet lifted?

DATA

Object	Estimated Mass
Key	30 g
Wrench	350 g

19. Stan works for a moving company. There are 36 boxes equally placed on 6 shelves. Draw a picture or bar diagram to find the number of boxes on each shelf.

20. **Higher Order Thinking** Rena knows a dollar coin has a mass of a little less than 10 grams. She estimates 1 kilogram of coins would be worth more than a million dollars. Is this reasonable? Explain.

21. Cody is thinking of an object that has a mass greater than 1 gram, but less than 1 kilogram. Name two objects that he could be thinking of.

Assessment Practice

22. Which metric units should you use to estimate the mass of a cookie?

Ⓐ Kilograms
Ⓑ Grams
Ⓒ Liters
Ⓓ Centimeters

23. Vimalesh is thinking of an object with a mass greater than 1 gram, but less than 1 kilogram. What object could Vimalesh be thinking of?

Ⓐ Chair
Ⓑ Car
Ⓒ Pen
Ⓓ Ladder

Name ____________________

Additional Practice 14-7
Measure Mass

Another Look!

Tanya estimated the mass of a box of nails to be 2 kilograms. Then she used a pan balance and metric weights to find its actual mass.

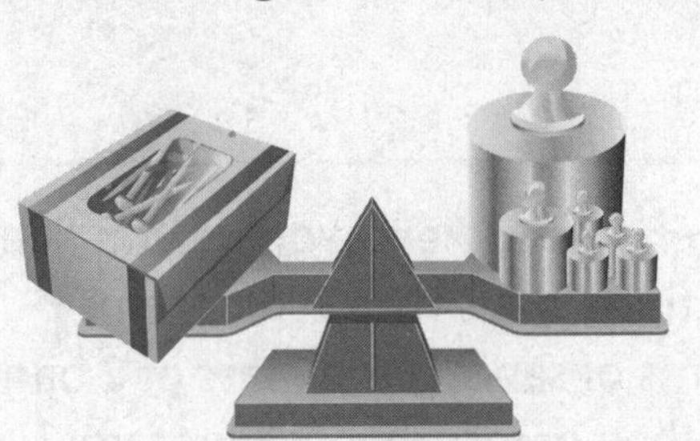

The box of nails balanced with one 1-kilogram weight, one 500-gram weight, and four 100-gram weights.

So, the mass of the box of nails is 1 kilogram 900 grams or 1,900 grams.

In **1–6**, write the total mass represented in each picture.

1.

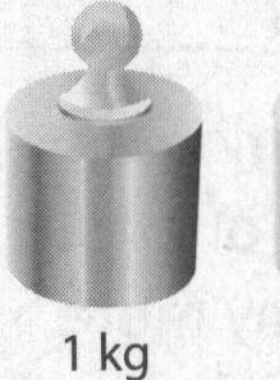

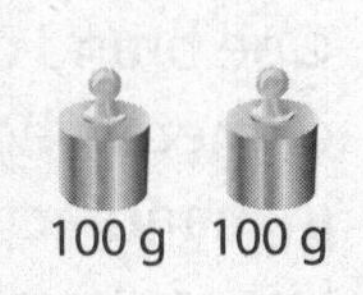

2.

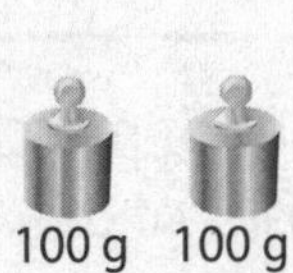

3.

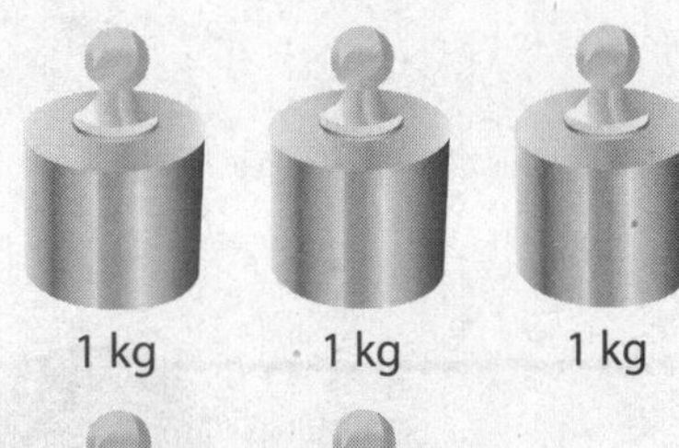

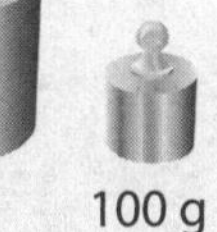

4.

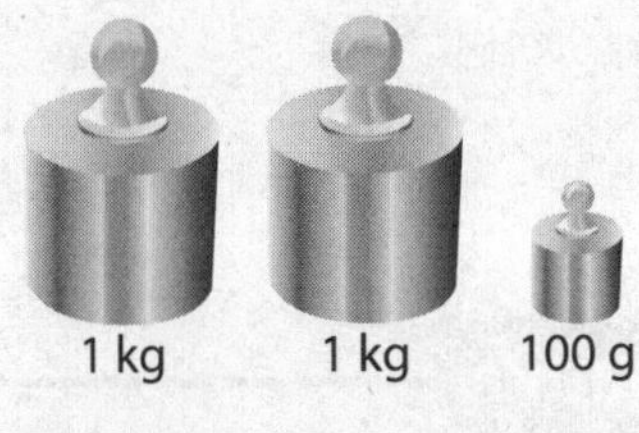

5.

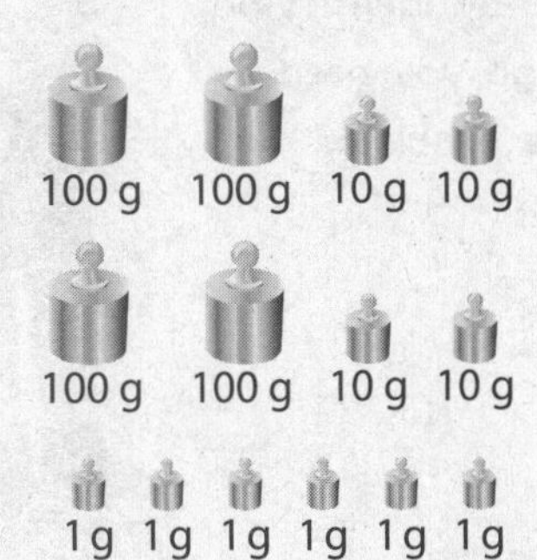

6.

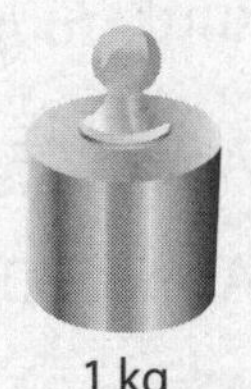

7. Ms. Walker has 15 kilograms of clay. She wants to give 3 students an equal amount of the clay. What is the mass of the clay that each student will get?

8. Higher Order Thinking Colby's dog gave birth to 6 puppies. Each puppy in the litter now has a mass of about 3 kilograms. About how much is the mass of the litter of puppies in kilograms?

9. Willie has 4 baseball caps. Two of the caps are blue. One of the caps is red and one is green. What fraction of the caps are blue?

10. Make Sense and Persevere Lynn filled each of three bags with 2 kilograms 450 grams of sand. Is the mass of 2 bags greater than or less than 5 kilograms? Explain how you know.

11. Kenisha packs 3 crates of merchandise. The crates have masses of 65 kilograms, 72 kilograms, and 42 kilograms. How many kilograms of merchandise does Kenisha pack?

12. One brand of car uses 772 kilograms of metal and 113 kilograms of plastic in manufacturing. How many more kilograms of metal are used than plastic?

Assessment Practice

13. An adult skunk has a mass of about 6 kilograms. There are 5 kits, or baby skunks, in a typical litter. Kits stay in the litter for about 8 months until they are fully grown. What is the mass of 5 adult skunks?

Ⓐ About 25 kilograms

Ⓑ About 30 kilograms

Ⓒ About 35 kilograms

Ⓓ About 40 kilograms

Name ______________________________

Additional Practice 14-8

Solve Word Problems Involving Mass and Liquid Volume

Another Look!

You can use different bar diagrams to solve problems.

Mrs. Jones bought 35 liters of juice for a school picnic. At the picnic, each class drank 5 liters of juice. No juice was left over. How many classes were at the picnic?

To find the number of classes, you can divide $35 \div 5$.

$35 \div 5 = 7$ There were 7 classes at the picnic.

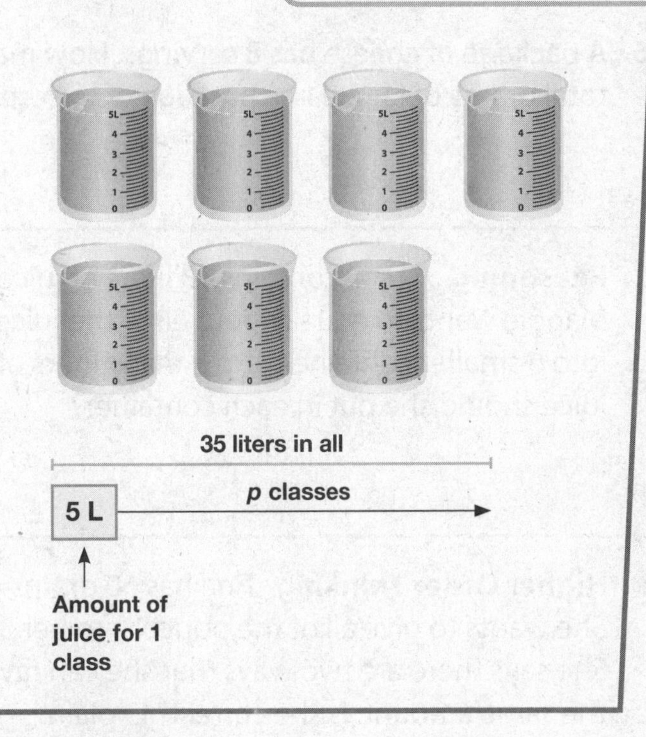

In **1** and **2**, use bar diagrams or equations to help solve.

1. Frank's bloodhound has a mass of 42 kilograms, and Dino's Labrador retriever has a mass of 39 kilograms. What is their total mass?

2. A small bicycle has a mass of 7 kilograms. The total mass of all the small bicycles at Mike's Bike Shop is 21 kilograms. How many small bicycles does Mike's Bike Shop have?

3. Donna has 6 first aid kits. Each kit is 8 kilograms. What is the total mass of all of Donna's first aid kits?

4. Chloe painted 4 bedrooms in her house. In each room, she used 10 liters of paint. How many total liters did she use?

Use the table for Exercises **5** and **6**. Use bar diagrams or equations to solve.

Total Fat (per serving)	
Food	**Amount of Fat (g)**
Cheddar Cheese	9
Honey Ham	2
Mixed Nuts	15

5. What is the sum of the number of grams of total fat per serving for cheddar cheese and mixed nuts?

6. A package of cheese has 8 servings. How many total grams of fat are in a package of cheese?

7. Reasoning A tank contains 18 liters of juice. Maggie wants to equally pour all of the juice into 6 smaller containers. How many liters of juice should she put in each container?

8. Number Sense George is thinking of a number less than 10 that has an odd product when multiplied by 5. What could George's number be?

9. Higher Order Thinking Tina has 60 grams of popcorn. She wants to give all of the popcorn to her 3 friends. She says there are two ways that she can give her friends the same amount. Is she correct? Explain.

Assessment Practice

10. Shawna placed a container outside to collect rain during a tropical storm. On Monday morning, there were 6 liters of rain. Three more liters were collected during the day. By Tuesday night, there were 14 liters of rain in the container. Mark the containers to show the amounts of rainfall collected each day. Then find how much more rain was collected on Tuesday than on Monday.

Ⓐ 3 liters

Ⓑ 4 liters

Ⓒ 5 liters

Ⓓ 6 liters

Name ____________________

Practice Video Tools Games

Additional Practice 14-9
Reasoning

Another Look!

Natalie finished listening to music at 4:30 P.M. She had listened to music for 45 minutes. Before that, Natalie spent 15 minutes reading. Before she read, she played soccer for 40 minutes. At what time did Natalie begin playing soccer? Use reasoning to decide.

Tell how you can show the relationships in the problem.

- I can identify the times and show them by drawing a picture.
- I can find the total time needed and work backward.

Solve the problem and explain your reasoning.

Natalie began at 2:50 P.M. I worked backward from 4:30 P.M. and used a number line to show my reasoning.

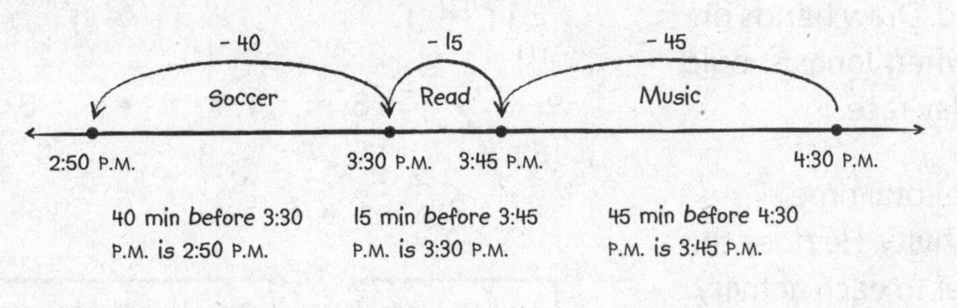

Reasoning

Will arrived at his mother's office at 11:00 A.M. It took him 30 minutes to walk from his home to the mall. Will was in the mall for 45 minutes. It took Will 15 minutes to walk from the mall to the office. At what time did Will leave home?

1. Describe the quantities you know.

2. Tell how you can show the relationships in the problem.

3. Solve the problem and explain your reasoning. You can use a picture to help.

Performance Task

Field Day

Jonas is planning Field Day at his school. The table shows the order of activities and how long each activity lasts. It takes 10 minutes to organize each activity before it starts. Students will have lunch at 12:00 P.M. Field Day must end at 2:35 P.M.

DATA

Activity	Length in Minutes
Tug-of-war	20
Bean bag toss	15
Egg relay race	20
800-yard dash	10

4. Make Sense and Persevere What time does Jonas need to start organizing the 800-yard dash? List the information that you need to use and then solve.

5. Model with Math The first clock shows the time Field Day must end. Draw hands on the second clock to show when Jonas should start organizing the egg relay race.

Organize egg relay race

6. Generalize Jonas finds the total time to organize and do each activity. He does this by adding the same number to each activity length. What number is this? Explain.

7. Reasoning What time should Field Day begin with Jonas organizing the tug-of-war? Explain.

Use reasoning to understand which numbers help you solve the problem.

Name ______________

Practice Video Tools Games

Additional Practice 15-1
Describe Quadrilaterals

Another Look!

Some quadrilaterals have special names because of their sides. Some have special names because of their angles. Here are some examples.

The same polygon can have more than one name.

Parallelogram	**Rectangle**	**Rhombus**	**Square**	**Trapezoid**
Opposite sides are the same length.	Parallelogram with 4 right angles	Parallelogram with 4 equal sides	Rhombus with 4 right angles	Exactly 1 pair of sides that never cross

In **1–4**, read the description and circle the correct quadrilateral. Write the name.

1. I have 4 right angles and all sides the same length. I am a ______________.

2. I have exactly 1 pair of sides that never cross. I am a ______________.

3. I have 4 right angles, but only my opposite sides are equal. I am a ______________.

4. I have all sides the same length, but I have no right angles. I am a ______________.

5. Is a trapezoid also a parallelogram? Explain why or why not.

____

____

6. Christine drew the shape shown below. Madison changes Christine's shape so that it has every side equal and every angle equal. What shape does Madison make?

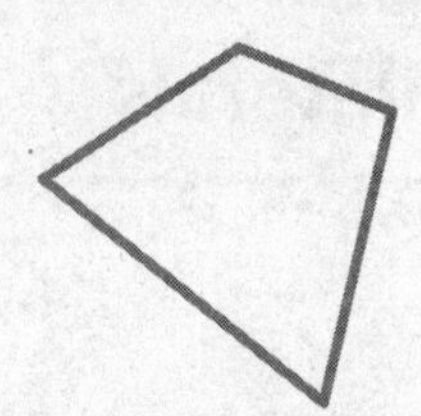

7. There are 20 slices of bread in a loaf. How many 2-slice sandwiches can you make with 1 loaf? Write a multiplication fact and a division fact you could use to solve this problem.

8. **enVision® STEM** Mari pushed a cube-shaped box to explore force. She examined the attributes of the box. Does a face of her box have a right angle? Explain.

9. **Be Precise** Mr. Rose asked his students to draw a concave quadrilateral with 4 unequal sides. Draw an example of this kind of quadrilateral.

In **10** and **11**, use the shape at the right.

10. **Higher Order Thinking** Melissa drew the shape at the right. What two quadrilaterals did she use to draw the shape? Draw a line to divide the shape into two quadrilaterals.

11. Suppose Melissa redrew the shape by turning it on its side. Would this change the names of the quadrilaterals she used? Explain.

12. A square and a rectangle are shown at the right. Which attributes do these shapes always have in common? Select all that apply.

- ☐ Number of sides
- ☐ Angle measures
- ☐ Number of angles
- ☐ Side lengths
- ☐ Right angles

Name ______________________

Additional Practice 15-2
Classify Shapes

Another Look!

What attribute do these two shapes have in common?

What is another shape that shares this attribute?

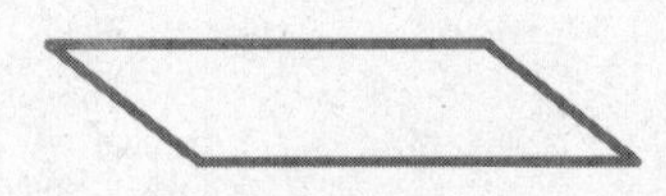

Think about attributes that shapes can have. What attribute do these shapes share?

The rhombus has 2 pairs of sides that are the same length.

The parallelogram also has 2 pairs of sides that are the same length.

A rectangle also has 2 pairs of sides that are the same length.

In **1–3**, use the groups below.

Group 1

Group 2

1. How do the shapes in Group 1 differ from those in Group 2?

2. How are the two groups alike?

3. What group of polygons do all the shapes belong to?

4. Draw a shape that is neither a square nor concave.

5. Draw a shape that is neither a trapezoid nor has a right angle.

6. Frida sorted polygons so Group 1 was only squares. Group 2 was only rectangles, not squares. Frida said all the shapes are parallelograms. Sam said they are all quadrilaterals. Who is right? Why?

7. **Be Precise** Can you draw a square that is **NOT** a rhombus? Explain.

8. **Number Sense** A bike helmet has a mass of 285 grams. Elena says that is about 300 grams. Is her estimate greater than, less than, or equal to the actual mass?

9. **Vocabulary** Define *convex shape*. Draw a convex shape.

10. **Higher Order Thinking** Hope makes 3 groups of shapes. What larger group do the shapes in A and B belong to? What larger group do the shapes in A and C belong to? What larger group do the shapes in B and C belong to?

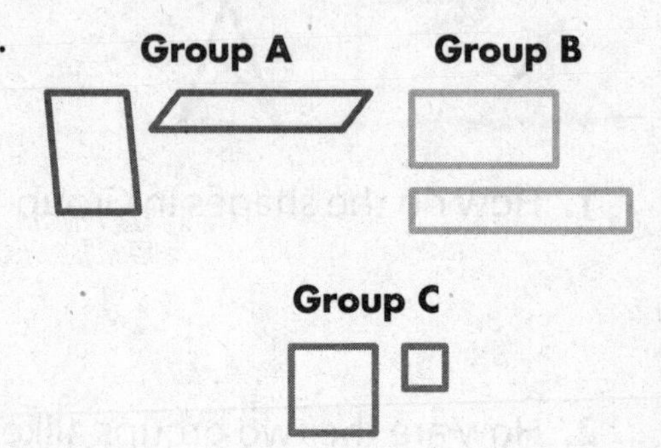

Assessment Practice

11. Which shape is a quadrilateral and a rectangle?

Ⓐ Rhombus

Ⓑ Parallelogram

Ⓒ Square

Ⓓ Trapezoid

12. Which shape could be sorted into a group of quadrilaterals or a group of parallelograms?

Ⓐ Hexagon

Ⓑ Triangle

Ⓒ Rhombus

Ⓓ Trapezoid

Name ____________________

Additional Practice 15-3
Analyze and Compare Quadrilaterals

Another Look!

List all the names and attributes of a square.

A square is a quadrilateral.
It has 4 sides.

A square is a parallelogram.
Its opposite sides are the same length.

A square is a rectangle.
It has 4 right angles and opposite sides are the same length.

A square is a rhombus.
It has 4 sides of the same length.

You can use structure to analyze and compare the attributes of a square with other polygons.

In **1–6**, list all the polygons shown at the right that fit the description. If no polygon fits the description, tell why.

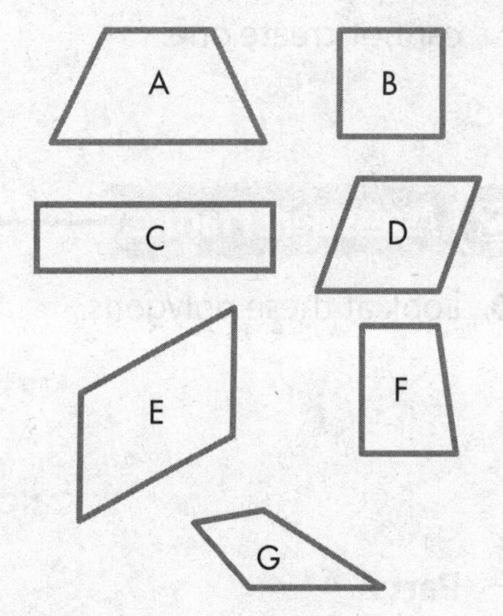

1. Is a square

2. Has at least one right angle but is not a square

3. Has no sides the same length

4. Is a square but not a rectangle

5. Is a parallelogram but not a rectangle

6. Is a rectangle with no angles the same size

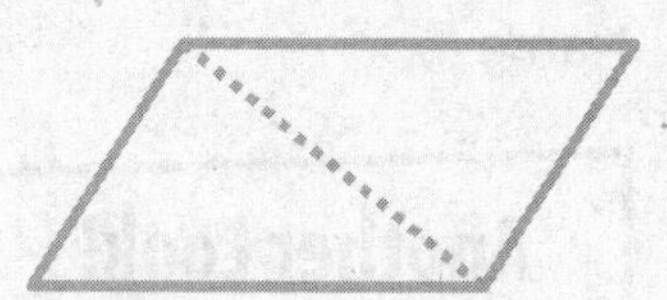

7. Critique Reasoning Mary claims that you can cut a parallelogram along its diagonal and get two pieces that are the same size and shape. Larry says that you cannot cut all parallelograms this way. Who is correct? Explain your thinking.

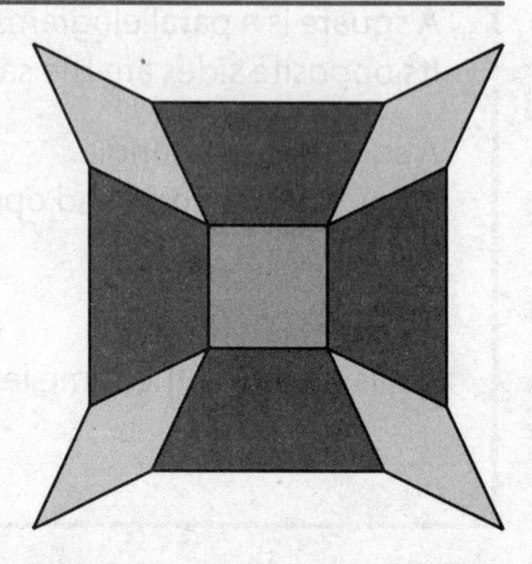

8. How are all the polygons in the mosaic alike and how are they different?

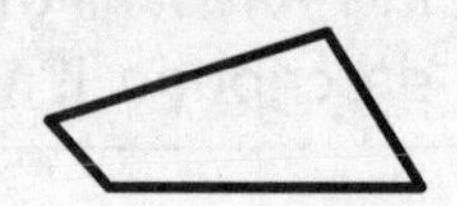

9. Higher Order Thinking Can you create a mosaic using the quadrilateral shown? The mosaic should not have any gaps or overlap. Draw your mosaic or tell why you cannot create one.

10. Look at these polygons.

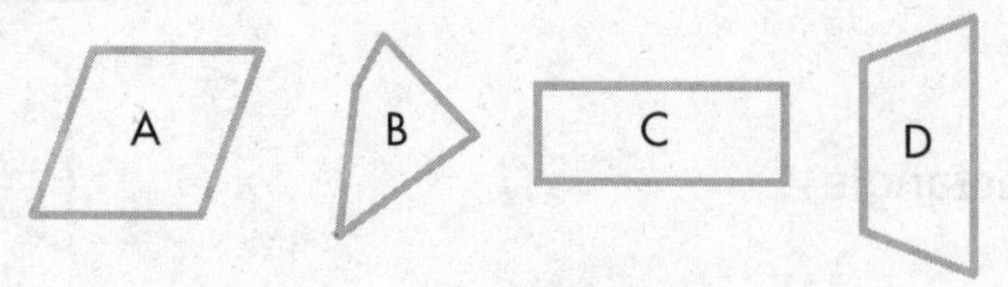

Part A

Name at least 2 attributes that A and C share.

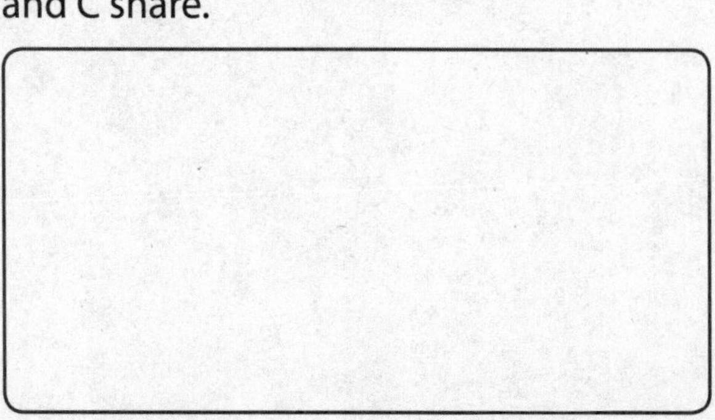

Part B

Tell how B is different from the other 3 polygons.

Name ___________________________

Additional Practice 15-4
Precision

Another Look!

Yoshi is thinking of a quadrilateral. All 4 sides are equal lengths and the shape has no right angles. Look at the array of shapes below. What shape is Yoshi thinking of?

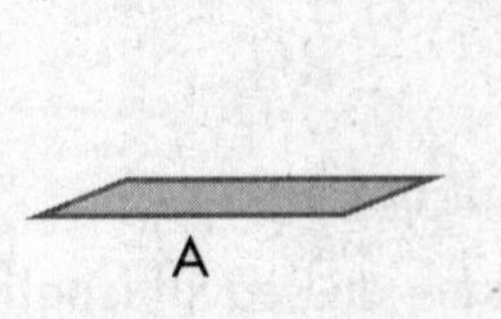

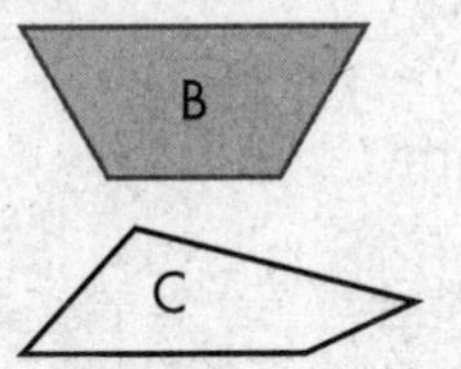

D
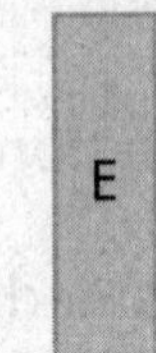

Tell how you can solve the problem with precision.

- I can correctly use the information given.
- I can draw pictures to identify possible answers.
- I can decide if my answer is clear and appropriate.

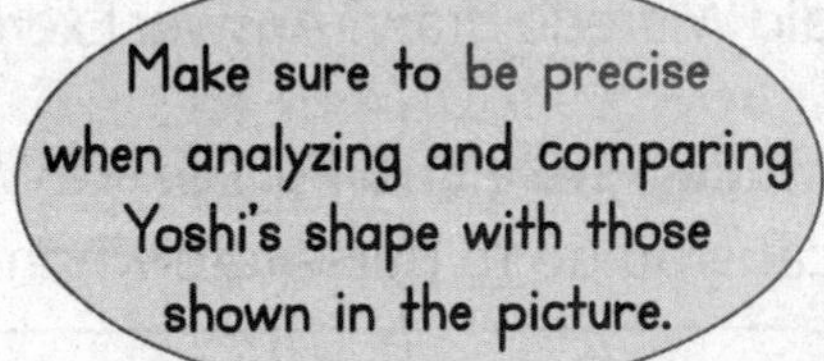

Be precise as you solve the problem.

All of the shapes are quadrilaterals. A, D, E, and F are parallelograms. A and E do not have 4 equal sides. D and F are rhombuses. F is a square with 4 right angles. Rhombus D is the only quadrilateral that fits all the clues.

Be Precise

Jacobi made a banner in the shape of a polygon that fits the rules at the right. What banner shape could Jacobi have made?

- It is a quadrilateral.
- Opposite sides are equal lengths.
- Two sides are longer than the other 2 sides.

1. What math words and numbers are important in this problem?

2. Draw and name a shape that matches the description of Jacobi's banner.

3. How can you check to make sure your answer is clear and correct?

Performance Task

The Name Game

Pairs of students in Mr. Kuan's class are playing the Name Game. One team member is given a list of attributes and has to draw a shape to match the description. The other team member must then name the shape. The first pair to complete the task wins.

Wilfredo was given a list with the information at the right.

- A quadrilateral
- No sides are equal length
- 2 right angles

He drew a shape and his partner, Olivia, named it. What shape did Wilfredo draw? Answer Exercises **4–7** to solve the problem.

4. Make Sense and Persevere What are you asked to do? What can you do to persevere when solving the problem?

5. Be Precise What math terms and numbers can help you solve the problem?

6. Use Structure What do you know about a quadrilateral? Use what you know to draw and name a shape that matches the information in the list.

7. Construct Arguments Is there more than one possible way for Wilfredo to draw the shape? Explain.

Name ______________________

Practice | Video | Tools | Games

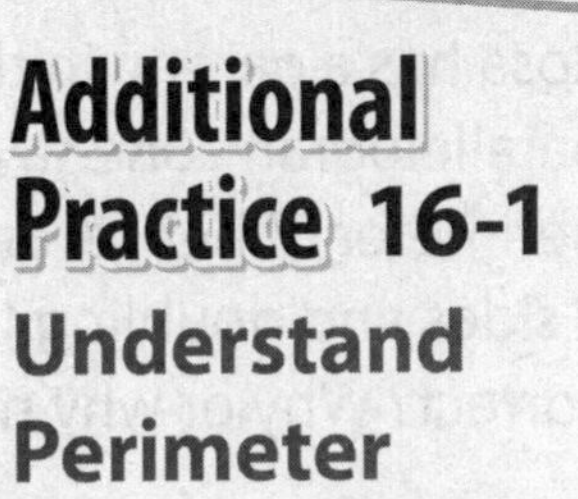

Additional Practice 16-1

Understand Perimeter

Another Look!

What is the perimeter of this figure?

Add the lengths of the sides.

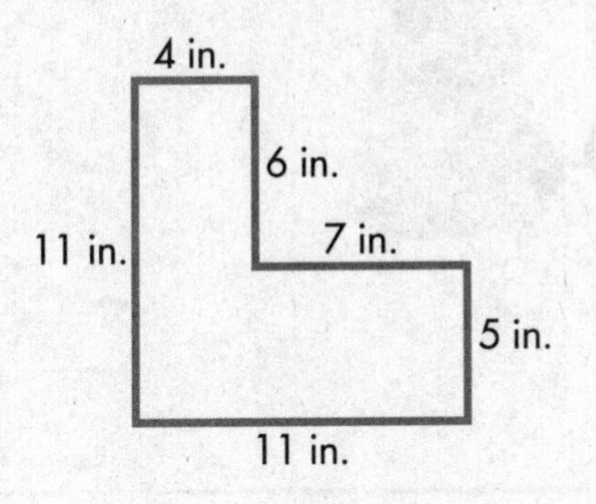

The perimeter of a figure is the distance around it.

$4 + 6 + 7 + 5 + 11 + 11 = 44$

The perimeter of the figure is 44 inches.

Leveled Practice In **1–3**, find the perimeter of each polygon.

1.

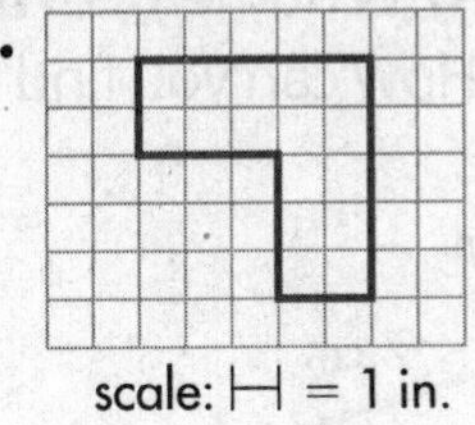

scale: ⊢⊣ = 1 in.

2.

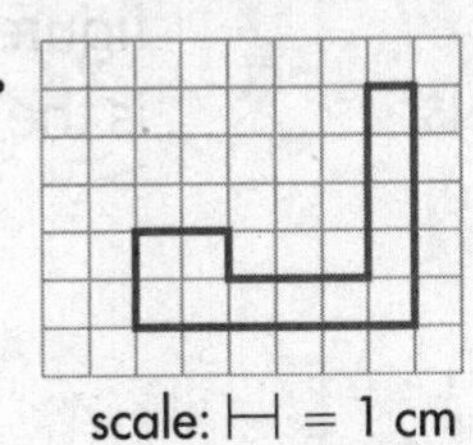

scale: ⊢⊣ = 1 cm

3.

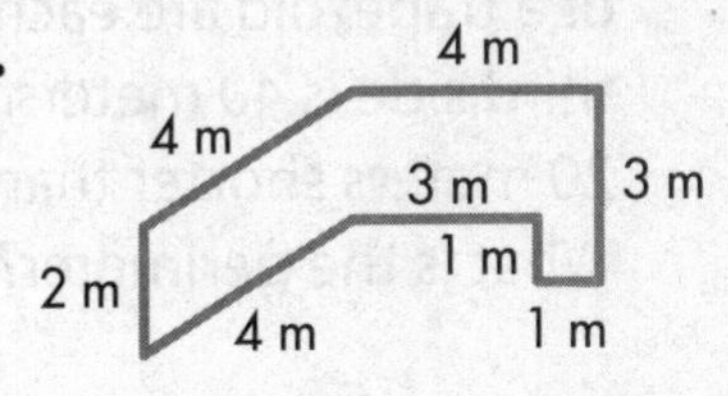

In **4–6**, draw a figure with the given perimeter.

4. 12 units

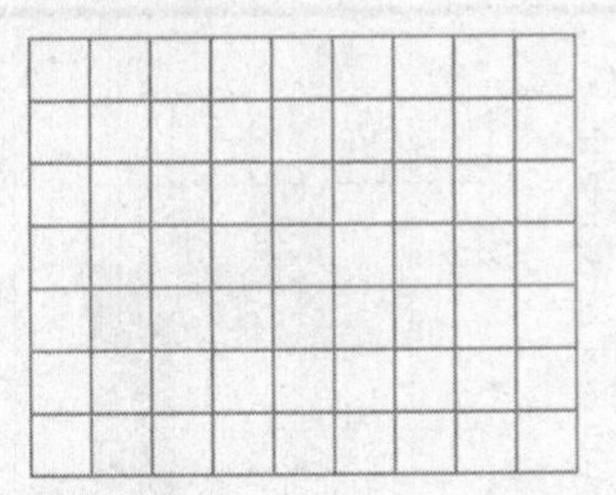

5. 18 units

6. 22 units

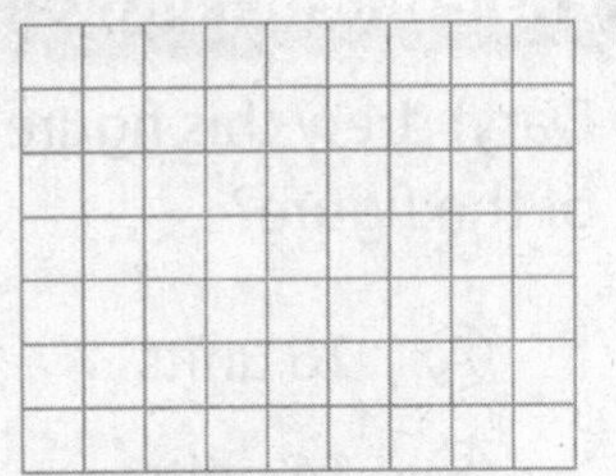

7. Rosa has a garden in the shape of a parallelogram. She says she can find the perimeter of her garden by adding the 2 sides and doubling the sum. Is Rosa correct? Why or why not?

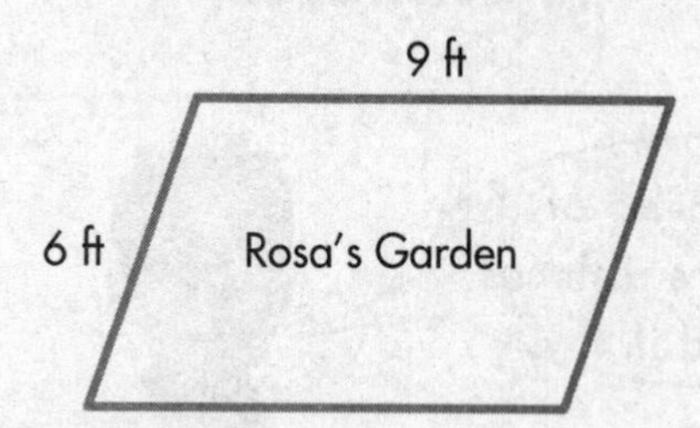

8. May bought 12 hats. What solid figure do the hats look like? What attributes help you decide?

9. **Vocabulary** Explain the difference between perimeter and area.

10. A plane figure has 2 sides that are each 5 inches and 2 sides that are each 3 inches. What is the perimeter of the plane figure?

11. **Make Sense and Persevere** Two sides of a trapezoid are each 25 meters. The third side is 40 meters. The fourth side is 20 meters shorter than the longest side. What is the perimeter? Explain.

12. **Higher Order Thinking** Ming drew this figure. Its perimeter is 47 centimeters. What is the missing length? How can you find it?

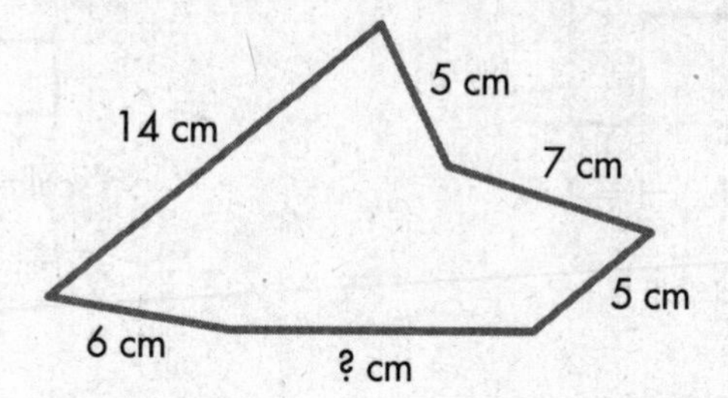

13. Daryl drew this figure on grid paper. What is the perimeter of the figure?

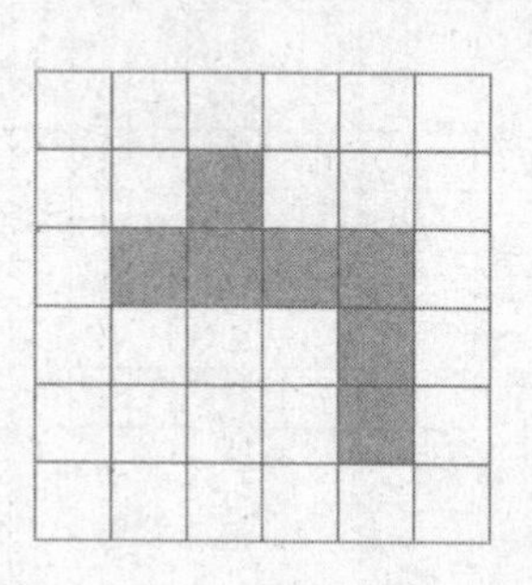

Ⓐ 16 units

Ⓑ 14 units

Ⓒ 12 units

Ⓓ 10 units

Name ______________________

Practice Video Tools Games

Additional Practice 16-2

Perimeter of Common Shapes

Another Look!

Use the attributes of these common shapes to find the missing side lengths. Then find the perimeters.

Rectangle

Opposite sides have the same length.

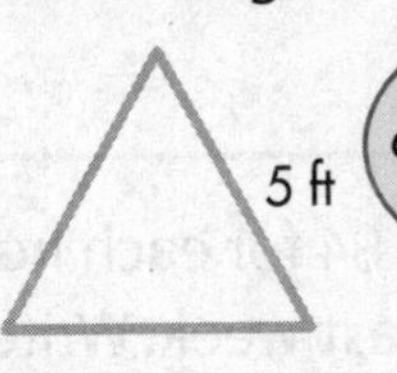

$(4 \times 2) + (5 \times 2) = 18$ in.

Square

All 4 sides have the same length.

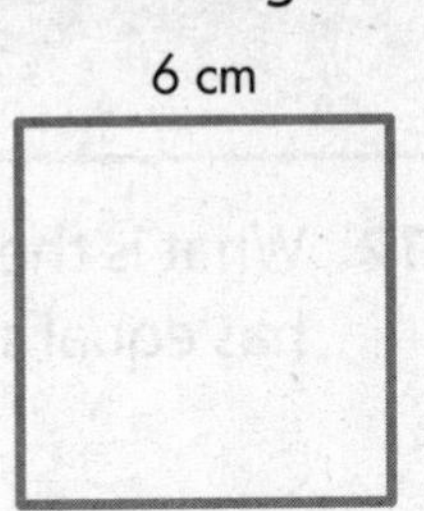

$6 \times 4 = 24$ cm

Equilateral Triangle

All 3 sides have the same length.

$5 \times 3 = 15$ ft

In **1–9**, find the perimeter of each polygon.

1. Square

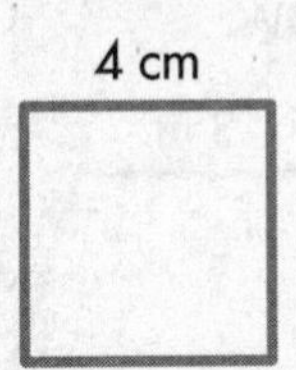

2. Rectangle

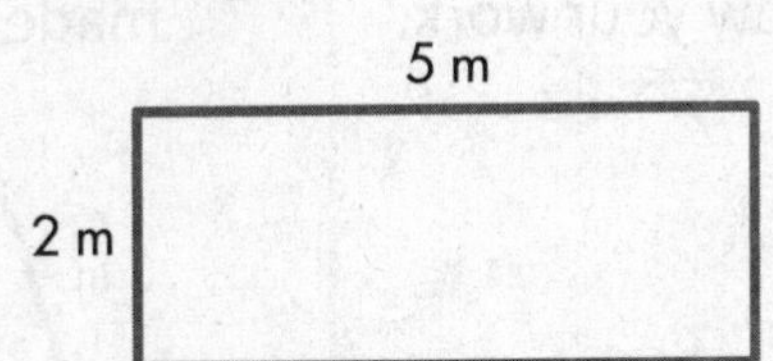

3. Equilateral Triangle

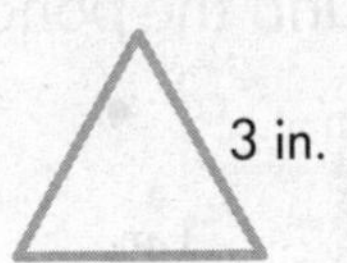

4. Parallelogram

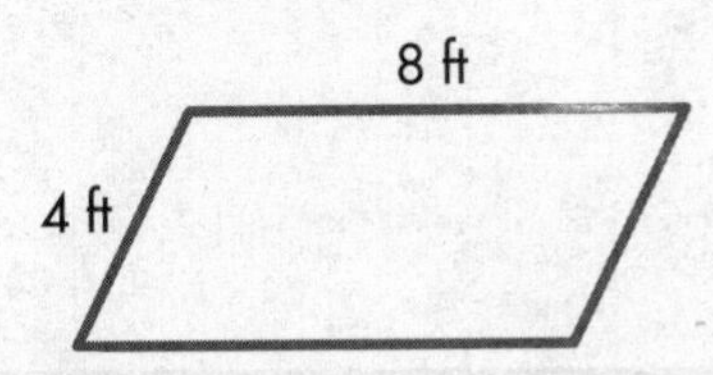

5. Rectangle

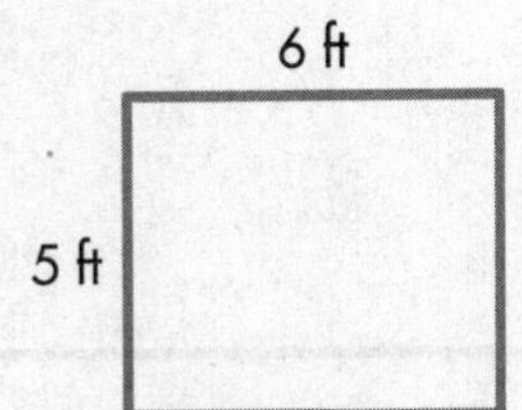

6. Equilateral Triangle

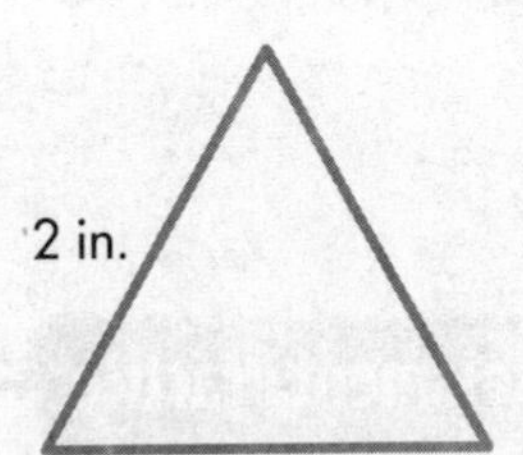

7. Equilateral Triangle

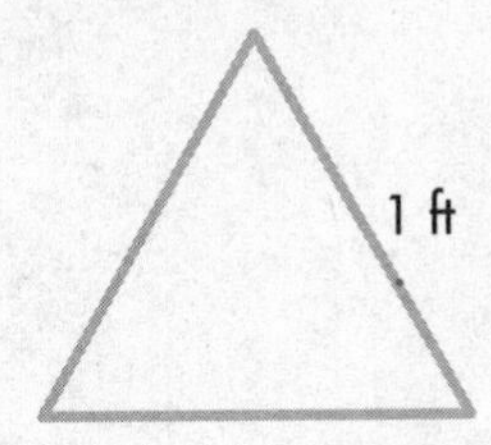

8. Square

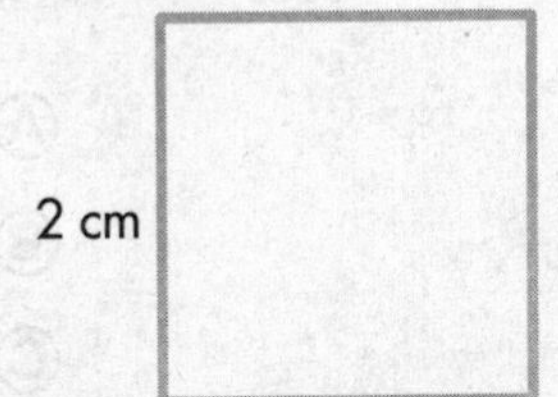

9. Rectangle

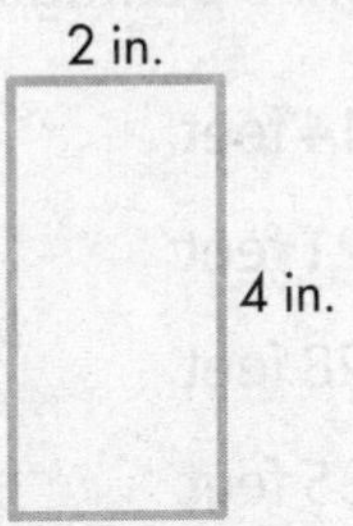

10. Reasoning The distance around the outside of this maze is the same as the perimeter of a rectangle. The picture shows the lengths of the sides of the rectangle. What is the perimeter of the maze? How did you find the answer?

11. Algebra Paolo earns $4 for each hour he tutors. He made $28 last week. Write an equation using h to represent the hours he tutored. Then solve the equation.

12. What is the perimeter of a hexagon that has equal sides of 12 centimeters?

13. enVision® STEM A pond is a habitat for many different kinds of plants and animals. Maria puts this fence around her pond. What is the perimeter of the fence around the pond? Show your work.

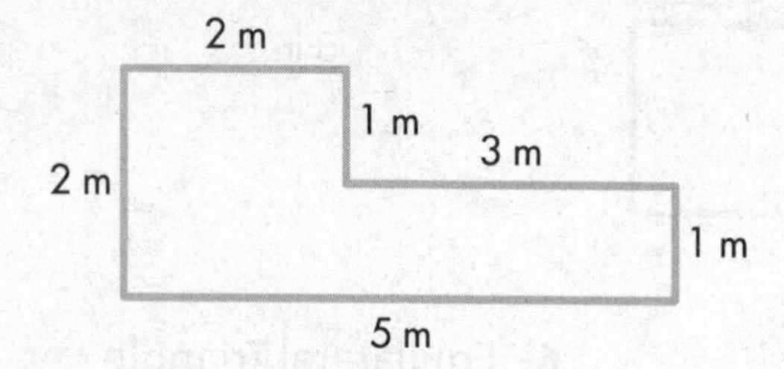

14. Higher Order Thinking Pete put these two trapezoids together along their 5-inch sides to make a hexagon. What was the perimeter of the hexagon Pete made? Explain how you know.

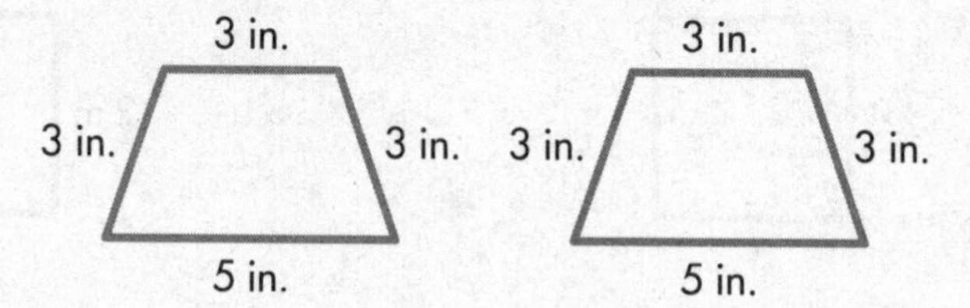

Assessment Practice

15. Nina draws a pentagon with side lengths of 7 feet each. What is the perimeter, in feet, of Nina's pentagon?

Ⓐ 14 feet
Ⓑ 21 feet
Ⓒ 28 feet
Ⓓ 35 feet

16. Debra draws a square. One side is 10 meters long. What is the perimeter of Debra's square?

Ⓐ 10 meters
Ⓑ 20 meters
Ⓒ 40 meters
Ⓓ 80 meters

Name ____________________

Practice Video Tools Games

Additional Practice 16-3

Perimeter and Unknown Side Lengths

Another Look!

The perimeter of the triangle is 14 meters. Another way to write the perimeter is by adding the lengths of its sides.

$5 + 6 + s =$ perimeter

So, $5 + 6 + s = 14$

$11 + s = 14$

Because $11 + 3 = 14$, $s = 3$ and the length of the unknown side is 3 meters.

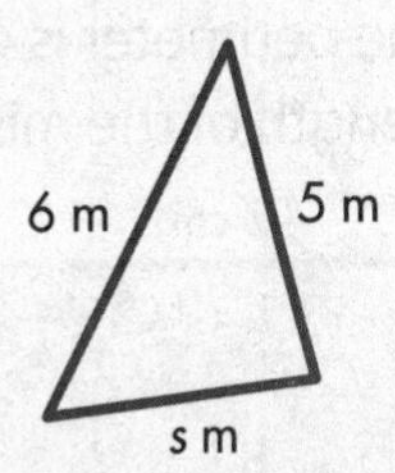

In **1–6**, find the length of the missing side for each polygon.

1. perimeter = 29 cm

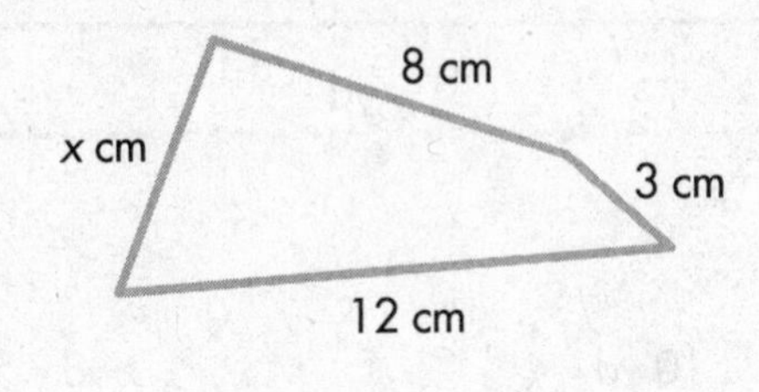

2. perimeter = 55 ft

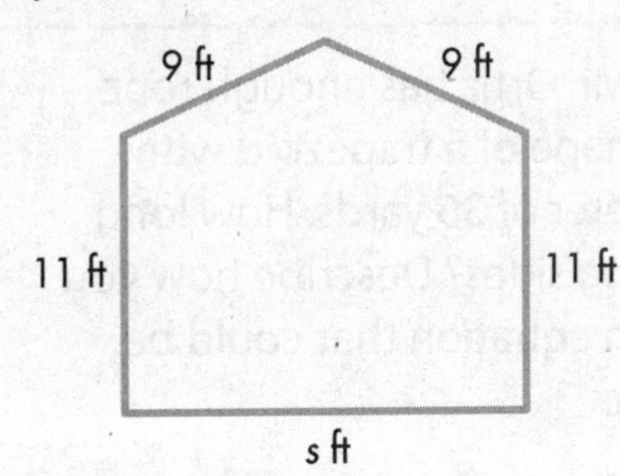

3. perimeter = 30 in.

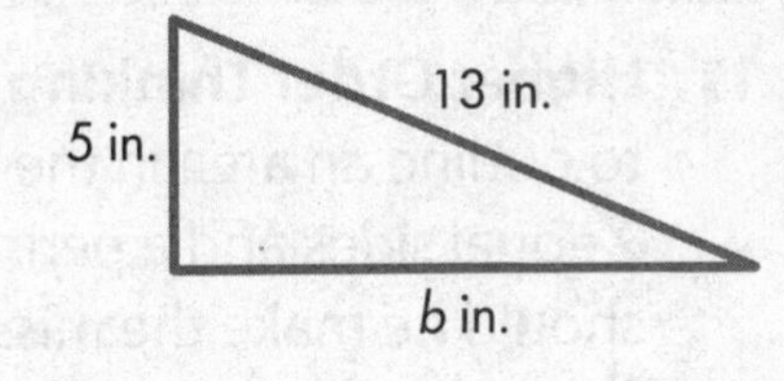

4. perimeter = 35 cm

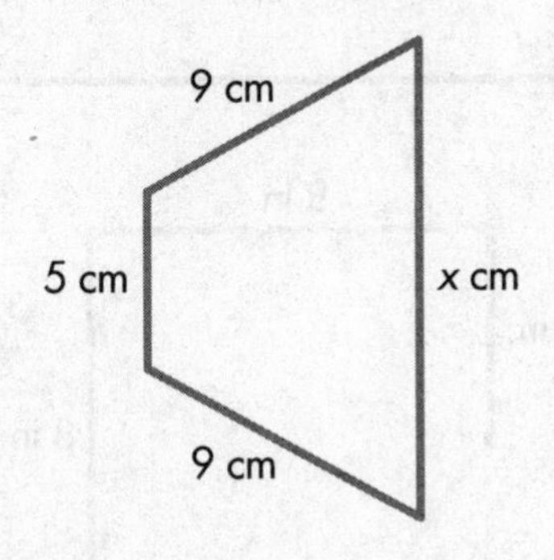

5. perimeter = 22 ft

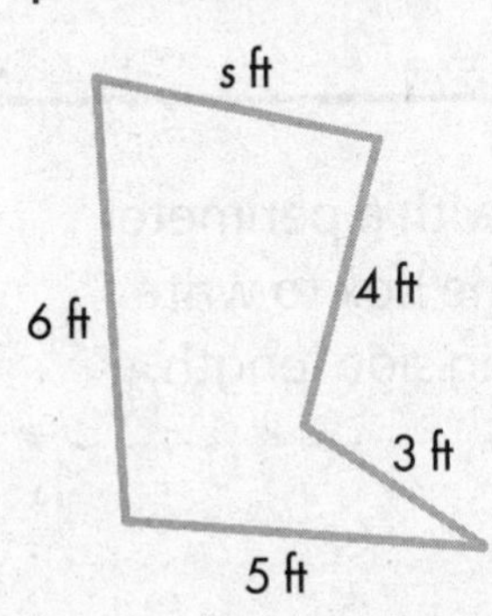

6. perimeter = 48 mm

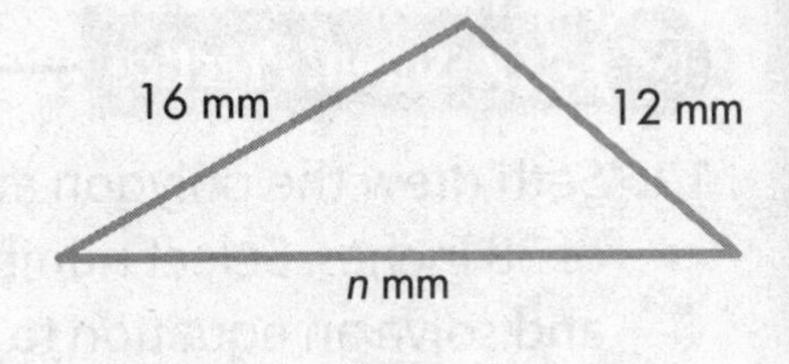

7. Reasoning A rectangle has a perimeter of 40 centimeters. One side is 12 centimeters. What are the lengths of the other 3 sides? Explain.

8. A square has a perimeter of 36 centimeters. What is the length of each side? Explain your answer.

9. Tracy measured the sides of a shape she drew. She forgot to label one side length, but knows the perimeter is 40 centimeters. What is the length of the missing side?

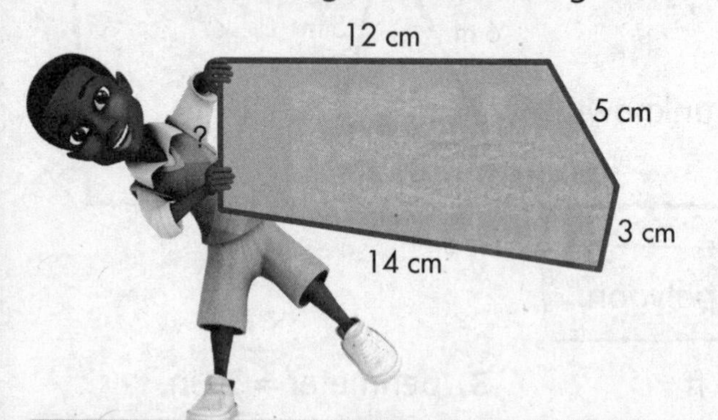

10. Arturo is putting 18 erasers into equal rows. He says there will be more erasers in 2 equal rows than in 3 equal rows. Is Arturo correct? Explain.

11. Higher Order Thinking Mr. Ortiz has enough rope to outline an area in the shape of a trapezoid with 2 equal sides and a perimeter of 36 yards. How long should he make the missing sides? Describe how you found the answer. Write an equation that could be used to solve the problem.

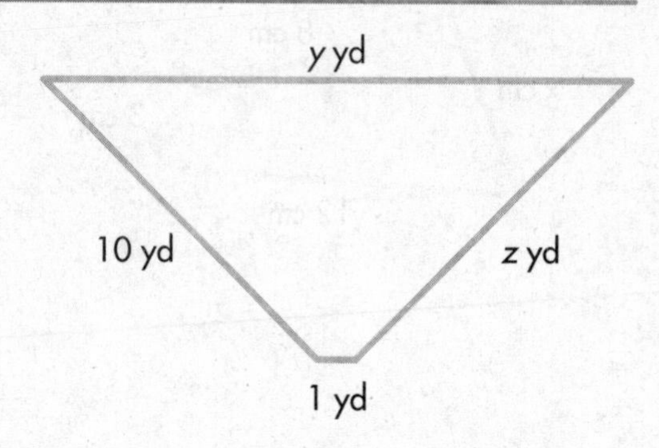

Assessment Practice

12. Seth drew the polygon at the right with a perimeter of 30 inches. Select numbers from the box to write and solve an equation to find missing side length.

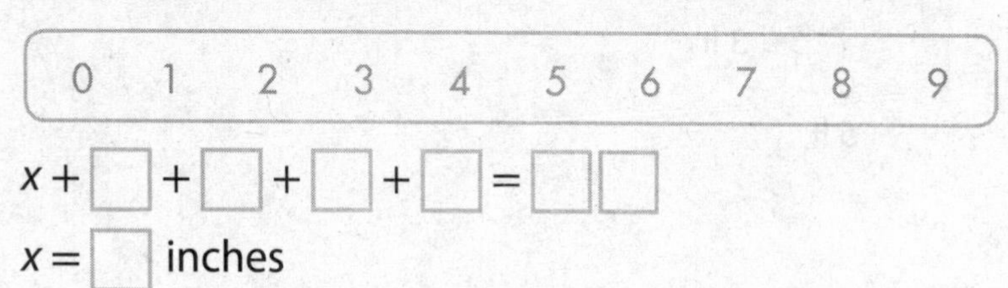

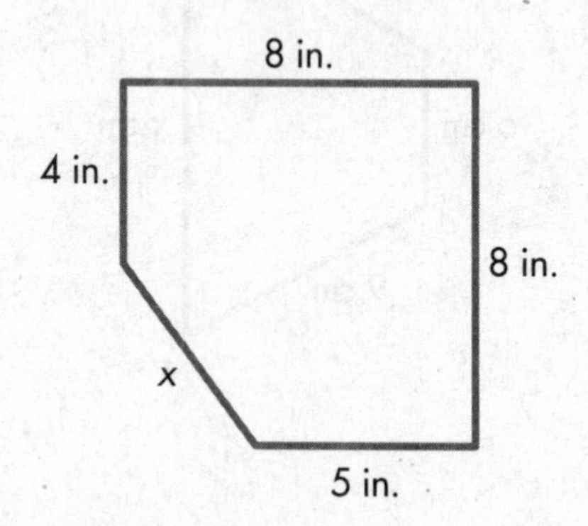

Name ________________

Practice

Video

Tools

Games

Additional Practice 16-4
Same Perimeter, Different Area

Another Look!

$A = 2 \times 6$
$A = 12$ sq cm
$P = 6 + 2 + 6 + 2$
$P = 16$ cm

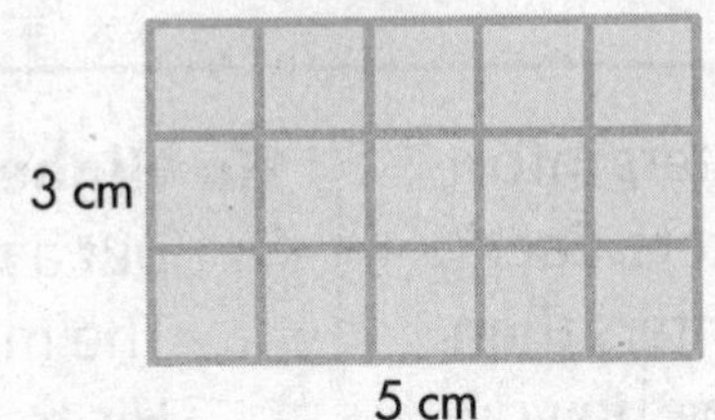

$A = 3 \times 5$
$A = 15$ sq cm
$P = 5 + 3 + 5 + 3$
$P = 16$ cm

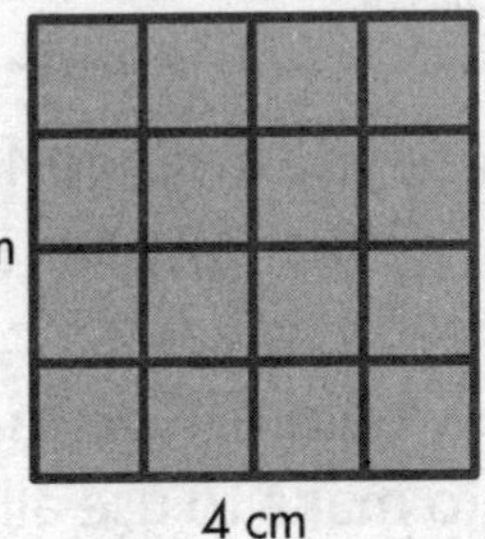

$A = 4 \times 4$
$A = 16$ sq cm
$P = 4 + 4 + 4 + 4$
$P = 16$ cm

Each of these rectangles has a different area. But they all have the same perimeter.

In **1–4**, use grid paper to draw two different rectangles with the given perimeter. Write the dimensions and the area of each rectangle. Circle the rectangle that has the greater area.

1. 12 meters

2. 28 inches

3. 20 feet

4. 24 centimeters

Leveled Practice In **5–7**, write the dimensions for a different rectangle with the same perimeter as the rectangle shown. Then tell which rectangle has the greater area.

5.

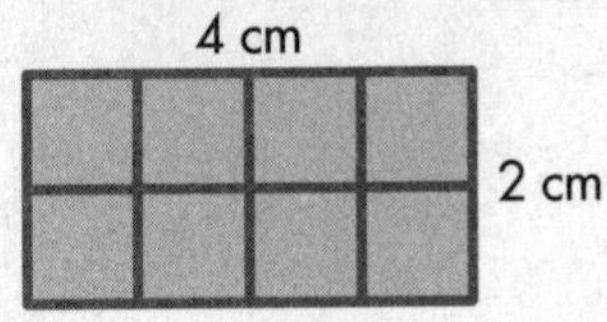

6.

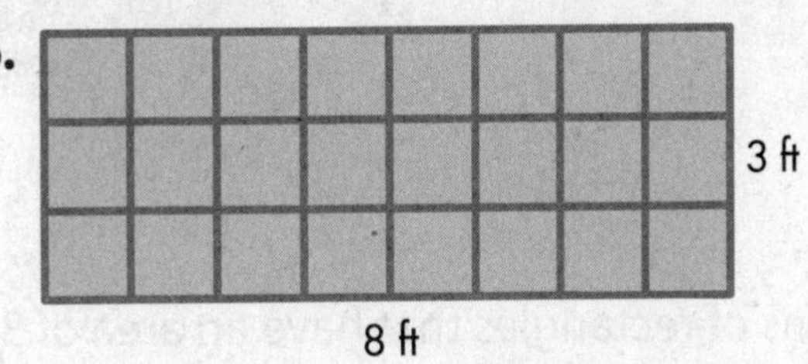

7.

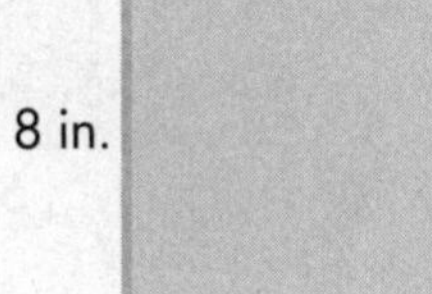

8. Make Sense and Persevere Lamar made a garden in the shape of a rectangle with an area of 36 square feet. Explain how you can find the perimeter of the garden.

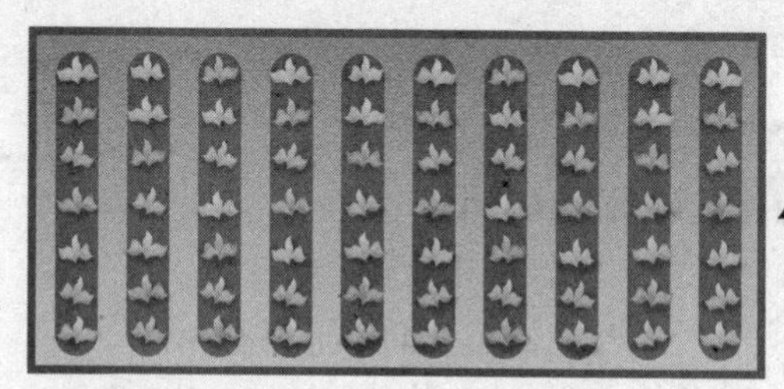

9. Suppose you arrange 48 counters into rows. The first row has 3 counters. Each row after that has 2 more counters than the row before. How many rows do you need to make to use all 48 counters?

10. Higher Order Thinking Jack wants to put a mat on the floor of his tree house. The mat has an area of 72 square feet. His tree house measures 8 feet by 8 feet. Does Jack have enough room in his tree house for the mat? How do you know?

Assessment Practice

11. Marisol draws a rectangle with a length of 12 inches and a width of 6 inches. Select all of the rectangles that have the same perimeter as Marisol's rectangle.

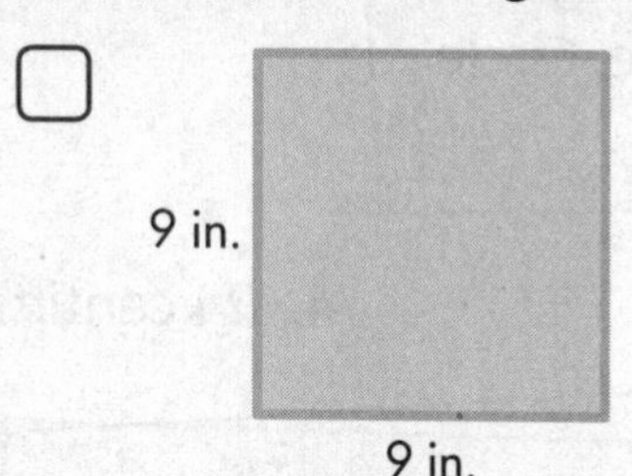

☐ 6 in. by 6 in.

☐ 6 in. by 9 in.

☐ 8 in. by 5 in.

☐ 4 in. by 14 in.

12. Select all the dimensions of rectangles that have an area of 36 square centimeters.

☐ $\ell = 9$ cm, $w = 4$ cm

☐ $\ell = 6$ cm, $w = 6$ cm

☐ $\ell = 4$ cm, $w = 6$ cm

☐ $\ell = 4$ cm, $w = 9$ cm

☐ $\ell = 3$ cm, $w = 10$ cm

Name ____________________

Practice

Video

Tools

Games

Additional Practice 16-5
Same Area, Different Perimeter

Another Look!

Phil has 18 square tiles with 1-foot sides. He uses the tiles to make 3 different rectangles. Each rectangle has an area of 18 square feet. What rectangles can he make? What is the perimeter of each rectangle?

Rectangle 1

1 row of 18 tiles
$A = 1 \times 18 = 18$ square feet

Find the perimeter:
$P = (2 \times 18) + (2 \times 1)$
$P = 36 + 2 = 38$ feet

Rectangle 2

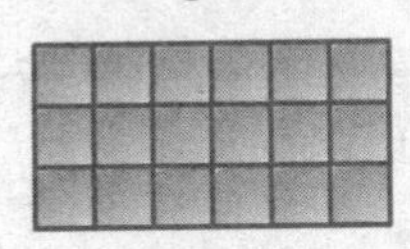

3 rows of 6 tiles
$A = 3 \times 6 = 18$ square feet

Find the perimeter:
$P = (2 \times 6) + (2 \times 3)$
$P = 12 + 6 = 18$ feet

Rectangle 3

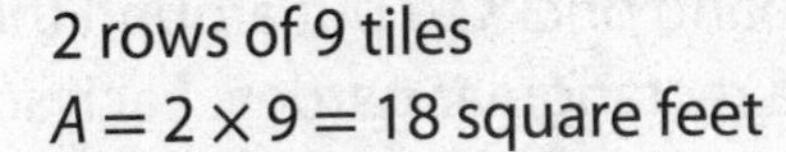

2 rows of 9 tiles
$A = 2 \times 9 = 18$ square feet

Find the perimeter:
$P = (2 \times 9) + (2 \times 2)$
$P = 18 + 4 = 22$ feet

Leveled Practice In **1–4**, write the dimensions of a different rectangle with the same area as the rectangle shown. Then tell which rectangle has the smaller perimeter.

1. 4 cm, 6 cm

2. 6 ft, 5 ft

3.

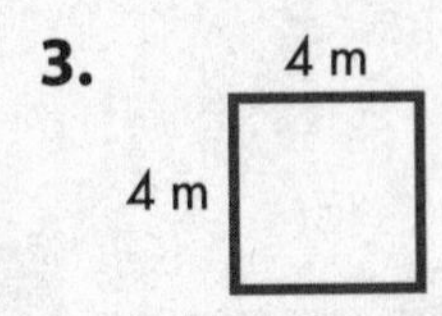

4.

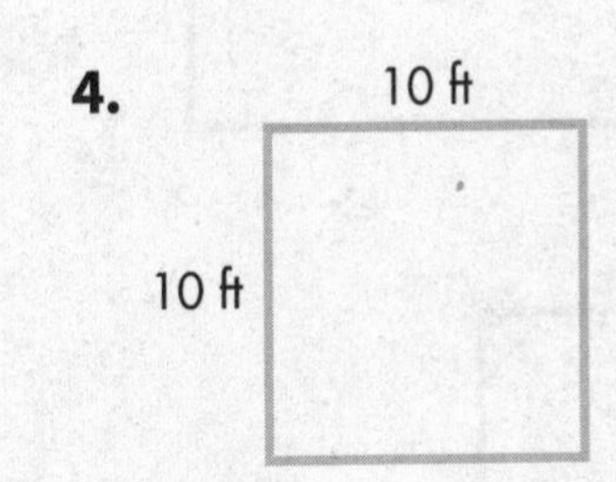

5. Wes has 20 feet of garden fencing. If he wants the smallest side of his garden to be 3 feet or longer, what possible rectangles can he make?

6. Mai drew the design shown below. Each rectangle in the design has the same area. Each rectangle is what fraction of the area of the complete design?

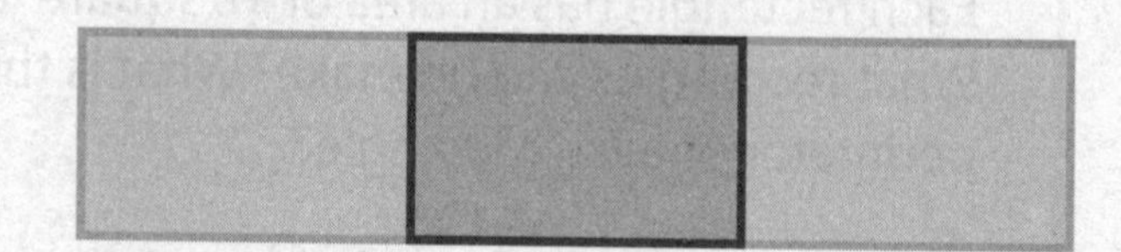

7. Reasoning Mari has 39 square feet of patio bricks to put around the edge of a rectangular garden. Each square brick has sides that are 1 foot long. What is the greatest perimeter that she can make with the bricks?

8. A-Z **Vocabulary** Jolanda started an art project at 9:00 A.M. and finished it at 9:50 A.M. The __________ for the project was 50 minutes.

9. Higher Order Thinking The area of a rectangle is 100 square inches. The perimeter of the rectangle is 40 inches. A second rectangle has the same area but a different perimeter. Is the second rectangle a square? Explain.

Think: Which math fact that you know has a product of 100?

Assessment Practice

10. Vimalesh draws a rectangle that is 5 inches wide by 6 inches tall. Which of the following rectangles has the same area but a different perimeter from Vimalesh's rectangle?

Ⓐ
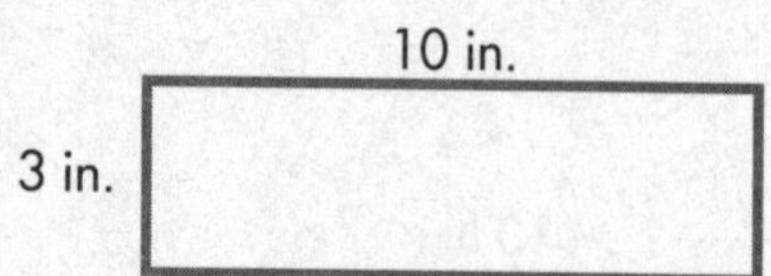

Ⓑ
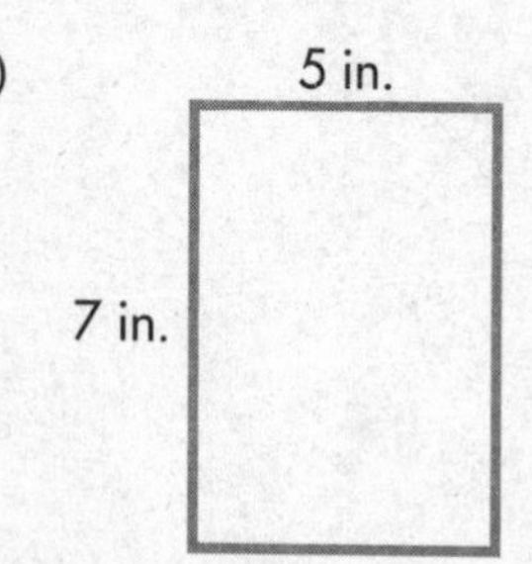

Ⓒ
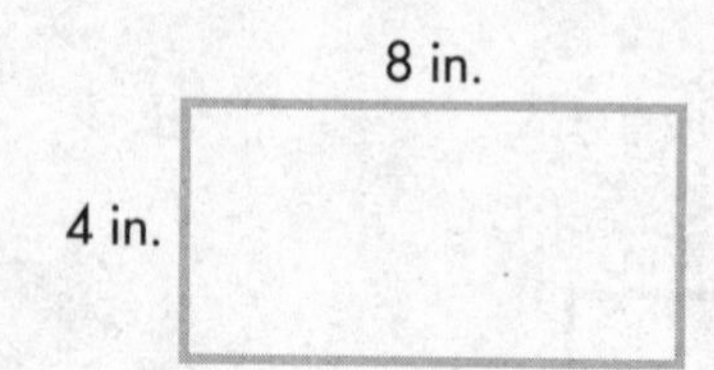

Ⓓ 20 in. 1 in.

Name ______________________

Practice Video Tools Games

Additional Practice 16-6
Reasoning

Another Look!

Marissa and Amy are making a rectangular garden 8 feet long and 6 feet wide. They plan to put a fence around the garden with fence posts 2 feet apart. Each corner has a fence post. How many fence posts will they need? How is the number of posts related to the number of sections?

Tell ways you can show the relationships in the problem.

- I can draw a picture to show relationships.
- I can give the answer using the correct unit.

Think about the different ways you can use reasoning to solve the problem.

Solve and explain your reasoning.

They need 14 posts. When I draw a picture I see that there are four 2-foot sections on each 8-foot side. So they need 5 posts for each length.

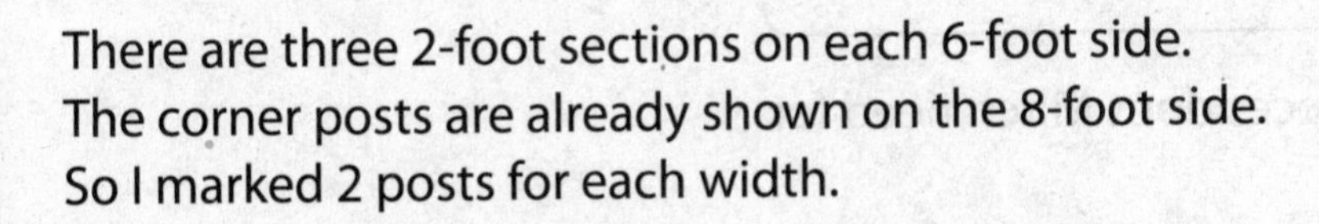

There are three 2-foot sections on each 6-foot side. The corner posts are already shown on the 8-foot side. So I marked 2 posts for each width.

$(5 \times 2) + (2 \times 2) = 14$ posts

The number of sections is equal to the number of posts.
$(4 \times 2) + (3 \times 2) = 14$ sections

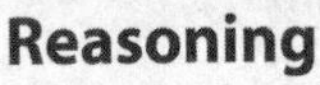

Reasoning
A farmer wants to build a straight fence with a post every 7 feet. Each end has a post. For a fence that is 49 feet long, how many posts will the farmer need?

1. Describe the quantities given.

2. Tell how you can show the relationships in the problem.

3. Solve and explain your reasoning.

Performance Task

Field Day

Mitch wants to build a sandbox in his backyard. He needs to decide on a design to use. He will border the sandbox with wood pieces that are 2 feet long. Each wood piece costs $3. Each square foot of sand will cost $2.

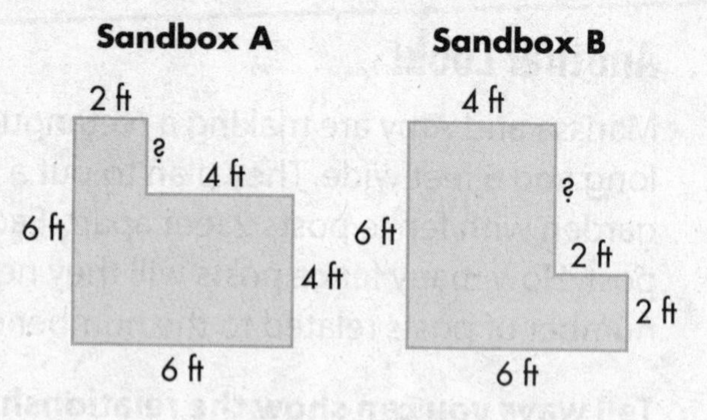

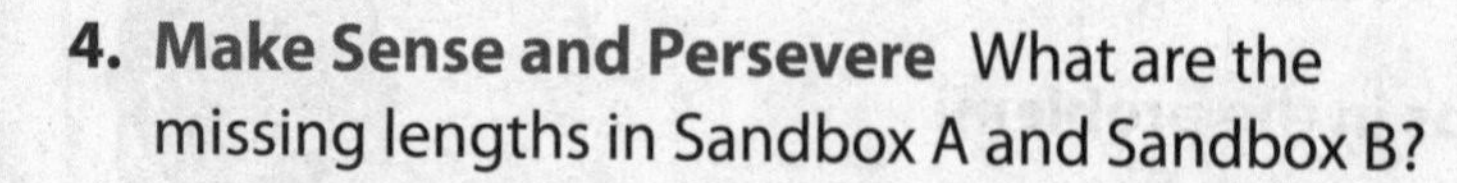

4. Make Sense and Persevere What are the missing lengths in Sandbox A and Sandbox B?

5. Be Precise How many wood pieces does Mitch need for Sandbox A?

6. Be Precise How many wood pieces does Mitch need for Sandbox B?

7. Use Structure How would the price of buying the wood for Sandbox A compare to the price of wood for Sandbox B? Explain how to solve without computing. Why?

8. Reasoning Which sandbox would cover a greater area? Explain how you know.

enVision® Mathematics

Photographs

Every effort has been made to secure permission and provide appropriate credit for photographic material. The publisher deeply regrets any omission and pledges to correct errors called to its attention in subsequent editions.

Unless otherwise acknowledged, all photographs are the property of Savvas Learning Company LLC.

Photo locators denoted as follows: Top (T), Center (C), Bottom (B), Left (L), Right (R), Background (Bkgd)

180 Jenoe/Fotolia.